D0206134

TRENDS
IN PUBLIC OPINION

TRENDS IN PUBLIC OPINION

A Compendium of Survey Data

Richard G. Niemi
John Mueller
Tom W. Smith

GREENWOOD PRESS
New York • Westport, Connecticut • London

ALBRIGHT COLLEGE LIBRARY

Library of Congress Cataloging-in-Publication Data

Niemi, Richard G.
    Trends in public opinion : a compendium of survey data / Richard
G. Niemi, John Mueller, and Tom W. Smith.
      p. cm.
    Bibliography: p.
    Includes indexes.
    ISBN 0-313-25426-5 (lib. bdg. : alk. paper)
    1. United States—Social conditions—1933-1945—Public opinion.
  2. United States—Social conditions—1945-1960—Public opinion.
  3. United States—Social conditions—1960-1980—Public opinion.
  4. United States—Social conditions—1980-　—Public opinion.
  5. Public opinion—United States.　6. Social surveys—United States—
Longitudinal studies.　I. Mueller, John E.　II. Smith, Tom W. (Tom
William), 1949-　.　III. Title.
  HN90.P8N53　1989
  303.3'8—dc20　　　89-2213

British Library Cataloguing in Publication Data is available.

Copyright © 1989 by Richard G. Niemi, John Mueller, and Tom W. Smith

All rights reserved. No portion of this book may be
reproduced, by any process or technique, without the
express written consent of the publisher.

Library of Congress Catalog Card Number: 89-2213
ISBN: 0-313-25426-5

First published in 1989

Greenwood Press, Inc.
88 Post Road West, Westport, Connecticut 06881

Printed in the United States of America

The paper used in this book complies with the
Permanent Paper Standard issued by the National
Information Standards Organization (Z39.48-1984).

10 9 8 7 6 5 4 3 2 1

303.3
N672t

225366

Contents

225366

List of Tables

Acknowledgments

The data reported in this book represent as much as fifty years worth of polling. Over this period, enormous amounts of time, energy, and resources have gone into the effort, and our first debt is to the organizations whose efforts made the collection of the data possible.

We would also like to thank the National Data Program for the Social Sciences for access to its social change archive and for special data runs from its General Social Surveys. For the use of certain data points about abortion, we would like to thank Judith Blake. Bruce L. Peterson and Sara P. Crovitz provided research assistance. A major debt is owed to Dana Loud for her expert typing, formatting, and reformatting of the tables. Her cheerful spirit as well as expert help made the project far more bearable than it might have been.

Richard G. Niemi

John Mueller

Tom W. Smith

TRENDS
IN PUBLIC OPINION

Introduction

Public opinion polls are ubiquitous and influential. In the 1988 presidential election campaign, for example, some 50 national polls were conducted from June to August alone (*Public Opinion*, 1988, 11(3):36-40). Though influence is harder to demonstrate, surveys are widely alleged to affect both electoral turnout and election outcomes. Other far-reaching influences are also suggested, such as the apparent use by Israel of American public opinion data in making military and other decisions (Gilboa, 1987).

Yet, for all this, polls are often difficult to interpret. Opinions can change with great speed and seemingly little provocation. Gaps may exist between opinions and behavior. More fundamentally, it is often difficult to determine just what public opinion is. Dramatic examples can be found of the sensitivity of opinions to question wording (Mueller, 1973, chap. 1; Schuman and Scott, 1987). Individuals sometimes respond to questions in almost random fashion (Converse, 1964). Parts of the public readily respond to questions asking about fictitious events (Bishop, Oldendick, Tuchfarber, and Bennett 1980).

These and other difficulties make responses to isolated survey questions are an inadequate guide to public opinion (Schuman, 1986). Instead, poll results must be used in a comparative manner. There are at least four such ways of analyzing public opinion data. The weakest form is to compare results with expectations. For example, if one has always assumed that news broadcasts are of great significance to the general public, it may be shocking to learn that, when telephoned within a few hours after a newscast, few television watchers can remember anything they saw. Such "surprises" are illuminating, but the surprise is mostly related to one's previous misconceptions and not to the precise numbers generated by the polling process.   Any of a wide variety of results would generate approximately the same shock.

A second form of comparison is to contrast responses from different groups within the population.   These may be a few standard democraphic groups (men versus women, blacks versus whites) or multiple groups designed specifically for this purpose ("informed" voters who prefer one presidential candidate versus informed voters who prefer another candidate versus uninformed voters versus nonvoters).   The analysis may be simple "crosstabs" or elaborate analyses using statistical controls.

A third form of comparative analysis seeks to understand public attitudes by looking at responses to different questions.   In May 1971, for example, 11 percent of a national sample favored withdrawal of U.S. troops from Vietnam by the end of the year "even if it threatened the lives or safety of United States POWs held by the North Vietnam," 29 percent favored withdrawal "even if it meant a Communist takeover of South Vietnam," and 68 percent favored having Congress vote for or against a proposal to require all troops to be withdrawn.   Multiple related questions are far superior to single items in determining what is actually being asked and how respondents feel about various components of the overall problem.

A fourth form--and the one on which we concentrate in this volume--is over-time comparisons.   Judging by the frequency of "trend analysis" in academic journals, the value of over-time analysis is gradually being recognized.   Yet there are at least three major problems for those interested in analyzing trends in public opinion.   First, pollsters are inclined to ask only about those topics that are most salient at a given time.   Among other things, this means that questions are often not asked early enough to establish initial baselines.   By the time an issue is clearly on the public agenda, it is likely that a good deal of change has already taken place.   Similarly, there are often large gaps between surveys about any particular topic.   A prime example is questions about civil liberties.   Stouffer conducted an important study of the topic in the early 1950s, but as McCarthyism faded, so did questions about the topic.   Not until 1973 did another study repeated the Stouffer questions (see chapter 5).

A second problem is that when appropriate questions are asked, the specific wording often changes from one survey to another.   Sometimes, of course, changes in society force wording changes, as when Newcomb and others (1967) found that questions used to determine political views in the late 1930s (for example, about the Spanish Civil War) were entirely inappropriate in his follow-up study in the 1960s.   Yet in many instances, questions are changed because of some perceived defect in the original wording. While the new question may indeed be an improvement, it renders over-time changes nearly impossible.[1]

Finally, even when questions are invariant, the results are often hard to find, especially with regard to earlier surveys and to items that were not a part of a continuous effort by one survey organization. In addition, when isolated results are found, it is often difficult to determine relevant information such as the size of the sample and the precise question wording.

Our purpose in this book is to provide easy access to a large, meaningful collection of questions that have been repeated in exactly or nearly exactly the same wording over an extended period of time. In the remainder of the introduction, we indicate the scope of the data included, cite additional sources of over-time data, and provide technical details on our major data source and on our manner of presentation of data. In the chapter introductions we summarize trends in the various areas surveyed as well as briefly discussing problems of interpretability of specific topics, including matters of timing, of question wording, and so on.

THE SCOPE OF THE BOOK

Our collection of over-time survey data is centered around the General Social Surveys (GSS). The General Social Surveys consist of an ongoing series of surveys conducted by the National Opinion Research Center (NORC) of the University of Chicago. They have been conducted every year since 1972 except for 1979 and 1981, with interviewing concentrated in March of each year. Each annual survey consists of approximately 1,500 face-to-face interviews with a nationally representative sample of the American public. Details of the survey design are presented below.

---

[1]Cf. Burns Roper's (1984, p. 6) obituary to George Gallup. Roper cited among Gallup's greatest contributions: "Third--and I was very slow to appreciate this one--was the tenacity with which George stuck to the wording of a question. As a prideful (possibly even biased) competitor, I always felt we could write a better question than Gallup at any point in time. And certainly, as the art of question writing developed, we could write a better question today than Gallup wrote ten years ago. As a result we were constantly improving our questions while Gallup stuck with the same mundane wording year after year. And, as a further result (I belatedly realized), Gallup has most of the trend data--invaluable trends data!"

GSS is an appropriate centerpiece for this collection because it is based on the principle that trend analysis is one of the most meaningful kinds of survey analysis. Operationally, this has meant two very important things. First, GSS has generally adopted previously used questions. This means that many of the time series extend back well before 1972. Second, since alterations in question wording usually destroy comparability, GSS has made a conscious effort to retain identical wordings over the seventeen years of its existence. There has been some experimentation, but it has typically taken the form of split-half samples so that at least half of a given year's sample is asked the original wording.

In addition to GSS, we have drawn on surveys from numerous other organizations. Data from the American Institute on Public Opinion (AIPO or Gallup) are especially frequent. For many years it was the only continuing organization doing nationwide surveys. In addition, even in its early years AIPO made an effort to preserve and document its data collection. Also of special interest are the pre-1970s data collected by the National Opinion Research Center. While these data have been widely used in monographs and articles, they have not been published in a single, comprehensive source.

A guiding principle in the selection of trends for this book is that identical or virtually identical questions be asked over an extended period of time. Recognizing that there is an element of subjectivity in judging what is "virtually" identical, we have been very conservative in our judgments. For the most part, the trends we report are based on invariant wordings. In some cases, however, it is possible to extend the series substantially with questions that use almost, but not quite, the same words. In a very few instances, such as the "most important problem" series (Table 1.24), a whole set of different questions is used because we think they tap the same underlying concept. In all cases, we document the exact wording used.

Insofar as possible, in each series we report, we have included every use of the identical question asked of a nationally representative sample. This coverage is made possible by the Roper search procedure (see below). There are, of course, numerous alternatively worded questions on the same topics (especially helpful is the appendix on previous usage found in GSS codebooks) and a number of important time series that we have not included (such as Gallup's and others' presidential popularity series). In the final section of this introduction we list the most important sources of additional time series data.

SURVEY DESIGNS AND PROCEDURES

The General Social Survey. GSS interviews have been
conducted in 1972-1978, 1980, and 1982-present, with plans
for continuing them at least through 1991. The interviews
are carried out in February-April, with the bulk of them conducted during March. All interviewing is conducted in person.
In 1973, interviews averaged 35 minutes; since 1984 they have
averaged 90 minutes. The surveys are administered by the
National Opinion Research Center of the University of Chicago.

The sample is a representative cross section of English-
speaking adults, 18 years and older, living in noninstitution-
al arrangements within the United States. For 1972-1974 the
sample design was multistage down to the segment level with
quotas applied at the final stage. The 1975-1976 sample was
experimental--half sampled as in previous years and half a
strict multistage probability sample (Stephenson, 1979). The
1977-1988 surveys are full, multistage probability samples.
In 1983 half the sample was from the 1970 NORC sample frame
and half from the 1980 frame. Since 1983, the 1980 sample
frame was employed for the whole survey.

The data from the interviews were processed according to
standard NORC procedures. Cleaning procedures, using a com-
bination of the coding specifications and interviewer instructions, were used to check for inconsistent or illegiti-
mate codes.

The heart of the survey consists of a core of replicating
questions. (In recent years there has also been an international module and a topical module.) Beginning in 1973, a
rotation scheme was introduced so that some items would appear
in two out of three surveys. Beginning in 1988, the scheme
was changed so that rotating items will appear in all surveys
but on a randomly chosen subsample consisting of two-thirds
of the cases. This change will ensure that all replicating
items will appear each year and that gaps will not appear in
the time series.

Further details about sample design, sampling error,
nonresponse rates, fieldwork, interviewer instructions, and
coding instructions are found in any of the cumulative codebooks. In addition, the GSS staff has produced numerous
methodological reports dealing with these and other subjects.
These are listed in *GSSNEWS*, an annual newsletter. *GSSNEWS*
is available upon request from General Social Survey, National
Opinion Research Center, 1155 East 60th St., Chicago, IL
60637.

Other Surveys. Other surveys cited in this volume are
more variable in their methods, if for no other reason than
their coverage of time. Before the early 1950s, most surveys
used some mixture of probability and old-fashioned quota

methods (less rigorous than the last-stage quotas used in the
1972-1976 GSS). There were other difficulties as well, such
as severe undersampling of southern blacks. As a consequence,
results of early surveys must be interpreted cautiously.
Descriptions of early sampling methods as well as of survey
procedures are relatively sparse. However, brief descriptions
of pre-1950s Gallup and NORC samples are found in *Survey Data
for Trend Analysis*, Appendixes A-B. The same volume also
contains Norval Glenn's (1974) perceptive essay on early sampling procedures along with his recommendations for proper
interpretation and possible reanalysis.

Descriptions of current survey practices are also less
detailed than would be desirable. Gallup (1972) has a fairly detailed, readily available description, though it is now
quite out-of-date. (A very brief description is given in
annual volumes of *The Gallup Poll* and in the monthly *Gallup
Report*.) NORC samples are described in brief papers available from the center. A good description of Harris surveys
in the 1960s and 1970s, along with a comparison of the com-
position of samples of several organizations, is found in
Presser (1981).

DATA PRESENTATION

The entries in this volume are mostly self-explanatory,
but a few comments are in order.

Mnemonic. Most of the questions begin with a mnemonic
of up to eight characters. These labels were devised to make
handling of GSS variables easier and more accurate and will
be familiar to users of those surveys. An index of mnemonics
is found at the end of the volume.

Question Wording. Insofar as possible, exact question
wordings are given. Occasionally, very minor changes--the
presence or absence of "a" or "the," for example--may be
undocumented. In order to simplify and shorten the presentation, common, often lengthy prefaces are replaced with el-
lipses after the initial item (e.g., Tables 3.2-3.27). The
table of contents, and usually the items themselves, make it
clear when a series is based on the same intial wording.

In a few instances, we show trends for alternative
wordings about the same subject. These make the point about
the sensitivity of public opinion to question wording but also
provide added insight into changes in opinion over time.

What cannot be captured in a large-scale compendium is
the questionnaire context, the nature of the items that preceeded the one in question. Most context effects are probably fairly small and large effects are fairly rare, but it is
something to keep in mind in detailed analyses of individual

survey entries (Schuman and Presser, 1981, chap. 2; Smith, 1988).

Month of Survey. GSS surveys are described as taking place in March, since that is when most of the interviews are conducted. Michigan election study surveys are listed as "autumn" because pre-election interviews begin in September and post-election interviews are not completed until December or later. Most surveys by commercial organizations are conducted in a much shorter period of time, so the month listed is a fairly precise indicator of the timing of the survey. Surveys that bridge the end of one month and beginning of another are listed according to the month that includes most of the survey dates.

Results. The results in each row--that is, for each survey reported--theoretically add to 100 percent. Use of whole numbers often leads to sums of 99 or 101 percent; on occasion, sums of 98 or 102 percent occur.

The percentages are based on all valid responses, including responses of "don't know" (DK). Distributions with "DK's" excluded can be found through simple repercentaging.

"Don't know" responses include those reported as "don't know," "no opinion," or "unsure." However, for issue questions for which there was an explicit filter, those reporting that they had "never thought about the issue" are listed separately.

Results are rounded to whole numbers, with a "0" indicating less than 0.5 percent (but more than zero cases). A "-" indicates zero cases.

N. The *N* reported is that on which the percentage is based. It is typically the number of cases in the sample minus missing data. Since "DK's" are included in the results, missing data are limited to NA's ("not ascertained" or "not answered," those for whom information should have been obtained but was not) and occasional "other" responses. In a few early surveys, the exact *N* could not be determined. In these cases, an approximate *N*, prefaced by "c," is given.

Where filter questions are involved, a line at the top of the table indicates whether the percentages are for the entire sample or for some subsample. In either case, the *N* remains the number of cases on which the percentages are based.

In the case of Gallup surveys conducted in 1961-1967, weighted *N*'s are sometimes reported. Weighted *N*'s are appropriate bases for percentages but would be inappropriate if one were to use them as a basis for tests of statistical significance.

Survey Organization. The following is a list of abbreviations used and the surveys or survey organizations they refer to. In most instances the survey number is indicated;

in a few cases, an abbreviated label is used to indicate the specific survey.

ABC/WP--American Broadcasting Corporation/*Washington Post* Poll
AIPO--American Institute of Public Opinion (Gallup Poll)
AUDITS--Audits and Surveys
BG--a special survey conducted by the Gallup Poll
BSSR--Bureau for Social Science Research, Columbia University
CBS/NYT--Columbia Broadcasting System/*New York Times* Poll
CNS--Continuing National Survey of the National Opinion Re-
    search Center
ELEC--National Election Studies, Institute for Social Re-
    search, University of Michigan
GO--Survey by Gallup organization, not part of AIPO series
GSS--General Social Surveys
HARRIS--The Harris Survey
LAT--*Los Angeles Times* Poll
NBC/AP--National Broadcasting Company/Associated Press Poll
NBC/WSJ--National Broadcasting Company/*Wall Street Journal*
NORC--National Opinion Research Center. This abbreviation
    refers to studies conducted by NORC other than the General
    Social Surveys
NUNN--Survey conduced by Response Analysis for Nunn, Crockett,
    and Williams, 1978
OPOR--Office of Public Opinion Research
ORCO--Opinion Research Corporation
PA--Potomac Associates
POS--Public Opinion Survey, by the Gallup Poll
RAC--Response Analysis Corporation
RFOR--Roper Organization, for *Fortune* magazine
ROPER--Roper Organization
SRC--Survey Research Center, University of Michigan
SRS--Survey Research Service of the National Opinion Research
    Center
STOUFFER--Surveys conducted by NORC and AIPO for Stouffer
    (1955)

ADDITIONAL SOURCES OF OVER-TIME SURVEY DATA

The following list includes published volumes and data respositories that are useful sources of over-time public opinion data:

American Public Opinion Index, Boston: Opinion Research
    Service, annual since 1981--A useful compilation because
    it lists small polls as well as the major national polls.
    However, it sometimes paraphrases question wording.

American National Election Studies Data Sourcebook, 1952-1978,
     Warren E. Miller, Arthur H. Miller and Edward J. Schneider,
     compilers; American Social Attitudes Data Sourcebook, 1947-
     1978, Philip E. Converse, Jean D. Dotson, Wendy H. Hoag,
     and William H. McGee, compliers. 1980. Cambridge: Harvard
     University Press--Compendia of results from studies con-
     ducted by the Institute for Social Research of the Univer-
     sity of Michigan. (Updated sourcebook may be published in
     the near future.) The election study staff also publishes
     the Continuity Guide, an index to repeated questions in the
     election study series.
The Gallup Poll--A multivolume set reporting selected poll
     results, including many breakdowns by demographic categor-
     ies. 1935-1971, 3 vols.; 1972-1977, 2 vols.; published
     annually since 1978 by Scholarly Resources, Wilmington,
     DE.
The Gallup Report--A monthly report of recent Gallup Poll re-
     sults. Reports often focus on a single theme and typically
     feature trends as well as detailed reports of current sur-
     veys.
The Harris Poll--Short news releases, published weekly or
     more often.
Inter-University Consortium for Political and Social Research
     --a partnership between the University of Michigan and over
     300 universities around the world. ICPSR maintains and
     disseminates more than a thousand sets of survey data and
     related data such as election results and congressional
     roll calls. The focus is on academic surveys, but some
     commercial polls (e.g., election day "exit" polls) are also
     maintained. Publishes an annual Guide to Resources and
     Services.
POLL (Public Opinion Location Laboratory) Database--a computer
     data base with over 100,000 questions from the Roper Cen-
     ter.
Public Opinion Quarterly--A journal of academic research on
     survey results and survey methodology. Trends are regu-
     larly reported in a section titled "The Polls."
Public Opinion--A magazine devoted chiefly to analysis of
     public opinion on current topics. The "Opinion Round-up"
     section reports survey data on one or more topics, with an
     emphasis on current surveys but with some trend data as
     well.
Public Opinion 1935-1946. Hadley Cantril and Mildred Strunk,
     compilers. 1951. Princeton: Princeton University Press.
Sourcebook of Harris National Surveys: Repeated Questions
     1963-1976. Elizabeth Martin, Diana McDuffee, and Stanley
     Press, compilers. 1981. Chapel Hill: Institute for Re-
     search in Social Sciences, University of North Carolina--
     an index to repeated questions in Harris surveys.

REFERENCES

Bishop, George G., Robert W. Oldendick, Alfred J. Tuchfarber, and Stephen E. Bennett. 1980. Pseudo Opinions on Public Affairs. *Public Opinion Quarterly*, 44:198-209.

Converse, Philip E. 1964. The Nature of Belief Systems in Mass Publics. In David E. Apter, ed. *Ideology and Discontent*. New York: Free Press.

Gallup, George. 1972. *The Gallup Poll*. New York: Random House.

Gilboa, Eytan. 1987. *American Public Opinion toward Israel and the Arab-Israeli Conflict*. Lexington, MA: Heath.

Glenn, Norval D. 1974. Trend Studies with Available Survey Data: Opportunities and Pitfalls. In *Survey Data for Trend Analysis*. Williamstown, MA: Roper Public Opinion Research Center.

Mueller, John. 1973. *War, Presidents and Public Policy*. New York: Wiley (reprinted 1985 by University Press of America).

Newcomb, Theodore M., Kathryn E. Koenig, Richard Flacks, and Donald P. Warwick. 1967. *Persistence and Change*. New York: Wiley.

Nunn, Clyde Z., Harry J. Crockett and J. Allen Williams. 1978. *Tolerance for Nonconformity*. San Francisco: Jossey-Bass.

Presser, Stanley. 1981. The Harris Data Center, Harris National Surveys, and Trend Analysis. In Elizabeth Martin, Diana McDuffee, and Stanley Presser, *Sourcebook of Harris National Surveys: Repeated Questions 1963-1976*. Chapel Hill: Institute for Research in Social Science, University of North Carolina.

Roper, Burns. 1984. Obituary to George Gallup. *AAPORNEWS*, 12:6.

Schuman, Howard. 1986. Ordinary Questions, Survey Questions. *Public Opinion Quarterly*, 50:432-442.

Schuman, Howard, and Jacqueline Scott. 1987. Problems in the Use of Survey Questions to Measure Public Opinion. *Science*, 236:957-959.

Schuman, Howard, and Stanley Presser. 1981. *Questions and Answers in Attitude Surveys*. New York: Academic Press.

Smith, Tom W. 1988. Timely Artifacts: A Review of Measurement Variation in the 1972-1988 GSS. GSS Methodological Report No. 56. National Opinion Research Center, University of Chicago.

Stephenson, C. Bruce. 1979. Probability Sampling with Quotas: An Experiment. *Public Opinion Quarterly*, 43:477-496.

Stouffer, Samuel A. 1955. *Communism, Conformity, and Civil Liberties*. Garden City, NY: Doubleday.

Survey Data for Trend Analysis. 1974. Williamstown, MA: Roper Public Opinion Research Center.

1

Politics

To many people, surveys are synonymous with political polling and have been since the inception of scientific polls in the 1930s. It is not surprising, therefore, that there exists a considerable amount of over-time data about political subjects. The time series are especially long and complete with respect to party identification and the nation's "most important problem." But very interesting time series also exist with respect to voting for certain kinds of individuals for president on both general and specific questions of governmental responsibilities. An additional concept--liberalism/conservatism--is mostly a recent discovery, though some early measurements exist.

Here we trace party identification in two series, the first beginning in 1952 and the second in 1972 (Table 1.1).[1] For more than twelve years, through 1964, there was relatively little movement in the distribution. The number of "apoliticals" declined as blacks, especially in the South, began to feel more involved in the party system,[2] but there were no significant changes in the proportions of Republicans, Democrats, and independents. By 1966, the number of independents

---

[1]Gallup data extend back to 1937, and by using recall questions about changes in the past, partisanship has been reconstructed back into the 1920s (Andersen, 1979). However, considerable caution is necessary in interpreting such extrapolations, because changes are often poorly remembered and because the recall questions tend to ignore changes involving the independent category (Niemi, Katz, and Newman, 1980).

[2]Prior to 1960, the partisanship question was evidently meaningless to as many as a fourth of southern blacks (Converse, 1966).

had begun to climb, reaching a high point in both series of close to 40 percent in the late 1970s.[3]

In the last eight to ten years, two important changes, and possibly a third, have taken place. First, the number of independents has declined, though it is still well above the levels of the 1950s. Second, along with the widely noted decline in partisan attitudes and behavior, a greater proportion of the electorate might again be regarded as apolitical (Miller and Wattenberg, 1983; Craig, 1985).

The third change is that the proportion of Republican identifiers may have gone up, at least relative to the proportion of Democratic identifiers. The possible resurgence of Republicans is much debated (see, for example, Norpoth, 1987). For one thing, the proportion of Republican versus Democratic partisans is affected in the short run by presidential elections (Borrelli, Lockerbie, and Niemi, 1987; Converse, 1976, pp. 123-130). Because all elections in the 1980s were won by Republicans, at least those polls conducted near the elections may show temporarily higher Republican percentages. In any event, judging by the series in Table 1.1, the reshuffling has been fairly minor, with self-identified Democrats still holding a commanding lead over Republicans.

Self-described liberalism or conservatism of the American population has been regularly determined only for about fifteen years. Gallup asked whether "you regard yourself as a liberal or conservative" as early as 1938, but the subject was seldom included in surveys; when it was, the question format varied. Hence, time series typically extend back only to the early to mid-1970s. Now, however, it is a staple of political surveys. (Multiple time series are reported in Robinson and Fleishman, 1988.)

In Tables 1.2 and 1.3, we present two versions of the question. One version (1.3) is filtered, inquiring whether respondents have thought much about the matter. With a fifth to as many as a third of the respondents admitting that they have not, the question is a reasonable one. Most surveys, however, implicitly assume that the concept has at least some degree of meaning for all respondents. In either case, there has been remarkably little change in the distributions over the past fifteen years, despite the Reagan victories on an explicitly conservative agenda and the success with which George Bush painted Michael Dukakis's liberalism as a strongly negative feature.

---

[3]Converse (1976) thoroughly analyzed the timing of the increase in the number of independents, tracing it to 1965.

Changing social attitudes are well documented by the
series of questions about whether one would vote for a woman,
a black, or other minority for president. What is perhaps
surprising in the first such table (1.4) is that in 1988
slightly more than 10 percent of the population still claim
that they would not vote for a "qualified" female. The distributions by sex are also quite fascinating. In the 1930s
and 1940s and into the 1950s, men were consistently more likely to say they would not vote for a woman. Since the late
1950s, in contrast, women themselves have been more likely to
say a female should not be president.

In other tables (1.5-1.13), the nation's changing attitudes and prejudices show through clearly. A large majority
--though never more than four-fifths--now say they would vote
for a qualified black.[4] A homosexual, at least in 1978, would
not fare well. In the 1960s, quite a few people said they
would not vote for a divorced male, but this attitude changed
in the 1970s, and in the 1980s little was made of the fact
that President Reagan had divorced and remarried. Religious
prejudices, at least insofar as presidential voting are concerned, have lessened over time, perhaps especially as a
result of John Kennedy's victory in 1960. With 25 percent of
the electorate in 1959 saying they would not vote for a
Catholic (1.10), one suspects that this is a case where what
people say and do are not always the same. It may be,
however, that an avowed atheist would still have a difficult
time being attracting votes (1.13).

The next two sets of tables show responses to questions
about perceived governmental policies and responsibilities.
In the 1930s, 1940s, and 1950s, questions about governmental
ownership of "basic" industries were seriously debated. And
if the results of surveys in the late 1930s are taken at face
value, more than half of all adults had some preference for
governmental ownership of electric power (1.14) and well over
a third favored governmental ownership of banks (1.16). By
1940, governmental ownership was less in vogue on these two
items, and there appeared to be a dip in support for at least
three of the items in the 1950s. Still, relatively high
levels of support for governmental ownership were sustained
right up until the time such questions were dropped in the
early 1960s.

More recent questions about the scope of governmental
responsibilities show an interesting pattern. If one looks
only at the last ten years, there is no systematic movement
on any of the items, but there was a substantial change in

---

[4]The decline in 1988 of willingness to vote for a qualified black candidate may reflect feelings specifically about
Jesse Jackson's candidacy.

the mid-1970s.   Both on the general question about "doing things that should be left to individuals" (1.18) and on three of the specific items (1.20-1.22), there was a decline in support for more governmental action.   Similarly, there was increased concern that the government was getting too powerful (1.19), at least until President Reagan entered office.   These changes are consistent with the view of the 1960s and 1970s as a time of expanding scope of government and of the 1980s as one of more self-reliance and contraction of government. The opposite is true, however, for the items about doctor and hospital bills (1.23).   Rising medical costs and perhaps an aging population have led to a desire for governmental action in this one domain.

The final series in this chapter is the fifty-year history of responses to question about the nation's most important problems.[5]   The specific questions have varied over the years--alternatively referring to "the government," "the U.S. government," "the government in Washington," "this country," and "the American people."   These changes notwithstanding, the responses reflect our international involvement in World War II, Korea, and Vietnam, numerous ups and downs of the economy, the civil rights struggles of the 1960s, and such specific events as Watergate and the oil crisis of 1973-1974. As such, it is an indelible record--unlike any other--of the concerns of the general population over a half century of history.

REFERENCES

Andersen, Kristi. 1979. *The Creation of a Democratic Majority*, 1928-1936. Chicago: University of Chicago Press.
Borrelli, Stephen, Brad Lockerbie, and Richard G. Niemi. 1987. Why the Democrat-Republican Partisanship Gap Varies from Poll to Poll. *Public Opinion Quarterly*, 51:115-119.
Converse, Philip E. 1966. On the Possibility of Major Political Realignment in the South. In Angus Campbell, Philip E. Converse, Warren E. Miller, and Donald E. Stokes. *Elections and the Political Order*. New York: Wiley.
Converse, Philip E. 1976. *The Dynamics of Party Support*. Beverly Hills, CA: Sage.
Craig, Stephen C. 1985. Partisanship, Independence, and No Preference: Another Look at the Measurement of Party Identification. *American Political Science Review*, 29: 274-290.

---

[5]Table 1.24 updates Part I of Smith (1985). See also Part II on regional, community, and personal problems.

Miller, Arthur H., and Martin P. Wattenberg. 1983. Measuring Party Identification: Independent or No Partisan Preference? *American Political Science Review*, 27:106-121.

Niemi, Richard G., Richard S. Katz, and David Newman. 1980. Reconstructing Past Partisanship: The Failure of the Party Identification Questions. *American Journal of Political Science*, 24:633-651.

Norpoth, Helmut. 1987. Underway and Here to Stay: Party Realignment in the 1980s? *Public Opinion Quarterly*, 51:376-391.

Robinson, John P., and John A. Fleishman. 1988. Ideological Identification: Trends and Interpretations of the Liberal-Conservative Balance. *Public Opinion Quarterly*, 52:134-145.

Smith, Tom W. 1985. America's Most Important Problems. Part I: National and International; Part II: Regional Community, and Personal. *Public Opinion Quarterly*, 49: 264-274, 403-410.

Table 1.1 Party Identification--1952-1988

PARTYID--Generally speaking, do you usually think of yourself as a Republican, Democrat, Independent, or what? [IF REPUBLICAN OR DEMOCRAT]: Would you call yourself a strong (Republican/Democrat) or not a very strong (Republican/Democrat)? [IF INDEPENDENT, NO PREFERENCE, OR OTHER]: Do you think of yourself as closer to the Republican or Democratic Party?

Michigan (National Election Studies) Series

	STRONG DEMOCRAT	NOT STRONG DEMOCRAT	INDEPENDENT NEAR DEMOCRAT	INDE- PENDENT	INDEPENDENT NEAR REPUBLICAN	NOT STRONG REPUBLICAN	STRONG REPUBLICAN	APOLIT- ICAL	N
Aut 1952	22	25	10	6	7	14	14	3	1784
Aut 1954	22	26	9	7	6	14	13	4	1130
Aut 1956	21	23	6	9	8	14	15	4	1757
Aut 1958	27	22	7	7	5	17	11	4	1808
Aut 1960	20	25	6	10	7	14	16	3	1911
Aut 1962	23	23	7	8	6	16	12	4	1287
Aut 1964	27	25	9	8	6	14	11	1	1550
Aut 1966	18	28	9	12	7	15	10	1	1278
Aut 1968	20	25	10	11	9	15	10	1	1553
Aut 1970	20	24	10	13	8	15	9	1	1501
Aut 1972	15	26	11	13	8	13	10	1	2694
Aut 1974	18	21	13	15	11	14	8	3	2505
Aut 1976	15	25	12	15	9	14	9	1	2850
Aut 1978	15	24	14	14	10	13	8	3	2283
Aut 1980	18	23	11	13	10	14	9	2	1613
Aut 1982	20	24	11	11	8	14	10	2	1418
Aut 1984	17	20	11	11	12	15	12	2	2236
Aut 1986	18	22	10	12	11	15	10	2	2166

	STRONG DEMOCRAT	NOT STRONG DEMOCRAT	INDEPENDENT NEAR DEMOCRAT	INDE- PENDENT	INDEPENDENT NEAR REPUBLICAN	NOT STRONG REPUBLICAN	STRONG REPUBLICAN	OTHER PARTY, REFUSED TO SAY	N
Mar 1972	20	27	10	10	6	14	8	4	1607
Mar 1973	15	26	13	10	9	15	8	4	1493
Mar 1974	17	25	14	10	7	15	7	4	1471
Mar 1975	17	24	14	14	8	16	6	1	1485
Mar 1976	15	27	14	16	7	14	6	0	1495
Mar 1977	18	26	13	12	9	15	7	1	1518
Mar 1978	14	25	13	14	9	16	7	1	1527
Mar 1980	13	26	13	17	8	15	8	1	1465
Mar 1982	16	25	13	13	10	14	9	1	1501
Mar 1983	15	24	14	12	9	16	9	1	1593
Mar 1984	18	19	14	11	11	17	9	2	1465
Mar 1985	16	23	10	10	10	17	12	1	1529
Mar 1986	17	23	11	13	10	16	10	1	1467
Mar 1987	19	21	11	11	10	17	10	1	1459
Mar 1988	16	21	12	13	9	19	10	0	1481
WHITES									
Mar 1972	15	26	11	11	7	16	9	4	1349
Mar 1973	13	24	13	10	10	16	9	4	1312
Mar 1974	15	24	14	10	8	16	8	4	1291
Mar 1975	14	23	15	15	9	17	7	1	1324
Mar 1976	14	26	14	17	8	15	7	0	1366
Mar 1977	16	26	13	12	9	16	8	0	1343
Mar 1978	12	25	13	14	9	17	8	1	1369
Mar 1980	10	25	14	17	9	16	8	1	1327
Mar 1982	12	24	14	14	10	15	10	1	1345

17

Table 1.1 (Continued)

	STRONG DEMOCRAT	NOT STRONG DEMOCRAT	INDEPENDENT NEAR DEMOCRAT	INDE-PENDENT	INDEPENDENT NEAR REPUBLICAN	NOT STRONG REPUBLICAN	STRONG REPUBLICAN	OTHER PARTY, REFUSED TO SAY	N
Mar 1983	13	24	13	12	9	18	10	1	1428
Mar 1984	15	19	14	11	12	18	10	2	1297
Mar 1985	13	22	10	10	11	19	14	1	1379
Mar 1986	14	22	11	13	11	18	11	1	1283
Mar 1987	14	21	11	12	10	19	12	1	1271
Mar 1988	12	20	12	12	11	21	11	0	1234
BLACKS									
Mar 1972	48	30	5	5	0	5	1	5	258
Mar 1973	34	35	11	7	2	4	3	5	181
Mar 1974	30	34	14	5	2	8	3	5	170
Mar 1975	42	29	8	11	1	6	2	1	161
Mar 1976	32	35	14	11	2	4	2	–	129
Mar 1977	37	31	11	12	2	3	3	–	175
Mar 1978	31	33	11	14	4	6	1	–	158
Mar 1980	38	32	9	13	3	4	1	1	138
Mar 1982	46	33	8	6	3	3	1	1	156
Mar 1983	34	28	16	13	4	2	–	1	165
Mar 1984	45	20	15	10	3	6	1	1	168
Mar 1985	41	31	12	7	4	2	1	–	150
Mar 1986	38	32	9	11	5	2	3	–	184
Mar 1987	47	22	11	10	4	5	1	–	188
Mar 1988	41	26	12	11	3	5	2	0	186

NOTE--GSS: In 1972-74 and 1976, those responding "Other" were not asked the "closer to" question. In 1975 and 1977-1988 and after, those answering "Other" and the new response, "No preference," were asked the "closer to" question.

Table 1.2 Liberal or Conservative Self-Identification--1974-1988

POLVIEWS--We hear a lot of talk these days about liberals and conservatives. I'm going to show you a seven-point scale on which the political views that people might hold are arranged from extremely liberal--point 1--to extremely conservative--point 7. Where would you place yourself on this scale?

	EXTREMELY LIBERAL	LIBERAL	SLIGHTLY LIBERAL	MODERATE	SLIGHTLY CONSERVATIVE	CONSERVATIVE	EXTREMELY CONSERVATIVE	DK	N
Mar 1974	1	14	14	38	15	11	2	5	1480
Mar 1975	3	12	13	38	16	10	2	5	1478
Mar 1976	2	13	12	37	15	13	2	6	1494
Mar 1977	2	11	14	37	16	12	3	5	1524
Mar 1978	1	9	16	36	17	12	2	5	1505
Mar 1980	2	8	14	40	18	12	3	2	1451
Mar 1982	2	9	15	39	14	13	4	4	1495
Mar 1983	2	8	12	40	18	13	2	4	801
Mar 1984	2	9	12	39	19	13	3	4	1462
Mar 1985	2	11	11	37	18	14	3	4	1525
Mar 1986	2	9	12	39	16	14	3	5	1468
Mar 1987	2	12	13	37	16	12	2	4	1437
Mar 1988	2	12	13	35	17	15	2	4	1472
WHITES									
Mar 1974	2	13	15	40	17	12	2		1256
Mar 1975	3	12	13	41	17	11	2		1253
Mar 1976	2	12	13	40	16	14	2		1292
Mar 1977	2	11	15	40	18	12	2		1296
Mar 1978	1	10	16	38	19	13	2		1297
Mar 1980	2	8	15	40	19	13	3		1292
Mar 1982	2	9	14	42	15	15	4		1289

19

Table 1.2 (Continued)

	EXTREMELY LIBERAL	LIBERAL	SLIGHTLY LIBERAL	MODERATE	SLIGHTLY CONSERVATIVE	CONSERVATIVE	EXTREMELY CONSERVATIVE	DK	N
Mar 1983	1	9	12	41	19	15	2		694
Mar 1984	2	9	13	40	21	14	2		1258
Mar 1985	2	10	12	39	19	15	3		1330
Mar 1986	2	9	12	42	18	16	3		1235
Mar 1987	2	12	13	40	17	14	2		1210
Mar 1988	2	11	12	37	18	17	2		1190
BLACKS									
Mar 1974	1	27	14	36	8	10	3		154
Mar 1975	7	19	21	29	12	7	4		144
Mar 1976	1	30	16	38	8	6	1		109
Mar 1977	7	17	15	33	13	11	4		157
Mar 1978	4	12	21	41	9	11	2		138
Mar 1980	8	10	11	44	12	10	5		137
Mar 1982	5	17	24	33	11	6	4		140
Mar 1983	8	8	16	42	16	5	5		76
Mar 1984	5	14	12	43	10	10	7		152
Mar 1985	6	17	14	39	11	7	6		132
Mar 1986	4	15	13	39	16	10	2		166
Mar 1987	5	21	17	33	16	7	2		168
Mar 1988	5	23	20	29	13	8	3		173

Table 1.3 Liberal or Conservative Self-Identification, Filtered Version--1972-1986

POLVIEWY--We hear a lot of talk these days about liberals and conservatives. I'm going to show you a seven-point scale on which the political views that people might hold are arranged from ex- tremely liberal--point 1--to extremely conservative--point 7. Where would you place yourself on this scale, or haven't you thought much about this?

	EXTREMELY LIBERAL	LIB	SLIGHTLY LIBERAL	MOD	SLIGHTLY CONS	CONS	EXTREMELY CONS	DK	HAVEN'T THOUGHT ABOUT IT	N	
Aut 1972	1	7	10	27	15	10	1	6	22	2155	ELEC72
Aut 1974	2	11	8	26	12	12	2	5	22	2478	ELEC74
Aut 1976	1	7	8	25	12	11	2	6	27	2841	ELEC76
Mar 1978	2	9	14	31	15	10	1	2	16	768	GSS
Aut 1978	2	8	10	27	14	11	2	4	23	2284	ELEC78
Aut 1980	2	6	9	20	13	13	2	4	32	1565	ELEC80
Aut 1982	1	6	8	22	13	12	2	2	34	1400	ELEC82
Aut 1984	2	8	9	23	14	13	2	4	26	2229	ELEC84
Aut 1986	1	6	11	28	15	13	2	3	21	2170	ELEC86

Table 1.4   Would You Vote for a Woman for President?--
             1936-1988

FEPRES--If your party nominated a woman for president, would
you vote for her if she were qualified for the job?

	YES	NO	DK	N	
1936[a]	31	65	4	c1500	AIPO
Jan 1937[a]	34	63	3	2834	AIPO66
Dec 1945[b]	33	55	12	2817	AIPO360
Sep 1949[c]	50	47	4	1440	AIPO448
Feb 1955[b]	52	44	4	1576	AIPO543
Sep 1958[d]	54	41	5	1506	AIPO604
Dec 1959[d]	57	39	4	1519	AIPO622
Aug 1963	55	40	4	1588	AIPO676
Apr 1967	57	39	4	1505	AIPO744
Mar 1969	54	39	7	1633	AIPO776
Jul 1971	66	29	5	1531	AIPO834
Mar 1972	70	25	5	1611	GSS
Mar 1974	78	19	3	1479	GSS
Mar 1975	78	19	3	1489	GSS
Aug 1975	74	23	4	1515	AIPO934
Mar 1977	77	20	3	1526	GSS
Mar 1978	79	18	3	1532	GSS
Jul 1978	75	20	5	1555	AIPO107G
Jul 1981	81	14	4	1076	BSSR
Mar 1982	83	13	3	1504	GSS
Mar 1983	84	13	3	1595	GSS
Apr 1983	80	16	4	1517	A213G
Jul 1984	78	17	5	1579	A239G
Mar 1985	80	17	3	1528	GSS
Mar 1986	84	13	3	1466	GSS
Mar 1988	86	12	3	985	GSS

WOMEN

	YES	NO	DK	N	
Jan 1937[a]	41	57	2	1420	AIPO66
Nov 1945[b]	37	51	12	1439	AIPO360
Sep 1949[b]	52	45	3	741	AIPO448
Feb 1955[b]	56	40	3	784	AIPO543
Sep 1958[c]	53	42	5	782	AIPO604
Dec 1959[c]	55	40	4	759	AIPO622
Aug 1963[c]	53	43	4	816	AIPO676
Apr 1967	53	44	3	759	AIPO744
Mar 1969	50	42	7	817	AIPO776
Jul 1971	66	28	5	774	AIPO834
Mar 1972	71	25	4	805	GSS
Mar 1974	77	19	4	791	GSS
Mar 1975	76	20	3	820	GSS
Mar 1977	75	22	3	835	GSS
Mar 1978	78	19	3	889	GSS
Jul 1978	76	20	5	763	AIPO107G
Mar 1982	84	13	3	866	GSS
Mar 1983	84	13	2	908	GSS
Mar 1985	78	19	3	844	GSS

Table 1.4 (Continued)

	YES	NO	DK	N	
Mar 1986	82	15	3	848	GSS
Mar 1988	84	13	3	549	GSS

MEN

	YES	NO	DK	N	
Jan 1937[a]	28	69	4	1414	AIPO66
Nov 1945[b]	29	58	13	1378	AIPO360
Sep 1949[b]	47	49	4	699	AIPO448
Feb 1955[b]	47	48	5	792	AIPO543
Sep 1958[c]	55	40	5	724	AIPO604
Dec 1959[c]	59	37	4	760	AIPO622
Aug 1963[c]	58	38	4	772	AIPO676
Apr 1967	61	34	5	746	AIPO744
Mar 1969	58	35	7	816	AIPO776
Jul 1971	65	29	6	757	AIPO834
Mar 1972	70	25	6	806	GSS
Mar 1974	78	19	2	688	GSS
Mar 1975	80	17	3	669	GSS
Mar 1977	80	18	2	691	GSS
Mar 1978	81	16	2	643	GSS
Jul 1978	75	21	4	792	AIPO107G
Mar 1982	83	14	3	638	GSS
Mar 1983	83	13	4	687	GSS
Mar 1985	82	14	3	684	GSS
Mar 1986	87	11	3	618	GSS
Mar 1988	88	10	2	436	GSS

[a]Would you vote for a woman for President if she qualified in every other respect?

[b]If the party whose candidate you most often support nominated a woman for President of the United States, would you vote for her if she seemed best qualified for the job?

[c]If the party whose candidate you most often support nominated a woman for President of the United States, would you vote for her if she seemed qualified for the job?

[d]If your party nominated a woman for President, would you vote for her if she seemed qualified for the job?

NOTE--Questions about presidential qualifications (Tables 1.4-1.13) were usually preceeded by a statement such as "Between now and 1960, there will be much discussion about the qualifications of the president." These have been omitted.

ALBRIGHT COLLEGE LIBRARY   225366

Table 1.5   Would You Vote for a Black for President?--
            1958-1988

RACPRES--If your party nominated a (Negro/black) for president, would you vote for him if he were qualified for the
job?

	YES	NO	DK	N	
WHITES ONLY					
Jul 1958[a]	37	53	10	1610	AIPO602
Sep 1958[a]	38	54	8	1510	AIPO604
Sep 1959[a]	49	46	5	1523	AIPO622
Aug 1961[a]	52	41	8	1532	AIPO649
Aug 1963[a]	48	45	7	1579	AIPO676
Jul 1965[a]	59	34	7	1590	AIPO714
Apr 1967[a]	53	41	6	1505	AIPO744
Mar 1969[a]	67	23	10	1634	AIPO776
Aug 1971[a]	70	24	7	1503	AIPO838
Mar 1972	69	25	6	1349	GSS
Mar 1974	78	18	4	1308	GSS
Mar 1975	77	17	6	1327	GSS
Mar 1977	75	22	4	1347	GSS
Mar 1978	80	16	4	1360	GSS
Jul 1978[b]	66	18	5	1394	AIP107G
Mar 1982	81	13	6	1347	GSS
Mar 1983	81	15	4	1428	GSS
Mar 1983[b]	77	16	7	c1365	AIPO211G
Mar 1985	80	16	4	1374	GSS
Mar 1986	84	14	6	1282	GSS
Mar 1988	75	19	5	858	GSS
BLACKS ONLY					
Mar 1974	93	4	4	171	GSS
Mar 1978	95	4	1	157	GSS
Mar 1982	97	3	-	156	GSS
Mar 1983	92	5	3	164	GSS
Mar 1985	95	1	3	150	GSS
Mar 1986	95	3	2	184	GSS
Mar 1988	98	2	-	125	GSS

[a]If your party nominated a generally well-qualified man for
president and he happened to be Negro, would you vote for
him?

[b]Same as in note a but uses black instead of Negro.

Table 1.6   Would You Vote for a Homosexual for President?--
             1978

If your party nominated a generally well-qualified man for
president and he happened to be a homosexual, would you vote
for him?

	YES	NO	DK	N	
Jul 1978	26	66	9	1555	AIPO107G

Table 1.7   Would You Vote for a Divorced Man for President?
             --1961-1978

If your party nominated a generally well-qualified man for
president and he happened to be divorced, would you vote for
him?

	YES	NO	DK	N	
Dec 1961[a]	76	17	7	2962	AIPO653
May 1963[a]	74	20	6	3865	AIPO671
Aug 1963	79	17	5	3559	AIPO676
Jul 1965	83	14	3	3524	AIPO714
Apr 1967	86	10	5	3516	AIPO744
Jul 1978	84	9	7	1555	AIPO107G

[a]Suppose a candidate for president is divorced. Would that
make any difference in your attitude toward voting for him,
provided he is well qualified otherwise?

Table 1.8   Would You Vote for a Baptist for President?--
1958-1967

If your party nominated a generally well-qualified man for president and he happened to be a Baptist, would you vote for him?

	YES	NO	DK	N	
Sep 1958	93	4	4	1497	AIPO604
Dec 1959	94	3	2	1523	AIPO622
Apr 1967	95	3	2	3519	AIPO744

Table 1.9   Would You Vote for a Jew for President?--
1937-1987

If your party nominated a generally well-qualified man for president and he happened to be a Jew, would you vote for him?

	YES	NO	DK	N	
Feb 1937[a]	46	47	8	2877	AIPO68
Jul 1958	62	28	10	1610	AIPO602
Sep 1958	63	29	7	1498	AIPO604
Dec 1959	72	22	6	1522	AIPO622
Aug 1961	68	23	9	3156	AIPO649
Aug 1963	77	17	6	3551	AIPO676
Jul 1965	80	15	5	3524	AIPO714
Apr 1967	82	13	5	3519	AIPO744
Mar 1969	87	7	6	1630	AIPO776
Jul 1978	81	13	6	1555	AIPO107G
Apr 1983	89	7	4	1517	AIPO213G
Aug 1987	89	6	5	1607	AIPO278G

[a]Would you vote for a Jew for president who was well qualified for this position?

Table 1.10   Would You Vote for a Catholic for President?--
1937-1983

If your party nominated a generally well-qualified man for
president and he happened to be a Catholic, would you vote
for him?

	YES	NO	DK	N	
Sep 1937[a]	60	30	10	2930	AIPO67
Mar 1940[b]	60	33	6	1646	AIPO188K
Mar 1940[a]	61	31	7	1602	AIPO188T
Jan 1955[c]	69	23	8	1456	AIPO542
May 1956[b]	72	22	5	1963	AIPO565
Apr 1958[b]	70	23	7	1435	AIPO598
May 1958[b]	72	23	6	1621	AIPO599
Jul 1958[b]	69	24	7	1619	AIPO602
Sep 1958	67	27	6	1494	AIPO604
Apr 1959	70	21	9	1724	AIPO612
Nov 1959	69	20	11	1500	AIPO620
Dec 1959	70	25	5	1520	AIPO622
May 1960[b]	71	21	8	3010	AIPO628
Aug 1961	82	13	5	3156	AIPO649
Aug 1963	84	13	3	3553	AIPO676
Jul 1965	87	10	3	3524	AIPO714
Apr 1967	90	8	2	3519	AIPO744
Mar 1969	89	7	5	1634	AIPO776
Jul 1978	91	5	4	1555	AIPO107G
Apr 1983	92	5	2	1517	AIPO213G

[a]Would you vote for a Catholic for president who was well
qualified for this position?

[b]As in note a except "...for president this year and
who...."

[c]As in note a except "...for president in 1956 and...."

Table 1.11 Would You Vote for a Quaker for President?--1967

If your party nominated a generally well-qualified man for president and he happened to be a Quaker, would you vote for him?

	YES	NO	DK	N	
Apr 1967	78	15	7	3519	AIPO744

Table 1.12 Would You Vote for a Mormon for President?--1967

If your party nominated a generally well-qualified man for president and he happened to be a Mormon, would you vote for him?

	YES	NO	DK	N	
Apr 1967	75	17	8	3519	AIPO744

Table 1.13 Would You Vote for an Atheist for President?--
         1958-1987

If your party nominated a generally well-qualified man for president and he happened to be an atheist, would you vote for him?

	YES	NO	DK	N	
Sep 1958	18	77	5	1497	AIPO604
Dec 1959	22	74	5	1517	AIPO622
Jul 1978	39	54	7	1555	AIPO107G
Apr 1983	42	51	6	1517	AIPO213G
Apr 1987	44	48	8	1607	AIPO278G

Table 1.14 Should the U.S. Government Own the Electric
Power Companies?--1937-1961

Do you think the United States government should own the
following things in this country:

Electric power companies?

	YES	NO	DK	N	
Jan 1937[a]	59	29	12	2855	AIPO66
Jan 1938[a]	55	34	11	1442	AIPO109A
Jan 1938[a]	54	35	12	1418	AIPO109B
Jul 1940[b]	30	49	20	1609	AIPO204K
Jul 1940[c]	32	52	16	1439	AIPO204T
Aug 1940[b]	32	44	24	1038	OPOR302K
Aug 1940[b]	34	44	21	1066	OPOR302T
May 1945[d]	29	50	21	1539	AIPO349T
Sep 1945[e]	26	63	11	1657	AIPO355K
Sep 1945[e]	28	60	12	1419	AIPO355T
Jan 1947	28	66	6	1463	AIPO387K
Jan 1947	27	66	7	1461	AIPO387T
Mar 1947[f]	26	58	16	1427	AIPO392K
Mar 1947[e]	24	62	14	1430	AIPO392T
May 1947[g]	27	65	7	1649	AIPO397K
May 1947[g]	26	66	8	1494	AIPO397T
Jun 1947[h]	25	57	17	1580	AIPO399
Nov 1947[i]	24	65	11	3529	NORC245
May 1948[j]	22	69	9	1534	AIPO419T
Dec 1948[j]	23	63	14	1489	AIPO434K
Dec 1948[j]	25	58	17	1477	AIPO434T
Sep 1953[g]	18	69	12	1526	AIPO520
Feb 1955[k]	25	68	7	3414	ORCO3842
Dec 1961[l]	25	60	15	1413	ORCO463S

[a]Would you prefer public (ownership) or private ownership of
the electric power industry?

[b]Do you think the government should own the electric companies?

[c]Do you think the electric companies should be owned by the
government, or by private business?

[d]Should the government own the electric power companies in
this country?

[e]Do you think the government should own the following things
in this country--electric power companies?

[f]Do you think the government should own the electric power
companies in this country?

[g]Do you think the United States Government should or should
not own the following things in this country--electric power
companies?

[h]Do you think the U.S. government should own the electric
power companies in this country?

Table 1.14 (Continued)

---

[i]Which do you think would be better for the people in this country--if the gas and electric companies were run by the government, or by private industry?

[j]Do you think the U.S. government should or should not own the following things in this country--electric power companies?

[k]What do you think about the government ownership and operation of the following kinds of business--electric power companies?

[l]What do you think about the government ownership and operation of the following kinds of business? Are you for or against the government ownership of the electric power companies?

Table 1.15   Should the U.S. Government Own the Coal Mines?--1936-1953

Do you think the United States government should own the following things in this country:

Coal Mines?

	YES	NO	DK	N	
Nov 1936[a]	27	64	9	c1500	AIPO
Aug 1944[b]	27	58	15	2521	NORC227
Sep 1945[c]	19	74	7	2258	AIPO355K
Sep 1945[c]	28	61	11	1419	AIPO355T
Jan 1947	30	65	5	1465	AIPO387K
Jan 1947	30	65	5	1461	AIPO387T
May 1947[d]	31	63	7	1650	AIPO397K
May 1947[d]	31	63	6	1495	AIPO397T
Nov 1947[e]	32	49	19	3529	NORC245
May 1948[f]	27	65	8	1535	AIPO419T
Dec 1948[f]	23	64	13	1486	AIPO434K
Dec 1948[f]	27	58	15	1478	AIPO434T
Sep 1953[d]	15	72	13	1528	AIPO520

---

[a]Do you favor government ownership of coal mines?

[b]After the war, do you think the government should or should not own coal mines?

[c]Do you think the government should own the following things in this country--mines?

[d]Do you think the United States government should or should not own the following things in this country--coal mines?

[e]Which do you think would be better for the people of this country--if the coal mines were run by the government, or by private business?

[f]Do you think the U.S. government should or should not own the following things in this country--coal mines?

Table 1.16   Should the U.S. Government Own the Banks?--1936-
1961

Do you think the United States government should own the
following things in this country:

Banks?

	YES	NO	DK	N	
Nov 1936[a]	36	56	8	c1500	AIPO
Dec 1936[a]	38	50	12	2620	AIPO60
Jul 1937[a]	47	39	14	2831	AIPO90
Aug 1937[b]	35	37	18	c1500	AIPO96
Jun 1945[c]	27	62	11	2937	AIPO348
Sep 1945[d]	26	64	10	1659	AIPO355K
Sep 1945[d]	23	65	12	1416	AIPO355T
Jan 1947[d]	26	69	5	1463	AIPO387K
Jan 1947[d]	22	71	7	1461	AIPO387T
May 1947[d]	21	71	8	1653	AIPO397K
May 1947[e]	25	68	7	1495	AIPO397T
Nov 1947[f]	28	55	17	3529	NORC245
May 1948[e]	19	72	9	1534	AIPO419T
Dec 1948[e]	20	67	13	1490	AIPO434K
Dec 1948	23	64	13	1477	AIPO434T
Sep 1953[e]	14	75	11	1528	AIPO520
Feb 1955[g]	16	77	7	3414	ORCO3842
Dec 1961[g]	21	63	16	1413	ORCO463S

[a]Do you favor government ownership of the banks?

[b]Would you like to have the government own and control the
banks?

[c]Do you believe that the government should own the banks?

[d]Do you think the (United States) government should own the
following things in this country--banks?

[e]Do you think the United States government should or should
not own the following things in this country--banks?

[f]Which do you think would be better for the people in this
country--if the banks were run by the government, or by private business?

[g]What do you think about the government ownership and operation of the following kinds of business: Are you for or
against government ownership of the banks of this country?

Table 1.17   Should the U.S. Government Own the Railroads?--
1936-1961

Do you think the United States government should own the
following things in this country:

Railroads?

	YES	NO	DK	N	
Nov 1936[a]	30	60	10	c1500	AIPO
Dec 1936[a]	29	55	16	2628	AIPO60
Jan 1936[b]	27	52	21	c1500	ROPER
Jan 1937[c]	25	58	17	2848	AIPO106
May 1938[d]	26	53	21	c1500	RFOR
Jul 1938[e]	27	60	13	3086	AIPO127
Aug 1940[a]	35	39	26	1036	OPOR302K
Aug 1940[d]	33	45	42	1068	OPOR302T
Aug 1944[f]	19	67	14	2521	NORC227
Jun 1945[g]	20	63	17	1584	AIPO349K
Sep 1945[h]	23	66	11	1659	AIPO355K
Sep 1945[h]	25	65	10	1419	AIPO355T
Jan 1947	25	70	5	1465	AIPO387K
Jan 1947	24	69	7	1461	AIPO387T
May 1947[i]	24	67	9	1652	AIPO397K
May 1947[i]	26	66	7	1497	AIPO397T
May 1948[j]	19	71	19	1532	AIPO419K
May 1948[j]	22	67	11	1508	AIPO419T
Dec 1948[j]	20	64	16	1489	AIPO434K
Dec 1948[j]	23	62	15	1477	AIPO434T
Sep 1953[i]	14	74	12	1528	AIPO520
Feb 1955[k]	15	78	7	3414	ORCO3842
Dec 1961[k]	22	62	16	1413	ORCO463S

[a]Do you favor government ownership of the railroads?

[b]Do you believe the government should take over the railroads?

[c]Do you believe the government should buy, own, and operate
the railroads?

[d]Do you think the federal government should buy, own, and
operate the railroads?

[e]Do you think the government should take over the railroads?
[f]After the war, do you think the government should or should
not own the railroads?

[g]Do you think the government should own the railroads in
this country?

[h]Do you think the government should own the following things
in this country--railroads?

[i]Do you think the United States government should or should
not own the following things in this country--railroads?

[j]Do you think the U.S. government should or should not own
the following things in this country--railroads?

[k]What do you think about the government ownership and operation of the following kinds of business--railroads?

Table 1.18   Is the Government Getting Too Powerful?--1964-1984

Some people are afraid the government in Washington is getting too powerful for the good of the country and the individual person. Others feel that the government in Washington is not getting too strong for the good of the country. Do you have an opinion on this? (IF YES) What is your feeling, do you think the government is getting too powerful or do you think the government is not getting too strong?

	GOVERNMENT GETTING TOO POWERFUL	DEPENDS	GOVERNMENT NOT GOTTEN TOO STRONG	DK	NO INTEREST	N	
Aut 1964a,b	30	3	36	3	28	1569	ELEC64
Aut 1966a,b	39	4	27	2	28	1286	ELEC66
Aut 1968b	40	3	30	2	24	1552	ELEC68
Aut 1970a,b	31	6	33	2	28	1490	ELEC70
Aut 1972b	42	4	27	2	26	1311	ELEC72
Aut 1976	49	3	20	0	28	2846	ELEC76
Aut 1978	43	2	14	1	41	2276	ELEC78
Aut 1980	49	2	15	1	34	1405	ELEC80
Aut 1984	32	1	22	1	44	973	ELEC84

a"Has not gotten too strong" was used instead of "is not getting too strong."

b"Have you been interested enough in this to favor one side over the other?" was used instead of "Do you have an opinion on this?".

Table 1.19 Is the Government Trying to Do Things that Should Be Left to Individuals?--1975-1987

HELPNOT--Some people think that the government in Washington is trying to do too many things that should be left to individuals and private businesses. Others disagree and think that the government should do even more to solve our country's problems. Still others have opinions somewhere in between. Where would you place yourself on this scale, or haven't you made up your mind on this?

	I STRONGLY AGREE THAT THE GOVERNMENT SHOULD DO MORE 1	2	I AGREE WITH BOTH ANSWERS 3	4	I STRONGLY AGREE THAT THE GOVERNMENT IS DOING TOO MUCH 5	DK	N	
Mar 1975	25	11	29	12	16	7	1487	GSS
Mar 1983	12	11	36	18	16	7	1595	GSS
Mar 1984	14	13	37	17	14	5	1449	GSS
Mar 1986	12	13	41	16	13	6	1467	GSS
Mar 1987	14	14	38	15	14	5	1460	GSS

Table 1.20 Should the Government Reduce Income Differences between Rich and Poor?--1973-1988

EQWLTH--Some people think that the government in Washington ought to reduce the income differences between the rich and the poor, perhaps by raising the taxes of wealthy families or by giving income assistance to the poor. Others think that the government should not concern itself with reducing this income differ-ence between the rich and the poor. Here is a card with a scale from 1 to 7. Think of a score of 1 as meaning that the government ought to reduce the income differences between rich and poor, and a score of 7 meaning that the government should not concern itself with reducing income differences. What score between 1 and 7 comes closest to the way you feel?

| | GOVERNMENT SHOULD REDUCE INCOME DIFFERENCES | | | | | | GOVERNMENT SHOULD NOT REDUCE INCOME DIFFERENCES | | | |
	1	2	3	4	5	6	7	DK	N	
Dec 1973	36	12	10	11	6	7	15	3	1489	NORC4179
Mar 1978	19	11	17	21	11	8	12	1	758	GSS
Mar 1980	17	9	16	20	12	7	16	3	1463	GSS
Mar 1983	20	11	16	17	11	8	14	2	1596	GSS
Mar 1984	21	12	15	17	13	8	12	2	1462	GSS
Mar 1986	23	9	17	21	11	6	12	1	1467	GSS
Mar 1987	19	9	17	21	13	6	14	1	1461	GSS
Mar 1988	19	10	18	20	12	8	11	2	994	GSS

Table 1.21 Should the Government Improve People's Standard of Living?--1975-1987

HELPPOOR--Some people think that the government in Washington should do every-thing possible to improve the standard of living of all poor Americans; they are at Point 1 on this card. Other people think it is not the government's responsibility, and that each person should take care of himself; they are at Point 5. Where would you place yourself on this scale, or haven't you made up your mind on this?

	I STRONGLY AGREE THAT THE GOVERN-MENT SHOULD IMPROVE LIVING STANDARDS 1	2	I AGREE WITH BOTH ANSWERS 3	4	I STRONGLY AGREE THAT PEOPLE SHOULD TAKE CARE OF THEMSELVES 5	DK	N	
Mar 1975	29	10	35	10	13	3	1490	GSS
Mar 1983	17	15	40	13	11	4	1593	GSS
Mar 1984	17	11	46	14	8	4	1462	GSS
Mar 1986	18	12	45	11	11	2	1466	GSS
Mar 1987	17	12	44	13	11	3	1459	GSS

Table 1.22 Does the Government Have a Special Obligation to Improve the Living Standards of Blacks?--1975-1987

HELPBLK--Some people think that (blacks/Negroes) have been discriminated against for so long that the government has a special obligation to help improve their living standards. Others believe that the government should not be giving special treatment to (blacks/Negroes). Where would you place yourself on this scale, or haven't you made up your mind on this?

	I STRONGLY AGREE THE GOVERNMENT IS OBLIGATED TO HELP BLACKS 1	2	I AGREE WITH BOTH ANSWERS 3	4	I STRONGLY AGREE THAT GOVERNMENT SHOULDN'T GIVE SPECIAL TREATMENT 5	DK	N	
Mar 1975	16	8	21	12	40	3	1488	GSS
Mar 1983	8	9	26	20	33	4	1592	GSS
Mar 1984	9	9	30	17	30	4	1450	GSS
Mar 1986	8	10	29	18	33	3	1466	GSS
Mar 1987	10	10	28	17	31	3	1459	GSS

Table 1.23 Is It the Government's Responsibility to Help People Pay for Doctors' and Hospital Bills?--1975-1987

HELPSICK--In general, some people think that it is the responsibility of the government in Washington to see to it that people have help in paying for doctors' and hospital bills. Others think that these matters are not the responsibility of the federal government and that people should take care of these things themselves. Where would you place yourself on this scale, or haven't you made up your mind on this?

	I STRONGLY AGREE IT IS THE RESPONSIBILITY OF GOVERNMENT TO HELP 1	2	I AGREE WITH BOTH ANSWERS 3	4	I STRONGLY AGREE PEOPLE SHOULD TAKE CARE OF THEMSELVES 5	DK	N	
Mar 1975	36	13	29	8	13	2	1484	GSS
Mar 1983	26	19	32	10	10	3	1593	GSS
Mar 1984	24	19	35	12	8	3	1449	GSS
Mar 1986	28	20	32	11	6	2	1463	GSS
Mar 1987	26	20	35	9	8	2	1461	GSS

Table 1.24 What is the Most Important Problem Facing the U.S. Today?--1935-1988

What do you think is the most important problem facing this (the) country today?

	FOREIGN AFFAIRS	DOMESTIC TOTAL	ECO-NOMIC	SOCIAL CONTROL	CIVIL RIGHTS	GOV-ERN-MENT	MISC. NAMED	UN-SPECI-FIED	NOT CLAS-SIFIED	DK	N CASES	N RES-PONSES	AIPO #
Sep 1935	11	89	61	4	-	11	11	2	-	-	NA	NA	NA
Dec 1936	24	76	58	2	-	2	14	-	-	-	NA	NA	NA
Dec 1937	27	66	46	-	-	5	3	12	-	7	NA	NA	106
Jan 1939	13	79	60	2	1	7	9	-	-	8	3063	3063	143
Apr 1939	35	61	49	1	0	2	7	1	0	4	3122	3122	155
Nov 1939	47	48	32	2	0	4	9	1	0	5	3192	3192	176
Aug 1940	52	42	26	3	0	7	5	-	-	6	3094	3094	205
Nov 1940	81	16	12	1	0	1	2	1	-	3	3065	3232	252
Nov 1941	75	13	7	-	-	-	-	0	-	12	NA	NA	254
Dec 1942	28	62	49	2	0	2	8	7	-	10	2935	3151	286
Mar 1945	24	66	51	6	5	-	3	-	-	10	3055	3318	342
Aug 1945	11	88	85	1	1	0	2	2	-	0	3106	3402	354
Oct 1945	12	88	83	1	1	0	3	-	0	0	3096	3561	357
Feb 1946	27	73	59	0	0	1	12	-	-	-	3122	3400	366
Jun 1946	14	86	79	0	0	1	5	0	0	0	3119	3362	374
Jan 1947	25	74	61	0	1	2	11	0	0	0	1468	1546	387
Jul 1947	46	46	35	1	1	-	8	1	1	6	3006	3210	401
Sep 1947	32	63	52	3	1	1	5	2	2	3	3056	3269	404
Mar 1948	68	23	10	-	-	-	2	12	6	3	2894	2926	415
Jun 1948	50	43	27	2	1	-	4	9	4	3	3154	3197	420
Jan 1949	46	49	35	2	1	1	6	4	-	5	3138	3267	435
Jun 1949	22	60	40	1	3	2	15	0	1	17	2765	3311	443T
Sep 1949	28	59	37	3	2	4	12	0	7	6	2896	3029	447
Nov 1949	32	57	47	0	1	2	6	0	2	9	2903	3087	449
Mar 1950	45	44	29	11	1	3	6	3	-	3	1458	1525	454
Sep 1951	56	40	24	4	0	4	4	4	1	3	1986	2093	480

39

Table 1.24 (Continued)

	FOREIGN AFFAIRS	DOMESTIC TOTAL	ECO-NOMIC	SOCIAL CONTROL	CIVIL RIGHTS	GOV-ERN-MENT	MISC. NAMED	UN-SPECI-FIED	NOT CLAS-SIFIED	DK	N CASES	N RES-PONSES	AIPO #
Jun 1952	54	43	26	7	0	6	1	2	–	3	2031	2258	494
Mar 1954	34	60	36	18	0	2	1	3	–	5	1562	1752	528
May 1954	49	28	19	0	1	3	1	4	14	9	1415	1524	530
Jun 1955	48	25	14	0	4	1	2	4	6	21	1462	1524	548
Oct 1955	41	38	20	1	2	5	2	7	4	17	1577	1662	555
Sep 1956	39	48	20	2	18	–	4	5	3	9	1979	2332	570
Sep 1956	44	43	19	3	12	0	3	5	3	10	2207	2439	571
Oct 1956	45	47	26	3	10	0	5	1	2	8	2223	2465	572
Oct 1956	47	43	25	2	9	–	5	4	2	10	2175	2415	573
May 1957	43	46	30	5	4	–	2	2	4	7	1570	1570	583
Aug 1957	37	51	23	5	18	–	3	2	2	10	1528	1805	588
Oct 1957	38	52	16	4	29	0	1	2	2	8	1558	1558	590
Dec 1957	50	40	21	5	4	1	5	4	0	10	1527	1527	593
Mar 1958	25	63	47	4	4	0	2	4	3	8	1609	1609	596
Jul 1958	33	52	37	2	6	1	2	4	5	10	1513	1513	601
Aug 1958	48	44	22	3	9	–	1	8	–	8	1563	1563	603
Sep 1958	53	40	16	2	16	–	1	4	–	6	1514	1514	604
Oct 1958	53	41	18	1	17	–	1	4	–	7	1665	1665	605
Oct 1958	46	46	24	1	14	–	1	6	–	8	1553	1553	606
Feb 1959	44	49	27	1	10	–	4	7	–	7	1616	1616	610
Mar 1959	48	46	28	3	7	–	1	8	–	6	1737	1737	612
Jul 1959	46	48	32	1	8	–	3	5	–	6	1532	1532	616
Sep 1959	55	38	23	4	5	–	1	5	–	8	5778	5778	618
Feb 1960	47	42	18	3	5	1	6	9	6	5	3135	3484	624
Apr 1960	40	48	20	2	16	1	3	6	5	7	2759	2900	627
May 1960	61	32	14	1	5	0	2	9	4	4	3044	3347	628
Jun 1960	53	31	11	1	6	0	1	12	10	6	2519	2779	629
Jun 1960	55	29	13	3	5	0	2	6	9	6	3254	3692	630
Jul 1960	57	30	12	3	6	0	2	7	8	6	2789	3275	631

			DOMESTIC											
	FOREIGN AFFAIRS	VIET-NAM	TOTAL	ECO-NOMIC	SOCIAL CONTROL	CIVIL RIGHTS	GOV-ERN-MENT	MISC. NAMED	UN-SPECI-FIED	NOT CLAS-SIFIED	DK	N CASES	N RES-PONSES	AIPO #
Jul 1960	60		28	14	2	6	0	2	3	9	4	3162	3485	632
Aug 1960	58		30	15	2	6	0	2	4	7	6	3077	3542	633
Aug 1960	57		28	13	3	7	0	3	2	9	6	3337	3789	634
Sep 1960	59		29	14	2	6	0	4	2	7	5	2906	3273	635
Sep 1960	59		27	16	2	4	0	2	4	9	6	3614	4480	636
Oct 1960	55		31	19	0	5	0	2	5	9	4	2988	3461	637
Feb 1961	42		43	34	2	5	0	2	1	9	5	2873	3310	641
May 1961	47	3[a]	32	21	2	5	0	3	1	17	4	3545	4415	644
Jul 1961	63	-	21	12	2	4	0	1	2	12	4	3158	3459	648
Dec 1961	60	-	24	12	2	4	0	4	4	10	6	2988	3409	653
Apr 1962	45	0	34	18	5	6	1	2	2	13	8	3403	3697	657
Jun 1962	35	1	44	23	6	8	0	3	4	13	8	3275	3759	660
Aug 1962	51	0	32	18	4	5	1	2	2	11	6	3350	3963	662
Sep 1962	65	-	30	13	1	8	-	8	-	-	5	3938	4163	663
Oct 1962	66	-	30	11	1	11	-	7	-	-	4	4248	4428	664
Nov 1962	72	-	17	9	1	2	1	5	4	6	6	4426	5265	665
Dec 1962	61	-	27	12	3	5	1	1	-	6	7	3193	3456	666
Mar 1963	61	-	33	17	-	4	-	-	12	-	7	NA	NA	669
Sep 1963	24	-	69	13	0	48	-	7	4	10	7	3230	3442	677
Mar 1964	28	2	54	13	1	30	-	6	4	8	8	3539	3943	688
Apr 1964	28	1	60	13	1	36	-	6	2	7	4	3509	4025	689
Jun 1964	24	6	64	8	1	42	-	10	2	6	4	3506	3922	694
Jul 1964	20	3	68	6	4	51	-	5	3	6	5	3515	4092	695
Aug 1964	41	10	48	6	4	30	-	6	6	6	5	3513	4214	696
Aug 1964	28	5	61	9	4	40	-	6	6	6	4	4003	4683	697
Sep 1964	33	5	56	10	4	29	3	4	2	-	5	3590	4233	698
Oct 1964	41	5	52	12	6	21	3	9	1	-	7	3503	4157	699
Feb 1965	52	25	42	8	7	22	1	4	-	-	5	3505	4043	706
Feb 1965[b]	52	-	43	5	1	21	-	2	14	-	6	1757	1757	POS 655

Table 1.24 (Continued)

	FOREIGN AFFAIRS	VIET-NAM	DOMESTIC								DK	N CASES	N RESPONSES	AIPO #
			TOTAL	ECO-NOMIC	SOCIAL CONTROL	CIVIL RIGHTS	GOVERN-MENT	MISC. NAMED	UN-SPECI-FIED	NOT CLAS-SIFIED				
Feb 1965[c]	20	–	70	26	–	–	–	28	15	–	11	1620	2140	POS 655
Feb 1965[d]	26	–	48	9	6	–	–	18	14	–	26	1620	1726	POS 655
Mar 1965	36	20	61	5	7	45	2	2	1	–	2	3500	4060	708
Mar 1965	53	19	43	7	8	19	1	4	4	–	4	3546	4220	711
Jul 1965	56	33	41	7	8	18	2	4	3	–	3	1590	1809	714
Aug 1965	57	35	39	6	7	19	2	4	2	–	4	3527	4030	715
Sep 1965	46	16	50	8	8	23	1	8	3	–	4	3555	4134	717
Oct 1965	55	31	42	7	10	15	2	6	1	–	4	3525	4116	719
Nov 1965	55	30	39	7	7	17	2	4	2	–	6	3521	3940	720
May 1966	57	42	39	16	8	8	3	4	1	–	4	1563	1706	728
Aug 1966	47	39	51	15	12	17	2	4	1	–	2	1509	1808	733
Oct 1966	54	45	43	15	6	16	1	4	1	–	3	1597	1847	735
Oct 1966	52	38	43	18	6	14	2	3	1	–	4	3510	3979	736
Jan 1967	58	46	39	15	6	9	2	5	2	–	3	3491	4183	740
Aug 1967	39	34	58	7	41	6	1	3	1	–	3	1627	1627	749
Oct 1967	52	43	47	10	18	11	3	4	1	–	1	1648	1776	753
Jan 1968	52	47	47	12	16	11	2	5	1	–	1	1502	1681	756
Jan 1968	38	38	59	7	17	23	–	4	8	–	3	NA	NA	761
Jul 1968	41	35	58	9	29	11	4	4	1	–	1	1526	1938	765
Jul 1968	44	40	55	8	22	17	3	5	1	–	1	1526	1785	766
Aug 1968	38	35	61	6	32	15	3	4	1	–	2	1507	1827	767
Sep 1968	39	34	59	8	30	15	3	4	0	–	2	1500	1785	769
Oct 1968	41	38	57	7	29	15	2	3	1	–	2	1605	1845	770
Jan 1969	44	36	54	10	18	20	2	6	1	–	2	1461	1666	773
May 1969	43	38	56	7	31	12	0	5	1	–	1	1539	1569	781
Jan 1970	33	28	66	16	22	11	1	15	1	–	1	1573	1776	797
May 1970	32	19	66	6	6	8	2	19	25	–	2	1509	1694	807
Jul 1970	28	20	70	14	32	8	1	14	0	–	2	1500	1780	811

	FOREIGN AFFAIRS	VIET-NAM	TOTAL	DOMESTIC						UN-SPECIFIED	NOT CLAS-SIFIED	DK CASES	N CASES	N RES-PONSES	AIPO #
				ECO-NOMIC	SOCIAL CONTROL	CIVIL RIGHTS	GOVERN-MENT	ENERGY	MISC. NAMED						
Sep 1970	33	21	65	10	36	9	2		7	1	—	2	1497	1814	814
Oct 1970	32	24	66	11	41	5	1		7	0	—	2	1507	1771	815
Feb 1971	34	25	65	22	20	6	1		14	1	—	2	1571	1731	824
Jun 1971	32	27	66	12	29	6	1		17	2	—	1	1591	1860	831
Aug 1971	22	18	77	35	21	5	2		12	2	—	2	1547	2037	836
Oct 1971	16	11	79	13	41	6	7		6	6	—	5	1558	1958	839
Nov 1971	20	13	78	37	22	5	2		11	1	—	2	1502	1851	840
Feb 1972	25	20	74	27	25	4	3		12	2	—	2	1542	1871	844
Apr 1972	30	23	68	22	25	4	4		13	2	—	2	1516	1918	851
Jun 1972	36	27	62	21	19	4	2		12	2	—	3	1526	1732	853
Jul 1972	25	21	74	21	28	4	4		13	2	—	1	1505	1751	855
Sep 1972	28	22	70	23	25	4	4		11	4	—	2	1516	1773	858
Oct 1972	31	25	66	26	22	3	3		11	2	—	3	1549	1848	859
Jan 1973	35	29	63	25	22	4	2		9	1	—	2	1517	1854	862
Feb 1973	9	3	89	39	25	6	2		16	1	—	2		1740	864
May 1973	9	3	89	40	22	3	12	2	10	1	—	3	1531	1698	870
May 1973	6	3	92	32	19	3	20	2	9	7	—	2	1548	1790	871
Sep 1973	6	1	92	57	12	1	11	3	7	1	—	3	1502	1841	877
Jan 1974	4	0	90	24	7	1	18	34	3	2	—	6	1589	1996	886
May 1974	4	0	92	46	12	1	23	4	5	1	—	4	1509	1760	906
Aug 1974	4	0	94	69	8	1	8	1	4	2	—	2	1590	1834	913
Sep 1974	2	—	96	75	7	1	8	2	3	2	—	2	1527	1709	915
Oct 1974	2	—	96	72	6	1	10	2	4	2	—	2	1586	1827	916
Feb 1975	4	0	96	61	14	1	7	6	5	2	—	—	1576	2118	924
Jul 1975	3	0	95	62	11	1	10	5	4	4	—	2	1561	1871	932

Table 1.24 (Continued)

	FOREIGN AFFAIRS	TOTAL	DOMESTIC ECO-NOMIC	SOCIAL CONTROL	CIVIL RIGHTS	GOVERN-MENT	ENERGY	MISC. NAMED	UN-SPECI-FIED	NOT CLAS-SIFIED	DK	N CASES	N RES-PONSES	AIPO #
Oct 1975	3	94	65	11	2	7	5	4	1	–	2	1553	1950	938
Dec 1975	7	91	61	15	1	5	2	4	2	–	2	1572	1929	943
Apr 1976	4	94	51	16	3	14	2	6	3	–	2	1549	2061	950
Sep 1976	8	90	64	9	1	9	1	5	1	–	3	1538	2074	960
Oct 1976	45	92	65	11	1	8	2	5	2	–	3	1550	2036	961
Feb 1977	9	90	47	15	2	3	10	10	3	–	1	1525	3300	970
Jul 1977	8	86	43	12	1	4	14	10	3	–	6	1516	1811	980
Sep 1977	6	92	50	12	2	2	15	9	3	–	3	1515	1826	986
Feb 1978	7	90	48	10	1	3	20	7	1	–	3	1546	1785	993
Apr 1978	7	90	62	9	1	3	7	6	2	–	2	1508	1828	999
May 1978	8	89	61	6	2	2	3	–	15	–	2	1555	NA	3G
Jul 1978	8	90	64	8	2	4	3	6	1	–	3	1530	1897	6G
Sep 1978	4	83	58	10	1	4	4	7	1	–	2	1534	1747	11G
Feb 1979	14	84	51	6	0	3	12	4	1	–	2	1511	1905	23G
May 1979	4	94	46	7	0	5	27	4	1	–	2	1589	1897	28G
Aug 1979	6	94	59	15	1	9	16	5	2	–	2	1539	2038	36G
Oct 1979	3	93	61	6	0	4	18	4	2	–	2	1552	1852	41G
Jan 1980	41	58	37	5	0	3	11	4	0	–	1	1597	1937	47G
Mar 1980	14	85	67	4	0	4	7	2	0	–	1	1571	1870	51G
Jun 1980	17	81	62	5	0	4	6	2	1	–	2	1583	1896	57G
Jul 1980	10	88	63	8	0	7	6	4	0	–	1	1548	1863	59G
Sep 1980	14	85	67	6	0	6	3	3	1	–	3	1602	1870	62G
Oct 1980	13	84	57	9	1	8	4	4	0	–	3	1593	1844	63G
Nov 1980	4	92	64	4	–	–	4	–	1	–	4	1556	NA	64G
J/F 1981	6	92	78	5	0	2	5	2	2	–	2	1609	1705	68G
May 1981	10	88	64	10	0	3	5	5	0	–	2	1519	1820	73G
Oct 1981	11	87	67	7	–	2	1	5	2	–	2	1508	1719	83G
Jan 1982	10	88	70	7	–	2	1	6	5	–	2	1484	1773	88G
Apr 1982	10	88	70	5	–	2	1	5	3	–	2	1543	1984	92G

Jun 1982	12	87	73	5	–	2	1	4	2	–	1504	1899	96G
Aug 1982	7	91	78	5	–	2	0	3	2	–	1543	2008	100G
Oct 1982	6	92	80	5	–	2	1	3	2	–	1543	1923	103G
Apr 1983	14	84	72	6	–	2	1	3	2	–	1509	1791	112G
Jul 1983	16	81	66	6	–	2	0	4	3	–	1567	1795	118G
Oct 1983	22	75	58	9	–	2	1	3	2	–	1513	1661	125G
Nov 1983	34	63	48	7	–	2	1	3	4	–	1504	1628	127G
Feb 1984	24	73	50	10	–	2	1	7	4	–	1610	1817	131G
Jun 1984	26	75	49	10	–	–	–	9	3	–	1522	1682	235G
Sep 1984	21	79	57	6	–	3	–	10	4	–	1521	NA	241G
Sep 1984	22	73	53	7	–	2	–	6	4	–	1518	NA	242G
Sep 1984	27	71	43	8	1	2	2	10	4	–	1590	1908	243G
Jan 1987	20	75	37	14	2	7	–	14	1	–	1562	1801	272G
Apr 1987	19	78	37	13	1	6	–	16	5	–	1571	1932	274G

aLaos
bProblems
cWorries
dFears

Questions:

A. What do you regard as the most vital issue before the American people today? (9/35, 12/36, 106)

B. What do you regard as the most important problem before the American people today? (143, 155)

C. What do you think is the most important problem before the American people today? (176, 205, 447)

D. What do you think is the most important issue before the country today? (252)

E. In your opinion, what is the most important problem the United States government must solve in the next few months? (254)

Table 1.24 (Continued)

F. Aside from winning the war, what do you think is the most important problem facing this country today? (286, 342)

G. Which problem here in the United States have you, yourself, been thinking about most during the last few days? (298)

H. What do you think will be the most important problem facing this country during the next year? (354, 357, 374T)

I. In your opinion, what is the most important problem the government must solve in the next few months? (366)

J. What do you think will be the most important problem facing this country in the next six months? (374K)

K. In your opinion, what is the most important problem the United States (U.S.) government must solve in the next year? (387, 449)

L. What do you think is the most important problem facing this (the) country today? (401, 404, 415, 420, 435, 443T, 494, 528, 570-664, 669-836, 840-274G)

M. What do you think is the most important problem facing the entire country today? (454, 480)

N. What do you regard as the biggest issue or problem facing the U.S. government today? (530)

O. What do you regard as the biggest issue or problem facing the government in Washington today? (548, 555)

P. Of the many problems facing this country, which one gives you the greatest worry or concern at this time? (665)

46

Q. Of the many problems which this country has, which one gives you the greatest worry or concern at this time? (666)

R. What are your chief worries these days--what things bother or upset you most? Now, what do you fear most? (POS655)

S. Now, how about the United States. Of ALL the problems--domestic and international--facing this country today, which ONE do you think is the most important? (POS655)

T. Turning to the next topic...what bothers or angers you the most about America today? (839)

47

2

International Affairs

Polling questions in the areas of foreign and international affairs tend to change from crisis to crisis, so that long-term trends are often difficult to document. For example, one might wish to assess the impact that the war in Vietnam had on international attitudes, as it is sometimes suggested that the war shattered a Cold War consensus that had prevailed earlier (see, for example, Holsti and Rosenau 1984). However, while the data show that a substantial variety of opinion on foreign policy existed in the post-Vietnam era, there is little comparable data from earlier periods to indicate whether opinion was any less divided at that time.

A trend line that does have a substantial history concerns the public's expectations about another world war (Table 2.1). As the Cold War became established by 1947, concerns that the United States would soon find itself in another big war grew (rising concern about Soviet intentions at the time is vividly documented in Table 2.14). There was a further growth in concern at the time of the Czech coup and the Berlin Blockade in 1948, but the Korean War, which began at the end of June 1950 and escalated with the dramatic entry of the Chinese in November, pushed the measure to near-unanimous levels. Other questions suggest that lowered, but lingering, fears of war persisted into the early 1960s and then tapered off in the post-1963 era of detente between the United States and the Soviet Union (Mueller, 1979). When the question in Table 2.1 was revived in 1976 and in the 1980s, fear of war had dropped to some of its lowest levels. The 1950s have become "happy days" in legend, but the public's fear of major war was far higher than in later, putatively less happy days.

The most frequently asked question about isolationism (Table 2.2) is a bit on the bland side, and it has shown little variation in the four decades during which it has been asked. There was perhaps some rise in internationalism in the

Kennedy era of the early 1960s, and the highest level the
question has ever reached was attained in June 1965 as American troops were being sent in large numbers to Vietnam. There
may have been some decline by the end of the Vietnam War in
the mid-1970s, with a rise to more usual levels by the 1980s.
The Vietnam effect is suggested more clearly in Tables 2.3-
2.5, which use questions that are more crisply worded. Data
in Table 2.6 suggest that the Korean War may have had a similar impact in its time (see also Free and Watts, 1980;
Mueller, 1977).

American support for staying in the United Nations has
not changed a great deal since the early 1950s, though there
may have been a temporary waning of enthusiasm in the mid-
1970s at the end of the Vietnam War and after the Yom Kippur
War of 1973 (Table 2.7). Growth of support for Communist
Chinese membership during the 1960s is documented in Tables
2.8 and 2.9.

Willingness to counter attacks on important allies fell
at the end of Vietnam (Tables 2.10 and 2.11), but rose again
later. A similar phenomenon at the end of the Korean War in
1953 is documented in 2.12.

As the United States moved into Vietnam, the public tended to see the blustering Chinese as a greater threat than the
Soviet Union, a substantial reversal from the period before
the 1962 Cuban Missile Crisis when the Soviet Union was seen
to be the big concern (Table 2.13).

A hefty array of data about American likes and dislikes
of other countries is presented in Tables 2.15-2.22. The
question about Russia (the Soviet Union) proves to be quite
a good Cold War indicator (2.15). Following the "-5" column,
shows that hostility was intense in the post-Korea era with
a substantial mellowing in the 1960s and early 1970s (despite
the Vietnam War). Hostility rose temporarily with the Soviet
intervention in Angola in 1975, and it soared after its intervention in Afghanistan at the end of 1979--though not to the
level of the mid-1950s. There has been a distinct mellowing
in the 1980s, especially after the beginning of the Gorbachev
era in 1985. Attitudes in the 1970s and 1980s toward Communism as a form of government followed a somewhat similar
pattern (2.23). (See also Russett and Deluca, 1981; Richman,
1982; Smith, 1983.)

Hostility toward the Chinese was very high in the wake
of the Korean War in 1954, but it had dropped greatly by the
time of President Nixon's visit there in 1972, and it has
steadily declined since (Table 2.20). Americans have yet to
sour on the Japanese despite trade disputes (2.16), and have,
if anything, become ever more friendly toward the British and
the Canadians (2.17, 2.18). In the 1980s Americans may have

become less friendly toward Israel while remaining at least as friendly toward Egypt (2.21, 2.22).

It is possible to compare attitudes toward the Korean and Vietnam War because comparable questions about American support for the wars were asked in each period. They are presented in Tables 2.24-2.26. Vietnam has a rival for the distinction of being America's most unpopular war: Korea was just as unpopular during the periods in which the wars were comparable in American casualties—decline was general in both as casualties mounted (2.24, 2.26). By this measure at least, the Tet offensive of early 1968 in Vietnam did not do a great deal to increase American disillusion with the war there—support was declining already and continued to do so. Moreover, the data suggest that televison coverage of the later war and the active protest against it did not cause support for the the war to drop to levels lower than those that would have been expected from the Korean experience (Mueller, 1973).

REFERENCES

Free, Lloyd, and William Watts. 1980. Internationalism Comes of Age...Again. *Public Opinion*, 3(2):46-50.

Holsti, Ole R., and James N. Rosenau. 1984. *American Leadership in World Affairs*. Boston: Allen & Unwin.

Mueller, John. 1973. *War, Presidents and Public Opinion*. New York: Wiley (reprinted 1985 by University Press of America).

_____. 1977. Changes in American Public Attitudes Toward International Involvement. In Ellen P. Stern, ed., *The Limits of Military Intervention*. Beverly Hills, CA: Sage.

_____. 1979. Public Expectations of War During the Cold War. *American Journal of Political Science*, 23:301- 329.

Richman, Alvin. 1982. Public Attitudes on Military Power, 1981. *Public Opinion*, 4(6):44-46.

Russett, Bruce M., and Donald R. Deluca. 1981. "Don't Tread on Me": Public Opinion and Foreign Policy in the Eighties. *Political Science Quarterly*, 96:381-399.

Smith, Tom W. 1983. American Attitudes Toward the Soviet Union and Communism. *Public Opinion Quarterly*, 47:277-292.

Table 2.1   Will the U.S. Fight Another (World) War within
Ten Years?--1946-1988

USWAR--Do you expect the United States to fight in another
(world) war within the next ten years?[a]

	YES	NO	DK	N	
Nov 1946	28	57	15	1263	NORC146
Apr 1947	48	42	10	1307	NORC149
Jun 1947	49	39	12	1273	NORC151
Jul 1947[b]	53	36	11	1486	AIPO400K
Oct 1947	57	34	9	1290	NORC152DU-1
Feb 1948[b]	54	32	14	1578	AIPO412T
Mar 1948[b]	67	19	14	1546	AIPO415K
Aug 1948[b]	56	27	17	1540	AIPO423K
Aug 1948[b]	59	27	14	1489	AIPO423T
Feb 1948	65	27	8	1271	NORC155DU-1
Jun 1948	58	34	8	1295	NORC158DU-1
Oct 1948	66	24	10	1257	NORC161DU-1
Nov 1948	62	29	9	1288	NORC162DU-1
Jan 1949	50	40	10	1261	NORC163DU-1
Mar 1949	55	33	12	1301	NORC164DU-1
Apr 1949	53	37	10	1281	NORC165DU-1
Jun 1949	50	41	9	1283	NORC166DU-1
Jun 1949	48	41	11	1284	NORC167DU-1
Aug 1949	47	44	9	1232	NORC168DU-1
Sep 1949	52	39	9	1273	NORC169DU-1
Oct 1949	58	31	11	1260	NORC170DU-1
Nov 1949	52	39	9	1288	NORC171DU-1
Jan 1950	55	35	10	1284	NORC273DU-1
Mar 1950	57	33	10	1270	NORC276-270
Apr 1950	67	24	9	1274	NORC280-281
Jun 1950	61	31	8	1276	NORC282-283
Jul 1950	80	13	7	1302	NORC287
Sep 1950	74	19	7	1284	NORC288
Oct 1950	66	26	8	1305	NORC291
Nov 1950	79	13	8	1275	NORC292
Dec 1950	83	10	7	1258	NORC295
Jan 1951	74	19	7	1236	NORC298
Mar 1951	64	27	9	1237	NORC300297N
Apr 1951	70	21	9	1289	NORC302
May 1951	67	23	10	1282	NORC307
Aug 1951	74	17	9	1292	NORC312
Oct 1951	71	21	8	1299	NORC313
Mar 1976	44	50	6	718	GSS
Mar 1985	43	51	6	778	GSS
Mar 1986	46	51	3	1443	GSS
Mar 1988	40	56	4	987	GSS

[a]Before the beginning of the Korean War in June 1950, the
question asked about "war," not "world war." Once Korea
began, "world" was added to make clear that it was not the
new form of "limited" war that was being asked about.

[b]Do you think the United States will find itself in another
war within, say, the next 10 years.

Table 2.2 Should the U.S. Take an Active Part in World
Affairs?--1945-1988

USINTL--Do you think it will be best for the future of this
country if we take an active part in world affairs, or if we
stayed out of world affairs?

	ACTIVE PART	STAY OUT	DK	N	
Oct 1945[a]	70	19	11	3074	AIPO357
Feb 1946[a]	75	20	5	3104	AIPO366
Nov 1946[a]	78	19	3	3194	AIPO384
Aug 1947[a]	65	26	9	2989	AIPO403K
Jun 1947	66	26	8	1273	NORC151
Mar 1947	68	25	7	537	NORCT-49
Mar 1948	70	24	6	1289	NORC156
Jun 1948	70	23	7	1301	NORC159
Sep 1949	67	25	8	1273	NORC169
Nov 1950	69	23	8	1340	AIPO467
Jan 1950	67	24	9	1284	NORC273
Dec 1950	66	25	9	1258	NORC295
Oct 1952	68	23	9	1306	NORC332
Feb 1953	73	22	5	1293	NORC337
Sep 1953	71	21	8	1262	NORC348
Apr 1954	69	25	6	1207	NORC355
Mar 1955	72	21	7	1225	NORC370
Nov 1956	71	25	4	1286	NORC399
Jun 1965	79	16	5	1464	SRS857
Mar 1973	66	31	3	1495	GSS
Mar 1975	61	36	4	1484	GSS
Mar 1976	63	32	5	1496	GSS
Mar 1978	64	32	4	1530	GSS
Oct 1982	54	35	12	1547	AIPO
Mar 1982	61	34	5	1501	GSS
Mar 1983	65	31	4	1592	GSS
Mar 1984	65	29	6	1449	GSS
Mar 1985	70	27	2	745	GSS
Mar 1986	65	32	4	1443	GSS
Mar 1988	65	32	4	982	GSS

[a]...would be best....

Table 2.3   Should the U.S. Go Its Own Way in International
                 Matters?--1964-1980

Since the United States is the most powerful nation in the
world, we should go our own way in international matters,
not worrying too much about whether other countries agree
with us or not.

	AGREE	DISAGREE	DK	N	
Oct 1964	19	70	11	3175	PA
1968	23	72	5		PA
1972	22	72	6		PA
1974	32	57	11		PA
1975	23	67	10		PA
May 1976	29	62	9	1071	PA
Feb 1980	26	66	8	1611	PA

Table 2.4   Should the U.S. Mind Its Own Business
                 Internationally?--1964-1980

The United States should mind its own business internation-
ally and let other countries get along as best they can on
their own.

	AGREE	DISAGREE	DK	N	
Oct 1964	18	70	12	3175	PA
1968	27	66	7		PA
1972	35	56	9		PA
1974	41	47	12		PA
1975	36	52	12		PA
May 1976	41	49	10	1071	PA
Feb 1980	30	61	9	1611	PA

Table 2.5 Should the U.S. Concentrate More on Its Own
             National Problems?--1964-1980

We shouldn't think so much in international terms but concentrate more on our own national problems and building up
our strength and prosperity here at home.

	AGREE	DISAGREE	DK	N	
Oct 1964	55	32	13	3175	PA
1968	60	31	9		PA
1972	73	20	7		PA
1974	77	14	9		PA
1975	71	18	11		PA
May 1976	73	22	5	1071	PA
Feb 1980	61	30	9	1611	PA

Table 2.6 Has the U.S. Gone Too Far in Concerning Itself
             with Other Parts of the World?--1947-1954

Do you feel that since the war this country has gone too far
in concerning itself with problems in other parts of the
world, or not?

	TOO FAR	NOT TOO FAR	DK	N	
Jun 1947	37	52	11	1273	NORC151
Mar 1948	34	55	11	1289	NORC156
Apr 1949	41	50	9	1281	NORC165
Oct 1949	48	41	11	1260	NORC170
Jun 1950	36	54	10	1276	NORC282
Dec 1950[a]	39	48	13	1258	NORC295
Oct 1952[b]	57	34	8	1751	ELEC52
Oct 1954[b]	43	47	8	1114	ELEC54

[a]"...since the end of World War II...."

[b]Some people feel that since the end of the last world war
this country has gone too far in concerning itself with problems in other parts of the world. How do you feel about
this? "Depends" were 2 percent in 1952, 3 percent in 1954;
qualified "too far" and "not too far" responses were 9 and 7
percent, respectively, in 1952, 6 and 6 percent in 1954.

Table 2.7   Should the U.S. Belong to the United Nations?--
                1951-1988

USUN--Do you think our government should continue to belong
to the United Nations, or should we pull out of it now?

	STAY IN	PULL OUT	DK	N	
Jan 1951[a]	78	12	10	1236	NORC298
May 1952[a]	85	6	9	1265	NORC325
Feb 1953[a]	84	10	6	1293	NORC337
Jun 1953[a]	84	10	6	1291	NORC341
Nov 1953[a]	74	13	13	1233	NORC349
Aug 1955	88	5	7	1262	NORC374
Apr 1956	88	6	6	1224	NORC386
Nov 1956	87	6	7	1286	NORC399
Jun 1965	85	6	8	1463	SRS857
Mar 1973	79	15	6	1496	GSS
Mar 1975	75	18	7	1488	GSS
Mar 1976	73	19	8	1497	GSS
Mar 1978	80	13	8	1529	GSS
Mar 1982	78	16	6	1504	GSS
Mar 1983	80	14	6	1596	GSS
Mar 1985	79	17	4	1529	GSS
Mar 1986	78	17	6	1447	GSS
Mar 1988	78	16	6	986	GSS

[a]"United Nations Organization"

Table 2.8 Should China Be Admitted to the United Nations?--
1954-1971

Do you think Communist China should or should not be admitted as a member of the United Nations?

	YES	NO	DK	N	
Jul 1954	7	78	15	1585	AIPO533
Jul 1954	8	80	12	1514	AIPO534
May 1955	10	67	23	1491	AIPO547
Aug 1955	17	71	12	1499	AIPO552
Jul 1956	11	74	15	2094	AIPO567
Dec 1956	15	69	15	1534	AIPO576
Feb 1957	13	70	17	1501	AIPO578
Jan 1958	17	67	16	1445	AIPO594
Aug 1958	20	63	17	1559	AIPO603
Mar 1961	19	65	16	3494	AIPO642
Sep 1961	18	65	17	3440	AIPO650
Jan 1964	14	70	15	3065	AIPO684
Jan 1964	20	57	23	3435	AIPO701
Feb 1965	22	64	14	3505	AIPO706
Dec 1965	22	67	11	3532	AIPO721
Mar 1966	25	55	20	3518	AIPO726
Sep 1966	25	56	19	3520	AIPO734
Jan 1969	34	53	13	1503	AIPO774
Sep 1970	35	49	16	1467	AIPO814
May 1971	46	37	17	1491	AIPO830

Table 2.9   If China Is Admitted to the United Nations, Should the U.S. Resign?--1955-1971

Suppose a majority of the members of the United Nations decide to admit Communist China to the United Nations. Do you think the United States should go along with the UN decision, or not?

	YES	NO	DK	N	
Aug 1955	31	53	16	1495	AIPO551
Jul 1956	38	46	15	2095	AIPO567
Feb 1961	59	25	16	2854	AIPO641
Sep 1961	44	39	17	3461	AIPO650
Feb 1964	42	44	14	3105	AIPO684
Feb 1965	49	35	16	3497	AIPO706
Dec 1965	46	41	12	3532	AIPO721
Mar 1966[a]	49	31	20	3513	AIPO726
Sep 1966[a]	53	33	13	3517	AIPO734
Jan 1969[b]	56	33	11	1503	AIPO774
May 1971	59	27	14	1491	AIPO830

[a]Suppose the United Nations votes to admit Communist China to the United Nations. Do you think the United States should go along with the UN decision, or not?

[b]Suppose a majority of the members of the United Nations votes to admit Communist China. Do you think the United States should go along with the decision, or not?

Table 2.10   Should the U.S. Defend Europe if Attacked by Soviets?--1972-1980

The United States should come to the defense of its major European allies with military force if any of them are attacked by Soviet Russia.

	AGREE	DISAGREE	DK	N	
Jun 1972	52	32	16		PA
Jan 1974	48	34	18		PA
1975	48	34	18		PA
May 1976	56	27	17	1071	PA
1978	62	26	12		PA
Sep 1979	64	26	10		PA
Feb 1980	70	17	13	1611	PA
Jul 1980	74	19	7		PA

Table 2.11   Should the U.S. Defend Japan if Attacked by
                 Soviets or China?--1972-1980

The United States should come to the defense of Japan with
military force if it is attacked by Soviet Russia or Communist China.

	AGREE	DISAGREE	DK		N
Jun 1972	43	40	17		PA
Jan 1974	37	42	21		PA
1975	42	39	19		PA
May 1976	45	37	18	1071	PA
1978	50	35	15		PA
Sep 1979	54	35	11		PA
Feb 1980	57	24	19	1611	PA
Jul 1980	68	28	4		PA

Table 2.12   If Communists Attack, Should the U.S. Help
                 Defend Countries as We Did in Korea?--1950-1956

If Communist armies attack any other countries in the world,
do you think the United States should stay out of it, or
should we help defend the countries, like we did in Korea?

	STAY OUT	DEPENDS	HELP DEFEND	DK	N	
Sep 1950	14	15	66	5	1284	NORC288
Dec 1950	28	15	48	9	1258	NORC295
Aug 1951	28	13	53	6	1292	NORC312
Dec 1951	30	13	52	5	1237	NORC315
Jun 1952	33	15	45	6	1285	NORC327
Oct 1952	31	18	45	6	1306	NORC332
Aug 1953	36	13	45	6	526	NORC347
Nov 1953	26	17	52	5	1233	NORC349
Oct 1955	28	14	52	6	527	NORC378
Nov 1956	24	20	52	4	1276	NORC399

**Table 2.13   Is Russia or China the Greater Threat?--
            1961-1964**

Looking ahead to 1970, which country do you think will be
the greater threat to world peace--Russia or Communist
China?

	RUSSIA	COMMUNIST CHINA	BOTH	DK	N	
Feb 1961	49	32	-	19	2864	AIPO641
Mar 1963	33	46	2	19	4328	AIPO669
Apr 1964	27	56	-	17	3450	AIPO689
Nov 1964	23	58	2	17	3371	AIPO701

Table 2.14   Is Russia Trying to Rule the World?--1946-1953

As you hear and read about Russia these days, do you believe
Russia is trying to build herself up to be <u>the</u> ruling power
of the world, or is Russia just building up protection
against being attacked in another war?

	RULING POWER	PROTEC- TION	DK	N	
May 1946	55	33	11	1586	AIPO371K
Jul 1946	58	29	13	2445	AIPO375
Mar 1948	76	15	9	1509	AIPO414K
May 1948	70	18	12	1618	AIPO419K
May 1949	70	14	17	1369	AIPO442
Nov 1949	72	19	10	1487	AIPO450K
Oct 1950[a]	83	9	8	2940	AIPO466
Nov 1950[a]	84	10	6	1344	AIPO467
Jul 1953[a]	78	10	12	1528	AIPO517

[a]"...or do you think Russia is just...."

Table 2.15 Like/Dislike Russia (Soviet Union)--1953-1988

RUSSIA--You will notice that the boxes on this card go from the highest position of "plus 5" for a country which you like very much, to the lowest position of "minus 5" for a country you dislike very much. How far up the scale or how far down the scale would you rate the following countries?

Russia?

	+5	+4	+3	+2	+1	-1	-2	-3	-4	-5	DK[a]	N	
Oct 1953	0	0	0	0	1	6	3	7	4	72	7	1488	AIPO521
Aug 1954	-	0	-	1	3	5	2	6	5	72	6	1593	AIPO535
Sep 1954	0	0	0	0	1	4	2	5	4	73	11	1466	AIPO537
Dec 1956	0	1	1	1	2	5	3	6	5	68	8	1558	AIPO576
Dec 1966	1	1	4	3	8	10	6	11	8	39	8	3542	AIPO738
May 1972	3	4	11	9	13	7	6	9	6	25	6	1541	AIPO852
Apr 1973b	3	4	7	7	15	12	6	8	6	23	9	1528	AIPO868
Jul 1973	4	5	9	9	20	11	6	7	4	16	10	1544	AIPO874
Mar 1974	3	3	12	10	17	11	5	8	4	22	5	1484	GSS
Mar 1975	3	3	12	10	16	10	5	8	5	21	7	1490	GSS
Jun 1976b	2	2	3	5	9	10	7	9	9	36	6	1544	AIPO954
Mar 1977	2	1	8	7	13	12	5	9	5	30	8	1530	GSS
Feb 1979b	3	3	7	8	12	10	5	10	7	32	6	1534	AIPO123G
Jan 1980b	1	1	3	4	5	7	6	10	9	53	2	1597	AIPO147G
Jan 1981	1	2	5	5	9	9	7	13	9	38	3	1609	AIPO168G
Mar 1982	1	1	4	4	10	10	6	9	6	43	4	1506	GSS
Sep 1982b	2	2	4	4	9	9	7	11	7	40	5	1500	AIPO204G
Mar 1983	1	1	4	5	12	12	7	13	7	34	4	1599	GSS
Mar 1985	2	1	3	4	11	11	8	11	7	36	6	1534	GSS
Mar 1986	1	1	7	7	16	13	7	11	6	26	4	1470	GSS
Mar 1988	3	2	9	10	20	10	5	9	4	22	6	988	GSS

NOTE--AIPO (all surveys): You notice that the 10 boxes on this card go from the highest position of plus 5--or something you like very much, to the lowest position of minus 5--

61

Table 2.15 (Continued)

	+5	+4	+3	+2	+1	-1	-2	-3	-4	-5	DK[a]	N

or something you dislike very much. Will you put your finger on any one of the 10 boxes which best tells how you feel about (each item).

[a]For Tables 2.15-2.22, includes DK and NA (not answered) responses. In some of the early surveys these two responses were distinguished. Since there were few NA's, they were later coded together.

[b]Soviet Union.

Table 2.16 Like/Dislike Japan--1966-1988

JAPAN--You will notice...How far up the scale or how far down the scale would you rate... Japan?

	+5	+4	+3	+2	+1	-1	-2	-3	-4	-5	DK	N	
Dec 1966	4	8	16	17	21	9	5	3	3	6	8	3542	AIPO738
May 1972	7	12	18	15	15	8	5	6	3	5	6	1541	AIPO852
Apr 1973	10	11	19	16	15	7	4	4	2	5	8	1528	AIPO868
Mar 1974	7	10	21	15	17	7	4	4	4	6	5	1484	GSS
Mar 1975	6	9	18	14	18	8	5	5	4	5	7	1490	GSS
Jun 1976	8	13	21	17	17	5	3	4	2	3	7	1544	AIPO954
Mar 1977	7	6	19	13	18	8	5	5	4	6	8	1530	GSS
Mar 1982	8	9	20	14	16	9	5	5	4	6	6	1506	GSS
Mar 1983	7	8	16	16	19	10	5	6	3	5	5	1599	GSS
Mar 1985	8	10	19	16	16	9	5	6	3	4	5	1534	GSS
Mar 1986	8	10	22	16	16	7	5	4	2	5	4	1470	GSS
Mar 1988	8	8	18	14	19	9	4	5	2	7	5	988	GSS

Table 2.17 Like/Dislike England--1953-1985

ENGLAND--You will notice...How far up the scale or how far down the scale would you rate... England?

	+5	+4	+3	+2	+1	-1	-2	-3	-4	-5	DK	N	
Oct 1953	10	11	20	13	13	6	5	4	3	3	10	1488	AIPO521
Aug 1954	10	10	15	14	18	8	4	3	3	6	10	1612	AIPO535
Oct 1954	11	7	19	11	14	6	4	5	2	5	15	1515	AIPO538
Dec 1956	13	10	22	12	11	6	3	4	2	6	19	1543	AIPO576
Dec 1966	10	12	23	17	16	5	4	3	1	2	7	3542	AIPO738
May 1972	24	22	20	12	10	2	1	2	0	2	5	1541	AIPO852
Apr 1973	19	21	19	13	10	3	1	2	1	1	9	1528	AIPO868
Mar 1974	17	20	24	14	10	4	2	2	1	2	4	1484	GSS
Mar 1975	16	16	25	13	13	4	2	2	1	2	6	1490	GSS
Jun 1976	17	15	32	13	10	2	1	1	1	2	7	1534	AIPO954
Mar 1977	18	17	21	13	13	4	2	1	1	2	8	1530	GSS
Mar 1982	21	19	23	13	12	3	2	2	1	1	5	1506	GSS
Mar 1983	21	19	22	13	13	3	2	2	1	1	4	1599	GSS
Mar 1985	21	19	24	14	11	2	1	1	1	1	5	751	GSS

Table 2.18 Like/Dislike Canada--1966-1988

CANADA--You will notice...How far up the scale or how far down the scale would you rate... Canada?

	+5	+4	+3	+2	+1	-1	-2	-3	-4	-5	DK	N	
Dec 1966	29	20	22	10	8	2	1	0	0	1	8	3542	AIPO738
May 1972	39	24	15	7	7	1	1	0	0	1	5	1541	AIPO852
Apr 1973	36	23	18	8	5	1	1	1	0	1	7	1528	AIPO868
Mar 1974	42	22	14	8	6	1	0	1	0	1	4	1484	GSS
Mar 1975	36	23	18	8	6	2	1	1	0	0	5	1490	GSS
Jun 1976	31	29	19	8	4	1	0	0	0	0	7	1544	AIPO954
Mar 1977	36	22	18	8	6	2	1	1	0	1	6	1530	GSS
Mar 1982	41	22	15	8	6	2	1	0	0	0	6	1506	GSS
Mar 1983	36	23	18	9	7	1	1	1	0	0	6	1599	GSS
Mar 1985	39	22	19	9	5	1	0	1	0	0	4	1534	GSS
Mar 1986	42	21	17	8	8	1	0	0	0	1	2	1470	GSS
Mar 1988	43	20	14	8	7	1	1	1	0	1	4	988	GSS

Table 2.19 Like/Dislike Brazil--1972-1985

BRAZIL--You will notice...How far up the scale or how far down the scale would you rate... Brazil?

	+5	+4	+3	+2	+1	-1	-2	-3	-4	-5	DK	N	
May 1972	4	6	15	16	23	8	4	5	2	3	13	1541	AIPO852
Mar 1974	6	8	17	13	22	9	3	2	1	2	14	1484	GSS
Mar 1975	5	7	14	15	23	10	5	4	2	2	14	1490	GSS
Jun 1976	4	5	13	19	26	10	4	3	2	2	12	1544	AIPO954
Mar 1977	6	6	13	13	22	10	5	4	2	4	14	1530	GSS
Mar 1982	5	8	13	14	24	10	5	3	2	2	15	1506	GSS
Mar 1983	5	4	10	16	30	13	5	3	1	2	12	1599	GSS
Mar 1985	4	6	13	13	28	11	5	4	2	3	12	751	GSS

Table 2.20 Like/Dislike China--1954-1988

CHINA--You will notice...How far up the scale or how far down the scale would you rate... China?

	+5	+4	+3	+2	+1	-1	-2	-3	-4	-5	DK	N	
Sep 1954	1	1	3	2	6	7	6	8	9	44	12	1327	AIPO537
May 1972	1	2	4	6	11	10	6	9	11	34	6	1541	AIPO852
Apr 1973	6	3	12	9	17	9	6	8	5	15	9	1528	AIPO868
Mar 1974	3	4	7	11	17	13	8	9	6	16	6	1484	GSS
Mar 1975	3	3	7	8	15	15	8	9	8	16	8	1490	GSS
Mar 1977	3	4	6	7	16	15	8	9	6	16	9	1530	GSS
Mar 1982	4	6	11	12	19	14	8	7	6	7	7	1506	GSS
Mar 1983	4	4	9	14	22	17	10	8	4	8	6	1599	GSS
Mar 1985	4	6	15	14	22	12	6	6	3	5	7	1534	GSS
Mar 1986	5	5	15	15	24	11	6	6	4	6	4	1470	GSS
Mar 1988	6	7	14	13	25	12	5	2	3	6	8	988	GSS

Table 2.21 Like/Dislike Israel--1956-1988

ISRAEL--You will notice...How far up the scale or how far down the scale would you rate... Israel?

	+5	+4	+3	+2	+1	-1	-2	-3	-4	-5	DK	N	
Dec 1956	7	5	9	11	17	10	5	4	2	4	26	1543	AIPO576
Dec 1966	7	6	12	13	25	11	3	2	2	1	17	3542	AIPO738
Mar 1974	13	10	16	12	17	9	4	4	2	6	7	1484	GSS
Mar 1975	10	8	14	11	18	11	6	5	3	5	8	1490	GSS
Jun 1976	9	9	14	14	20	10	5	4	2	4	9	1544	AIPO954
Mar 1977	12	10	13	11	18	10	5	4	3	4	10	1530	GSS
Mar 1978	15	11	22	11	16	7	2	3	1	3	9	1509	NORC4269
Mar 1982	11	8	14	11	16	12	7	5	3	4	8	1506	GSS
Mar 1983	9	8	11	11	18	13	7	7	4	6	6	1599	GSS
Mar 1985	11	8	14	13	17	10	6	5	3	5	8	1534	GSS
Mar 1986	11	9	12	12	19	10	6	5	4	7	5	1470	GSS
Mar 1988	10	6	10	9	16	13	8	8	3	10	8	988	GSS

Table 2.22 Like/Dislike Egypt--1956-1988

EGYPT--You will notice...How far up the scale or how far down the scale would you rate... Egypt?

	+5	+4	+3	+2	+1	-1	-2	-3	-4	-5	DK	N	
Dec 1956	2	2	5	8	14	13	9	9	5	9	25	1543	AIPO576
Dec 1966	3	3	8	10	22	15	8	6	2	4	18	3542	AIPO738
Apr 1973	4	3	6	7	15	16	9	9	6	11	13	1528	AIPO868
Mar 1974	4	6	9	10	19	13	8	7	5	9	9	1484	GSS
Mar 1975	3	3	8	10	21	15	8	8	5	9	10	1490	GSS
Jun 1976	3	3	8	12	23	17	8	7	4	6	11	1544	AIPO954
Mar 1977	5	4	10	11	22	17	6	5	4	5	12	1530	GSS
Mar 1982	5	8	15	13	22	10	4	5	2	4	10	1506	GSS
Mar 1983	5	6	13	13	24	13	6	6	3	3	8	1599	GSS
Mar 1985	5	6	13	13	25	11	6	5	2	4	9	1534	GSS
Mar 1986	4	5	10	14	24	14	7	6	3	6	6	1470	GSS
Mar 1988	6	5	11	10	23	14	6	6	2	6	11	988	GSS

Table 2.23   Is Communism a Bad/Good Kind of Government?--
             1973-1988

COMMUN--Thinking about all the different kinds of govern-
ments in the world today, which of these statements comes
closest to how you feel about communism as a form of government?

	WORST KIND	BAD, NOT WORST	OK FOR SOME	GOOD FORM	DK	N	
Mar 1973	43	27	24	3	4	1501	GSS
Mar 1974	49	26	19	3	3	1480	GSS
Mar 1976	51	26	20	1	3	1497	GSS
Mar 1977	53	24	20	1	2	1526	GSS
Mar 1980	57	26	13	1	3	1465	GSS
Mar 1982	59	25	12	1	2	1501	GSS
Mar 1984	60	25	11	2	2	1467	GSS
Mar 1985	57	26	13	1	2	1529	GSS
Mar 1987	55	28	14	1	2	1456	GSS
Mar 1988	48	31	16	2	3	971	GSS

Table 2.24   Was Korea a Mistake?--1950-1953

Do you think the United States made a mistake in going into
the war in Korea or not?

	YES	NO	DK	N	
Aug 1950[a]	19	66	15	1341	AIPO460
Dec 1950[a]	49	39	12	1369	AIPO469
Feb 1951	49	41	10	1403	AIPO471
Mar 1951	44	43	13	2101	AIPO473
Apr 1951	37	45	18	1266	AIPO474
Jun 1951	43	39	18	1997	AIPO476
Aug 1951	42	47	11	2057	AIPO478
Mar 1952	50	37	13	1922	AIPO487
Oct 1952	46	36	18	3097	AIPO506
Oct 1952	42	37	20	3114	AIPO507
Jan 1953	36	50	14	1558	AIPO510

[a]In view of the developments since we entered the fighting
in Korea, do you think the United States made a mistake in
deciding to defend Korea (South Korea), or not?

Table 2.25 Was the U.S. Right to Go into Korea?--1950-1953

Do you think the United States was right or wrong in sending American troups to stop the Communist invasion of South Korea?

	RIGHT	WRONG	DK	N	
Jul 1950[a]	75	21	4	1302	NORC287
Sep 1950	81	13	6	1284	NORC288
Dec 1950	55	36	'9	1258	NORC295
Feb 1951	57	32	11	1236	NORC298
Mar 1951	60	30	10	1237	NORC300
Apr 1951	63	27	10	1289	NORC302
May 1951	59	30	11	1282	NORC307
Aug 1951	60	30	10	1292	NORC312
Dec 1951	54	36	9	1281	NORC314
Jan 1952	56	34	9	1237	NORC315
Mar 1952	50	40	10	1260	NORC320
Jun 1952	55	38	7	1293	NORC327

[a]Do you approve or disapprove of the decision to send American troops to stop the Communist invasion of South Korea?

As you look back on the Korean war, do you think the United States did the right thing in sending troops to stop the Communist invasion, or should we have stayed out of it entirely?

Sep 1953	64	28	8	1262	NORC348

Table 2.26   Was Vietnam a Mistake?--1965-1973

In view of the developments since we entered the fighting in Vietnam, do you think the U.S. made a mistake sending troops to fight in Vietnam?

	YES	NO	DK	N	
Aug 1965	24	61	15	3525	AIPO716
Mar 1966	25	59	16	3555	AIPO725
May 1966	36	49	15	3519	AIPO728
Sep 1966	35	48	17	3532	AIPO734
Nov 1966	31	51	18	3525	AIPO737
Jan 1967	32	52	16	3491	AIPO740
Apr 1967	37	50	13	3519	AIPO744
Jul 1967	41	48	11	1518	AIPO748
Oct 1967	46	44	10	1585	AIPO752
Dec 1967	45	46	9	1549	AIPO755
Jan 1968	45	45	12	1500	AIPO757
Feb 1968	50	42	8	1501	AIPO758
Apr 1968	48	40	12	1504	AIPO760
Aug 1968	53	35	12	1526	AIPO766
Sep 1968	54	37	9	1500	AIPO769
Jan 1969	52	39	9	1503	AIPO774
Sep 1969	58	32	10	1560	AIPO788
Jan 1970	57	33	10	1573	AIPO797
Mar 1970	58	32	10	1551	AIPO803
May 1970	56	36	8	1509	AIPO807
Jan 1971	59	31	10	1502	AIPO821
May 1971	61	28	11	1639	AIPO830
Jan 1973	60	29	11	1549	AIPO862

3

Taxation and Spending

Americans have been asked quite regularly since 1947 whether
they consider their federal taxes to be too low, and it will
come as no surprise to discover that just as regularly they
have been strongly inclined to think not (Table 3.1). However, there has been some fluctuation in the proportions that
believe their taxes to be "too high" and "about right."

Protest against high taxes generally rose in the immediate postwar period, reaching a peak in 1952 and 1953 during
the Korean War and, perhaps not coincidentally, at a time when
Republicans were returned to the White House. Thereafter
people registered more contentment with their tax burden, and
the percentages holding taxes to be too high dipped during the
early 1960s, when the Kennedy administration was trying with
some difficulty to get a tax cut bill accepted. The percentage feeling taxes were too high then rose, reaching high
levels again by 1969. It held at that level until the early
1980s and has declined markedly since. These fluctuations may
have been influenced not only by the exact levels of federal
spending and tax rates, but also by inflation and by feelings
about the distribution of the tax load (Ladd, et al, 1979).
When prices are rising painfully, people seek relief, and the
idea of cutting taxes gains new appeal (Hansen, 1983).

Data on the public's spending priorities during the period since 1971 are presented in Tables 3.2-3.28. As the percentage of people insisting that their federal taxes are too
high has declined in the 1980s, so the percentage favoring
expanded expenditures has increased somewhat--despite very
substantial White House rhetoric to the contrary. However,
the public is selective about where the spending increases
should go.

Support for increased spending for space exploration
stood at very low levels in the years after the Americans
finally made it to the moon, but rose later (3.2, 3.3).

There has been an increased willingness to spend more for environmental concerns during the later 1980s after a dip in the late 1970s and early 1980s (3.4, 3.5).   A similar pattern holds for spending on health measures (3.6, 3.7) and, to a degree, on drug problems (3.12, 3.13), on helping blacks (3.16), and on welfare (3.23).[1]

There has been no clear parallel rise (though there has been no notable decrease either) in willingness to spend on big cities (3.8, 3.9), on crime and law enforcement (3.10, 3.11), on foreign aid (3.21, 3.22), on parks and recreation (3.28), and, it appears, on social security (3.26).

Any increased willingness to spend on education during the 1980s has been small, but there was a previous rise in the early 1970s (3.14, 3.15).   Meanwhile, data from the 1980s charts reduced enthusiasm for spending on such classic public works projects as highways and bridges (3.25) and mass transportation (3.27).

More extensive data are available for defense spending, and they reveal substantial fluctuations since 1951 (3.18-3.20).   Support for defense spending was high during the Korean War.   This support declined by 1960 and dropped substantially by 1969 (unfortunately, there appear to be no comparable data to cover the period of the Vietnam buildup that took place between those two dates).   From 1969 to the middle 1970s there occurred the decline of the Vietnam War, notable detente with the Soviet Union, and the growth of improved relations with China--and support for defense spending remained low. Support for increased defense spending grew during the late 1970s over concerns about a renewed Cold War and about the Soviet military buildup (3.19). This support bolted upward in 1980 as the Soviets invaded Afghanistan and as Ronald Reagan launched his campaign for the presidency.   But defense spending support dropped precipitously again in 1981 and has declined in the years since as the Cold War mellowed (see also 2.15) and as Reagan has responded to public concerns and his own rhetoric by, indeed, raising defense spending substantially.

This discussion has concentrated on comparing attitudes toward spending as they have changed over time.   It is far more difficult to compare different spending questions in the same year to determine what the public's priorities are at a given point in time.   This is because the degree to which respondents are willing to spend money on something is determined substantially by what the questioner chooses to call it (Smith, 1987; Rasinski, 1988).

---

[1]On the question of whether these and other changes signal a generally growing conservatism in the U.S., see Chafetz and Ebaugh (1983).   See also AuClaire (1984).

In 1988, for example, 68 percent were willing to boost spending to "halt the rising crime rate" but only 54 percent wanted to spend more on "law enforcement" (3.10, 3.11); 46 percent wanted to spend to "solve the problems" of the big cities, but only 21 percent wanted to "assist" them (3.16, 3.17); and only 23 percent wanted to spend more on "welfare" but fully 68 percent supported increased "assistance to the poor" (3.23, 3.24). It is also clear that responses can be substantially influenced by question form and order: a 1974 survey found a 10 percentage point increase in support for defense cutbacks when the question positioned *implied* trade-offs with other spending priorities (Mueller 1977, p. 325; see also Smith, 1987).

Thus while the polls do suggest that in 1988 the public was more willing to cut, say, expenditures for foreign aid than for defense, and more willing to cut defense than education or "assistance to the poor," it would be unwise to lean too heavily on the precise numbers. They are quite changeable by creative question formulators.

REFERENCES

AuClaire, Philip Arthur. 1984. Public Attitudes Toward Social Welfare Expenditures. *Social Work*, 29:139-144.

Chafetz, Janet Saltzman, and Helen Rose Fuchs Ebaugh. 1983. Growing Conservatism in the United States? An Examination of Trends in Political Opinion between 1972 and 1980. *Sociological Perspectives*, 26:275-298.

Hansen, Susan B. 1983. *The Politics of Taxation*. New York: Praeger.

Ladd, Everett Carll, Jr., Marilyn Potter, Linda Basilick, Sally Daniels, and Dana Suszkin. 1979. The Polls: Taxing and Spending. *Public Opinion Quarterly*, 43:126-135.

Mueller, John E. 1977. Changes in American Public Attitudes Toward International Involvement. In Ellen P. Stern, ed., *The Limits of Military Intervention*. Beverly Hills, CA: Sage.

Rasinski, Kenneth A. 1988. The Effect of Question Wording on Public Support for Government Spending. NORC: GSS Methodological Report No. 54.

Smith, Tom W. 1987. That Which We Call Welfare by Any Other Name Would Be Sweeter. *Public Opinion Quarterly*, 51:75-83.

Table 3.1 Do You Pay Too Much in Federal Income Tax?--
1947-1988

TAX--Do you consider the amount of federal income tax which
you have to pay as too high, about right, or too low?

	TOO HIGH	ABOUT RIGHT	TOO LOW	PAYS NONE (VOLUN-TEERED)	DK	N	
Mar 1947[a]	53	40	1		6	2309	AIPO392
Nov 1947[b]	61	31	1		7	1139	AIPO408
Mar 1948[c]	57	39	1		3	1235	AIPO414
Mar 1949[c]	42	52	1		5	945	AIPO439
Mar 1950[d]	53	38	0		8	1005	AIPO452TPS
Feb 1951[e]	52	43	2		3	1078	AIPO471
Feb 1952[f]	71	26	0		3	1657	AIPO486
Jan 1953[g]	60	37	-		3	1291	AIPO511
Feb 1956	55	35	1		9	2012	AIPO560
Apr 1957	61	31	0		7	1654	AIPO581
Mar 1959	51	40	2		7	1519	AIPO611
Feb 1961	46	46	1		8	2863	AIPO641
Feb 1962	48	45	-		7	1511	AIPO655
Jun 1962	47	45	1		7	3255	AIPO660
Jan 1963	52	38	1		1	4367	AIPO667
Feb 1964	56	35	1		9	3474	AIPO686
Feb 1966	52	39	0		9	3510	AIPO724
Mar 1967	58	37	1		3	3522	AIPO742
Mar 1969	69	25	1		6	1633	AIPO776
Feb 1973	64	30	1		6	1517	AIPO864
Mar 1976	64	26	1	7	3	774	GSS
Mar 1977	65	28	1	2	4	1523	GSS
Mar 1980	68	27	0	-	5	1449	GSS
Mar 1982	69	26	0	1	4	1496	GSS
Mar 1984	63	33	1	2	2	1459	GSS
Mar 1985	60	32	0	4	3	1531	GSS
Jun 1985	63	32	1	-	4	1540	AIPO254G
Mar 1987	59	35	1	2	4	1452	GSS
Mar 1988	55	39	1	2	3	975	GSS

[a]Asked of 79% who "filed and paid an income tax by March 15
of this year."

[b]77% who pay a federal income tax.

[c]81% as in note a.

[d]67% who "had to pay a federal income tax on money earned
last year."

[e]78% as in note d.

[f]83% who have to pay federal income tax.

[g]81% as in note f.

Others asked of all respondents.

Table 3.2 Are We Spending Too Much, Too Little, about Right on the Space Exploration Program?--1971-1988

NATSPAC--We are faced with many problems in this country, none of which can be solved easily or inexpensively. I'm going to name some of these problems, and for each one I'd like you to tell me whether you think we're spending too much money on it, too little money, or about the right amount. First, are we spending too much, too little, or about the right amount on

Space exploration program?

	TOO LITTLE	ABOUT RIGHT	TOO MUCH	DK	N	
Sep 1971	6	23	66	5	1497	ROPER524
Sep 1971	6	23	66	5	1497	ROPER524
Mar 1973	7	29	58	5	1503	GSS
Dec 1973	3	24	66	6	1768	ROPER003
Mar 1974	8	28	61	4	1480	GSS
Dec 1974	7	28	56	9	2005	ROPER75-1B
Mar 1975	7	30	58	4	1490	GSS
Dec 1975	9	28	55	9	2002	ROPER76-1B
Mar 1976	9	28	60	2	1496	GSS
Dec 1976	11	33	46	9	2000	ROPER77-1B
Mar 1977	10	34	50	6	1530	GSS
Dec 1977	12	34	43	10	2001	ROPER78-1
Mar 1978	12	35	47	6	1532	GSS
Dec 1978	13	32	44	10	1742	ROPER79-1C
Dec 1979	15	33	42	10	2003	ROPER80-1C
Mar 1980	18	35	39	8	1466	GSS
Dec 1980	19	33	36	12	2000	ROPER81-1B
Dec 1981	18	37	36	9	1439	CBS-NYT
Dec 1981	14	38	41	7	2000	ROPER82-1B
Mar 1982	12	41	40	6	1505	GSS
Aut 1982[a]	12	36	46	6	1400	ELEC82
Dec 1982	12	37	44	6	2000	ROPER83-1
Mar 1983	14	40	40	6	1598	GSS
Dec 1983	10	45	38	7	2000	ROPER841
Mar 1984	12	43	39	6	487	GSS
Mar 1985	11	44	41	4	748	GSS
Mar 1986	11	43	41	4	727	GSS
Mar 1987	16	38	40	6	484	GSS
Mar 1988	18	42	34	6	714	GSS

[a]"...whether the federal government is spending...."

Table 3.3   Are We Spending Too Much, Too Little, about Right
on Space Exploration?--1984-1988

NATSPACY--Warefaced with many problems in this country, none
of which can be solved easily or inexpensively. I'm going
to name some of these problems, and for each one I'd like
you to tell me whether you think we're spending too much
money on it, too little money, or about the right amount.
First, are we spending too much, too little, or about the
right amount on

Space exploration?

	TOO LITTLE	ABOUT RIGHT	TOO MUCH	DK	N	
Mar 1984	10	40	46	4	489	GSS
Mar 1985	10	43	43	4	780	GSS
Mar 1986	9	47	39	5	733	GSS
Mar 1987	16	44	36	4	973	GSS
Mar 1988	20	36	38	7	754	GSS

Table 3.4   Are We Spending Too Much, Too Little, about Right
               on Improving and Protecting the Environment?--
               1971-1988

NATENVIR--We are faced with many problems...are we spending
too much, too little, or about the right amount on

Improving and protecting the environment?

	TOO LITTLE	ABOUT RIGHT	TOO MUCH	DK	N	
Oct 1971	56	25	5	14	1495	ROPER524
Mar 1973	61	26	7	6	1498	GSS
Dec 1973	45	30	15	9	1766	ROPER003
Mar 1974	59	27	8	7	1476	GSS
Dec 1974	49	30	11	9	2005	ROPER75-1B
Mar 1975	53	31	10	6	1490	GSS
Dec 1975	48	30	13	9	2002	ROPER76-1B
Mar 1976	55	31	9	5	1494	GSS
Dec 1976	50	31	12	7	2000	ROPER77-1B
Mar 1977	48	34	11	7	1524	GSS
Dec 1977	49	31	12	8	2001	ROPER78-1
Mar 1978	52	33	10	5	1528	GSS
Dec 1978	44	35	13	7	1796	ROPER79-1C
Dec 1979	45	35	14	6	2003	ROPER80-1C
Mar 1980	48	31	15	6	1465	GSS
Dec 1980	47	32	14	7	2000	ROPER81-1B
Dec 1981	48	36	10	7	2000	ROPER82-1B
Mar 1982	50	32	12	6	1504	GSS
Aut 1982	42	38	11	10	1411	ELEC82
Dec 1982	47	37	10	6	2000	ROPER83-1
Mar 1983	54	31	8	6	1592	GSS
Dec 1983	48	38	7	6	2000	ROPER841
Mar 1984	59	33	4	4	485	GSS
Mar 1985	56	32	8	4	747	GSS
Mar 1986	59	29	5	6	725	GSS
Mar 1987	65	25	5	5	482	GSS
Mar 1988	65	26	5	4	714	GSS

Table 3.5   Are We Spending Too Much, Too Little, about Right
               on the Environment?--1984-1988

NATENVIY--We are faced with many problems...are we spending
too much, too little, or about the right amount on

The environment?

	TOO LITTLE	ABOUT RIGHT	TOO MUCH	DK	N	
Mar 1984	57	30	8	5	487	GSS
Mar 1985	60	27	7	6	780	GSS
Mar 1986	58	30	7	6	732	GSS
Mar 1987	60	28	7	5	973	GSS
Mar 1988	64	25	4	6	750	GSS

Table 3.6 Are We Spending Too Much, Too Little, about Right
on Improving and Protecting the Nation's Health?
--1971-1988

NATHEAL--We are faced with many problems...are we spending
too much, too little, or about the right amount on

Improving and protecting the nation's health?

	TOO LITTLE	ABOUT RIGHT	TOO MUCH	DK	N	
Oct 1971	55	30	4	11	1491	ROPER524
Mar 1973	61	31	5	3	1497	GSS
Dec 1973	57	32	5	7	1761	ROPER003
Mar 1974	64	28	5	3	1477	GSS
Dec 1974	60	27	5	8	2005	ROPER75-1B
Mar 1975	63	28	5	4	1485	GSS
Dec 1975	57	29	6	8	2002	ROPER76-1B
Mar 1976	60	31	5	3	1491	GSS
Dec 1976	55	31	7	6	2000	ROPER77-1
Mar 1977	56	33	7	5	1526	GSS
Dec 1977	58	28	6	7	2001	ROPER78-1
Mar 1978	55	34	7	4	1532	GSS
Dec 1978	60	27	7	7	1815	ROPER79-1C
Dec 1979	59	29	7	5	2003	ROPER80-1C
Mar 1980	55	34	8	4	1467	GSS
Dec 1980	58	31	6	6	2000	ROPER81-1B
Dec 1981	56	33	6	6	2000	ROPER82-1B
Mar 1982	56	32	6	5	1504	GSS
Aut 1982	49	36	6	9	1412	ELEC82
Dec 1982	56	35	5	4	2000	ROPER83-1
Mar 1983	57	34	5	4	1591	GSS
Dec 1983	56	33	5	6	2000	ROPER841
Mar 1984	58	31	7	4	486	GSS
Mar 1985	58	33	6	3	749	GSS
Mar 1986	59	34	4	3	726	GSS
Mar 1987	68	26	4	2	481	GSS
Mar 1988	66	28	3	3	714	GSS

Table 3.7 Are We Spending Too Much, Too Little, about Right
on Health?--1984-1988

NATHEALY--We are faced with many problems...are we spending
too much, too little, or about the right amount on

Health?

	TOO LITTLE	ABOUT RIGHT	TOO MUCH	DK	N	
Mar 1984	55	32	8	4	488	GSS
Mar 1985	55	32	10	2	780	GSS
Mar 1986	59	31	7	3	730	GSS
Mar 1987	64	27	6	3	971	GSS
Mar 1988	68	24	5	3	754	GSS

Table 3.8   Are We Spending Too Much, Too Little, about Right
on Solving the Problems of the Big Cities?--
1971-1988

NATCITY--We are faced with many problems...are we spending
too much, too little, or about the right amount on

Solving the problems of the big cities?

	TOO LITTLE	ABOUT RIGHT	TOO MUCH	DK	N	
Oct 1971	41	22	10	26	1488	ROPER524
Mar 1973	48	27	12	12	1499	GSS
Dec 1973	42	25	10	22	1517	ROPER003
Mar 1974	50	24	11	15	1474	GSS
Dec 1974	43	24	10	22	2005	ROPER75-1B
Mar 1975	47	25	12	16	1479	GSS
Dec 1975	37	24	20	19	2002	ROPER76-LB
Mar 1976	43	26	20	12	1492	GSS
Dec 1976	40	24	18	17	2000	ROPER77-1B
Mar 1977	40	26	19	14	1525	GSS
Dec 1977	42	26	15	18	2001	ROPER78-1
Mar 1978	39	30	19	13	1531	GSS
Dec 1978	36	28	19	17	1933	ROPER79-1C
Dec 1979	38	32	17	13	2003	ROPER80-1C
Mar 1980	40	26	21	13	1464	GSS
Dec 1980	38	28	19	15	2000	ROPER81-1B
Dec 1981	43	28	14	15	2000	ROPER82-1B
Mar 1982	43	24	20	14	1502	GSS
Aut 1982	37	27	16	19	1407	ELEC82
Dec 1982	42	30	12	16	2000	ROPER83-1
Mar 1983	41	29	16	14	1591	GSS
Dec 1983	38	33	17	12	2000	ROPER841
Mar 1984	44	31	12	13	485	GSS
Mar 1985	39	33	16	12	747	GSS
Mar 1986	44	31	16	10	720	GSS
Mar 1987	38	33	13	16	482	GSS
Mar 1988	46	29	10	15	713	GSS

Table 3.9   Are We Spending Too Much, Too Little, about Right
on Assistance to Big Cities?--1984-1988

NATCITYY--We are faced with many problems...are we spending
too much, too little, or about the right amount on

Assistance to big cities?

	TOO LITTLE	ABOUT RIGHT	TOO MUCH	DK	N	
Mar 1984	18	37	33	12	485	GSS
Mar 1985	18	33	37	12	781	GSS
Mar 1986	15	38	33	14	732	GSS
Mar 1987	20	30	30	14	970	GSS
Mar 1988	21	34	28	16	753	GSS

Table 3.10 Are We Spending Too Much, Too Little, about
Right on Halting the Rising Crime Rate?--
1971-1988

NATCRIME--We are faced with many problems...are we spending
too much, too little, or about the right amount on

Halting the rising crime rate?

	TOO LITTLE	ABOUT RIGHT	TOO MUCH	DK	N	
Oct 1971	61	19	4	16	1460	ROPER524
Mar 1973	65	25	5	6	1497	GSS
Dec 1973	62	24	5	9	1757	ROPER003
Mar 1974	67	23	5	5	1481	GSS
Dec 1974	66	20	5	10	2005	ROPER75-1B
Mar 1975	66	23	5	6	1484	GSS
Dec 1975	64	20	7	9	2002	ROPER76-1B
Mar 1976	66	21	8	5	1489	GSS
Dec 1976	71	18	5	6	2000	ROPER77-1B
Mar 1977	66	22	6	6	1524	GSS
Dec 1977	65	23	5	8	2001	ROPER78-1
Mar 1978	64	25	6	4	1526	GSS
Dec 1978	65	21	6	7	1796	ROPER79-1C
Dec 1979	68	21	4	7	2003	ROPER80-1C
Mar 1980	69	21	6	4	1463	GSS
Dec 1980	73	17	5	6	2000	ROPER81-1B
Dec 1981	72	19	3	6	2000	ROPER82-1B
Mar 1982	72	19	5	5	1496	GSS
Aut 1982	59	25	5	10	1405	ELEC82
Dec 1982	68	23	4	5	2000	ROPER83-1
Mar 1983	67	24	5	4	1591	GSS
Dec 1983	64	25	4	6	2000	ROPER841
Mar 1984	68	25	5	3	484	GSS
Mar 1985	63	28	5	4	747	GSS
Mar 1986	64	27	5	4	725	GSS
Mar 1987	68	24	4	4	478	GSS
Mar 1988	68	23	4	5	712	GSS

Table 3.11 Are We Spending Too Much, Too Little, about
Right on Law Enforcement?--1984-1988

NATCRIMY--We are faced with many problems...are we spending
too much, too little, or about the right amount on

Law enforcement?

	TOO LITTLE	ABOUT RIGHT	TOO MUCH	DK	N	
Mar 1984	55	36	7	3	487	GSS
Mar 1985	57	34	6	4	778	GSS
Mar 1986	51	39	7	4	732	GSS
Mar 1987	51	39	6	3	970	GSS
Mar 1988	54	36	6	4	752	GSS

Table 3.12   Are We Spending Too Much, Too Little, about
Right on Dealing with Drug Addiction?--
1971-1988

NATDRUG--We are faced with many problems...are we spending
too much, too little, or about the right amount on
Dealing with drug addiction?

	TOO LITTLE	ABOUT RIGHT	TOO MUCH	DK	N	
Oct 1971	62	21	4	13	1493	ROPER524
Mar 1973	66	22	6	6	1493	GSS
Dec 1973	57	28	5	10	1759	ROPER003
Mar 1974	60	28	6	6	1478	GSS
Dec 1974	55	27	7	11	2005	ROPER75-1B
Mar 1975	55	29	8	8	1482	GSS
Dec 1975	56	26	9	10	2002	ROPER76-1B
Mar 1976	59	27	8	7	1493	GSS
Dec 1976	57	26	7	9	2000	ROPER77-1B
Mar 1977	55	29	9	7	1520	GSS
Dec 1977	54	27	7	12	2001	ROPER78-1
Mar 1978	55	31	9	5	1527	GSS
Dec 1978	55	25	9	10	1740	ROPER79-1C
Dec 1979	60	27	6	7	2003	ROPER80-1C
Mar 1980	60	25	8	7	1460	GSS
Dec 1980	63	23	6	8	2000	ROPER81-1B
Dec 1981	61	25	5	9	2000	ROPER82-1B
Mar 1982	57	27	8	8	1502	GSS
Aut 1982	54	29	6	11	1407	LEC82
Dec 1982	60	28	5	8	2000	ROPER83-1
Mar 1983	60	30	5	5	1591	GSS
Dec 1983	58	27	5	9	2000	ROPER841
Mar 1984	63	27	6	4	485	GSS
Mar 1985	62	28	5	4	748	GSS
Mar 1986	58	32	6	4	726	GSS
Mar 1987	65	28	4	2	482	GSS
Mar 1988	68	24	4	3	713	GSS

Table 3.13   Are We Spending Too Much, Too Little, about
Right on Drug Rehabilitation?--1984-1988

NATDRUGY--We are faced with many problems...are we spending
too much, too little, or about the right amount on

Drug rehabilitation?

	TOO LITTLE	ABOUT RIGHT	TOO MUCH	DK	N	
Mar 1984	47	38	9	6	489	GSS
Mar 1985	53	30	8	8	779	GSS
Mar 1986	53	32	9	6	734	GSS
Mar 1987	56	30	8	6	969	GSS
Mar 1988	57	29	8	6	754	GSS

Table 3.14   Are We Spending Too Much, Too Little, about
Right on Improving the Nation's Education
System?--1971-1988

NATEDUC--We are faced with many problems...are we spending
too much, too little, or about the right amount on

Improving the nation's education system?

	TOO LITTLE	ABOUT RIGHT	TOO MUCH	DK	N	
Oct 1971	44	37	9	10	1488	ROPER524
Mar 1973	49	38	9	4	1499	GSS
Dec 1973	44	39	9	8	1752	ROPER003
Mar 1974	51	37	9	4	1474	GSS
Dec 1974	46	38	8	8	2005	ROPER75-1B
Mar 1975	49	35	11	5	1487	GSS
Dec 1975	49	35	8	7	2002	ROPER76-1B
Mar 1976	50	37	9	3	1495	GSS
Dec 1976	48	35	10	7	2000	ROPER77-1B
Mar 1977	48	39	10	4	1527	GSS
Dec 1977	54	31	9	6	2001	ROPER78-1
Mar 1978	52	34	11	4	1530	GSS
Dec 1978	49	34	9	8	1786	ROPER79-1C
Dec 1979	53	35	8	5	2003	ROPER80-1C
Mar 1980	53	33	10	4	1463	GSS
Dec 1980	52	33	9	7	2000	ROPER81-1B
Dec 1981	56	33	7	5	2000	ROPER82-1B
Mar 1982	56	32	8	4	1504	GSS
Aut 1982	55	31	7	6	1411	ELEC82
Dec 1982	56	34	5	5	2000	ROPER83-1
Mar 1983	60	31	6	3	1593	GSS
Dec 1983	59	32	5	5	2000	ROPER84-1
Mar 1984	64	31	3	2	483	GSS
Mar 1985	60	31	5	3	746	GSS
Mar 1986	60	33	4	3	726	GSS
Mar 1987	62	30	6	3	483	GSS
Mar 1988	64	29	4	3	711	GSS

Table 3.15   Are We Spending Too Much, Too Little, about
Right on Education?--1984-1988

NATEDUCY--We are faced with many problems...are we spending
too much, too little, or about the right amount on

Education?

	TOO LITTLE	ABOUT RIGHT	TOO MUCH	DK	N	
Mar 1984	64	27	7	2	488	GSS
Mar 1985	65	26	7	2	781	GSS
Mar 1986	66	27	5	2	732	GSS
Mar 1987	65	28	5	2	970	GSS
Mar 1988	68	25	5	2	755	GSS

Table 3.16 Are We Spending Too Much, Too Little, about
          Right on Improving the Conditions of
          Blacks?--1973-1988

NATRACE--We are faced with many problems...are we spending
too much, too little, or about the right amount on

Improving the conditions of blacks?

	TOO LITTLE	ABOUT RIGHT	TOO MUCH	DK	N	
Mar 1973	33	39	22	6	1499	
Mar 1974	31	42	21	7	1477	GSS
Mar 1975	27	41	24	8	1486	GSS
Mar 1976	27	41	25	7	1491	GSS
Mar 1977	25	42	25	8	1525	GSS
Mar 1978	24	43	25	7	1529	GSS
Mar 1980	24	44	24	8	1462	GSS
Mar 1982	28	44	20	8	1498	GSS
Aut 1982	30	39	17	14	1407	ELEC82
Mar 1983	29	43	18	9	1592	GSS
Mar 1984	35	43	16	6	485	GSS
Mar 1985	31	43	20	7	749	GSS
Mar 1986	34	43	16	8	724	GSS
Mar 1987	35	43	15	7	479	GSS
Mar 1988	35	41	16	8	714	GSS

Table 3.17 Are We Spending Too Much, Too Little, about
          Right on Assistance to Blacks?--1984-1988

NATRACEY--We are faced with many problems...are we spending
too much, too little, or about the right amount on

Assistance to blacks?

	TOO LITTLE	ABOUT RIGHT	TOO MUCH	DK	N	
Mar 1984	24	42	24	10	486	GSS
Mar 1985	26	40	25	9	781	GSS
Mar 1986	23	45	26	6	733	GSS
Mar 1987	26	43	22	9	972	GSS
Mar 1988	25	40	23	12	753	GSS

Table 3.18   Should the Government Spend More, Less, or about
the Same on the Armed Forces?--1951-1955,
National Defense?--1960-1976?

During the coming year, do you think we should cut down the
amount we are spending on our rearmament program, keep it
about the same, or spend even more on our armed forces?

	SPEND MORE	KEEP SAME	CUT DOWN	DK	N	
Apr 1951	44	39	8	9	1289	NORC302
Dec 1952	31	52	11	6	1283	NORC334
Oct 1955[a]	26	60	8	6	527	NORC378

[a]"arms program" instead of "rearmament program"

There is much discussion as to the amount the government in
Washington should spend for national defense and military
purposes. How do you feel about this--do you think we are
spending too little, too much, or about the right amount?

	TOO LITTLE	ABOUT RIGHT	TOO MUCH	DK	N	
Apr 1960[a]	21	45	18	16		AIPO625
Jul 1969	8	31	52	9		AIPO784
Nov 1969			46			AIPO793
Mar 1971	11	31	49	9		AIPO
Feb 1973	8	40	42	10		AIPO
Sep 1973	13	30	46	11		AIPO
Sep 1974	12	32	44	12		AIPO
Feb 1976	22	32	36	10		AIPO

[a]"...the country should spend for national defense. How..."

Table 3.19   Are We Spending Too Much, Too Little, about
               Right on Military, Armaments and Defense?--
               1971-1988

NATARMS--We are faced with many problems...are we spending
too much, too little, or about the right amount on

          The military, armaments and defense?

	TOO LITTLE	ABOUT RIGHT	TOO MUCH	DK	N	
Oct 1971	15	33	35	17	1488	ROPER524
Mar 1973	11	45	38	6	1496	GSS
Dec 1973	14	40	32	14	1762	ROPER003
Mar 1974	17	45	31	7	1479	GSS
Dec 1974	13	42	32	13	2005	ROPER75-1B
Mar 1975	17	46	31	7	1484	GSS
Dec 1975	20	41	27	13	2002	ROPER76-1B
Mar 1976	24	42	27	7	1492	GSS
Dec 1976	22	44	22	12	2000	ROPER77-1B
Mar 1977	24	45	23	8	1527	GSS
Dec 1977	23	40	24	13	2001	ROPER78
Mar 1978	27	44	22	8	1529	GSS
Dec 1978	31	35	23	11	1728	ROPER79-1C
Dec 1979	41	35	16	9	2003	ROPER80-1C
Mar 1980	56	26	11	6	1465	GSS
Dec 1980	56	24	12	9	2000	ROPER81-1B
Dec 1981	29	38	27	7	2000	ROPER82-1B
Mar 1982	29	36	30	5	1497	GSS
Aut 1982	19	39	35	8	1411	ELEC82
Dec 1982	19	37	38	6	2000	ROPER83-1
Mar 1983	24	38	32	6	1595	GSS
Dec 1983	21	40	32	7	2000	ROPER84-1
Mar 1984	17	41	38	3	486	GSS
Mar 1985	14	42	40	3	747	GSS
Mar 1986	16	38	40	5	726	GSS
Mar 1987	15	41	41	4	480	GSS
Mar 1988	16	40	38	6	712	GSS

Table 3.20   Are We Spending Too Much, Too Little, about
               Right on National Defense?--1984-1988

NATARMSY--We are faced with many problems...are we spending
too much, too little, or about the right amount on

          National defense?

	TOO LITTLE	ABOUT RIGHT	TOO MUCH	DK	N	
Mar 1984	18	39	38	5	487	GSS
Mar 1985	16	39	41	5	781	GSS
Mar 1986	16	45	35	4	734	GSS
Mar 1987	20	40	36	4	972	GSS
Mar 1988	18	39	37	7	753	GSS

Table 3.21   Are We Spending Too Much, Too Little, about
Right on Foreign Aid?--1971-1988

NATAID--We are faced with many problems...are we spending
too much, too little, or about the right amount on

Foreign aid?

	TOO LITTLE	ABOUT RIGHT	TOO MUCH	DK	N	
Oct 1971	4	13	70	13	1487	ROPER524
Mar 1973	4	20	70	5	1503	GSS
Dec 1973	2	14	76	8	1766	ROPER003
Mar 1974	3	17	76	4	1481	GSS
Dec 1974	4	15	73	7	2005	ROPER75-1B
Mar 1975	5	17	73	5	1489	GSS
Dec 1975	3	14	75	8	2002	ROPER76-1B
Mar 1976	3	18	75	4	1494	GSS
Dec 1976	3	20	67	9	2000	ROPER77-1B
Mar 1977	3	24	66	7	1527	GSS
Dec 1977	4	19	69	8	2001	PER78-1
Mar 1978	4	24	67	6	1532	GSS
Dec 1978	4	17	71	8	1936	ROPER79-1C
Dec 1979	5	18	72	5	2003	ROPER80-1C
Mar 1980	5	20	70	5	1466	GSS
Dec 1980	5	19	69	6	2000	ROPER81-1B
Dec 1981	5	19	69	7	2000	ROPER82-1B
Mar 1982	5	18	72	5	1502	GSS
Aut 1982	4	16	72	8	1406	ELEC82
Dec 1982	3	15	75	7	2000	ROPER83-1
Mar 1983	4	17	74	5	1595	GSS
Mar 1984	4	21	70	5	486	GSS
Mar 1985	7	24	65	4	745	GSS
Mar 1986	6	19	71	4	726	GSS
Mar 1987	7	20	69	4	481	GSS
Mar 1988	5	22	68	5	715	GSS

Table 3.22   Are We Spending Too Much, Too Little, about
Right on Assistance to Other Countries?--
1984-1988

NATAIDY--We are faced with many problems...are we spending
too much, too little, or about the right amount on

Assistance to other countries?

	TOO LITTLE	ABOUT RIGHT	TOO MUCH	DK	N	
Mar 1984	4	16	77	3	488	GSS
Mar 1985	7	20	69	4	776	GSS
Mar 1986	4	16	75	4	734	GSS
Mar 1987	5	20	72	3	968	GSS
Mar 1988	4	19	73	4	750	GSS

Table 3.23 Are We Spending Too Much, Too Little, about
Right on Welfare?--1971-1988

NATFARE--We are faced with many problems...are we spending
too much, too little, or about the right amount on

Welfare?

	TOO LITTLE	ABOUT RIGHT	TOO MUCH	DK	N	
Oct 1971	18	19	53	11	1474	ROPER524
Mar 1973	20	24	51	4	1497	GSS
Dec 1973	18	24	48	9	1762	ROPER003
Mar 1974	22	32	42	4	1481	GSS
Dec 1974	19	23	49	9	2005	ROPER75-1B
Mar 1975	23	29	43	5	1484	GSS
Dec 1975	17	22	53	9	2002	ROPER76-1B
Mar 1976	13	22	60	4	1493	GSS
Dec 1976	13	21	59	7	2000	ROPER77-1B
Mar 1977	12	23	60	5	1524	GSS
Dec 1977	15	20	58	7	2001	ROPER78-1
Mar 1978	13	25	58	4	1529	GSS
Dec 1978	13	20	60	6	1820	ROPER79-1C
Dec 1979	13	25	57	5	2003	ROPER80-1C
Mar 1980	13	26	57	4	1463	GSS
Dec 1980	16	21	58	6	2000	ROPER81-1B
Dec 1981	20	23	52	5	2000	ROPER82-1B
Mar 1982	20	28	48	4	1505	GSS
Aut 1982	19	23	50	8	1407	ELEC82
Dec 1982	22	26	45	7	2000	ROPER83-1
Mar 1983	21	28	47	4	1594	GSS
Dec 1983	20	31	43	6	2000	ROPER84-1
Mar 1984	24	33	40	3	484	GSS
Mar 1985	19	33	45	4	749	GSS
Mar 1986	22	34	40	4	726	GSS
Mar 1987	21	31	44	4	481	GSS
Mar 1988	23	32	42	3	709	GSS

Table 3.24 Are We Spending Too Much, Too Little, about
Right on Assistance to the Poor?--1984-1988

NATFAREY--We are faced with many problems...are we spending
too much, too little, or about the right amount on

Assistance to the poor?

	TOO LITTLE	ABOUT RIGHT	TOO MUCH	DK	N	
Mar 1984	62	24	11	3	485	GSS
Mar 1985	63	25	10	2	781	GSS
Mar 1986	61	27	9	2	734	GSS
Mar 1987	66	23	9	2	972	GSS
Mar 1988	68	23	7	2	752	GSS

Table 3.25 Are We Spending Too Much, Too Little, about
           Right on Highways and Bridges?--1984-1988

NATROAD--We are faced with many problems...are we spending
too much, too little, or about the right amount on

        Highways and bridges?

	TOO LITTLE	ABOUT RIGHT	TOO MUCH	DK	N	
Mar 1984	46	43	7	4	973	GSS
Mar 1985	41	46	8	5	1524	GSS
Mar 1986	35	52	8	5	1459	GSS
Mar 1987	35	52	8	5	1450	GSS
Mar 1988	36	52	8	4	1459	GSS

Table 3.26 Are We Spending Too Much, Too Little, about
           Right on Social Security?--1982-1988

NATSOC--We are faced with many problems...are we spending
too much, too little, or about the right amount on

        Social security?

	TOO LITTLE	ABOUT RIGHT	TOO MUCH	DK	N	
Aut 1982	46	33	12	9	1403	ELEC82
Mar 1984	51	36	9	5	968	GSS
Mar 1985	52	38	7	3	1527	GSS
Mar 1986	56	36	6	3	1456	GSS
Mar 1987	55	35	6	4	1449	GSS
Mar 1988	53	38	6	4	1467	GSS

Table 3.27   Are We Spending Too Much, Too Little, about
Right on Mass Transportation?--1984-1988

NATMASS--We are faced with many problems...are we spending
too much, too little, or about the right amount on

Mass transportation?

	TOO LITTLE	ABOUT RIGHT	TOO MUCH	DK	N	
Mar 1984	34	46	11	9	972	GSS
Mar 1985	30	48	12	10	1528	GSS
Mar 1986	28	50	12	9	1457	GSS
Mar 1987	29	47	13	11	1451	GSS
Mar 1988	28	49	10	12	1459	GSS

Table 3.28   Are We Spending Too Much, Too Little, about
Right on Parks and Recreation?--1984-1988

NATPARK--We are faced with many problems...are we spending
too much, too little, or about the right amount on

Parks and recreation?

	TOO LITTLE	ABOUT RIGHT	TOO MUCH	DK	N	
Mar 1984	32	58	6	3	974	GSS
Mar 1985	31	58	7	4	1530	GSS
Mar 1986	29	60	6	5	1459	GSS
Mar 1987	30	61	6	4	1453	GSS
Mar 1988	29	61	6	5	1468	GSS

4

Confidence in Institutions

Great social and political institutions rest ultimately not upon their legal powers, their bureaucratic structure, or their internal resources, but on the goodwill of the people. To function effectively institutions must have the faith and trust or confidence of those whom they serve. Governmental bodies need the support and loyalty of the citizenry, businesses the loyalty of their customers, and labor unions and voluntary associations the loyalty of their members. Without popular confidence institutions lose their ability to function effectively--governments topple, businesses go bankrupt, and organizations lose members and dwindle away.

Measures of confidence in institutions are middle-range indicators of support. They do not tap underlying confidence in the sociopolitical system, such as in our democratic form of government or our free enterprise system; nor do they focus on the day-to-day job performance of specific incumbents as presidential popularity measures do. Instead they strike somewhere between these two extremes, focusing on the actual functioning of major institutions without emphasizing particular actors. While these items have been subjected to certain methodological criticisms (Turner and Kraus, 1978), extensive methodological review and experimentation have shown them to be reliable and valid measures (Smith, 1981; Lipset and Schneider, 1983; Smith and Peterson, 1985). The items do appear to undergo some sharp, short-term fluctuations, but these shifts seem to be closely related to historical events and objective conditions, rather than being measurement artifacts or random noise.

Overall, the early 1970s were a bear market for public confidence in most American institutions. In the political and economic realms, as well as some other areas, confidence generally declined. Then in the late 1970s or early 1980s confidence in most institutions bottomed out and usually a modest recovery occurred (Lipset and Schneider, 1983; Citrin, Green, and Reingold, 1987; Miller, 1983).

In the political realm confidence questions refer to the three main branches of government, the executive branch of the federal government, the United States Supreme Court, and the Congress. Confidence in the Supreme Court has always exceeded that of the two elected branches of government (Table 4.2). In addition, confidence has remained fairly stable over the last decade and a half, although there is some indication that support has fluctuated with the popularity of the Court's decisions (Caldeira, 1986). Congress has generally ranked lowest in public confidence (Table 4.3). Confidence fell from 24 percent in 1973 to 9 percent in 1980 before partially recovering to around 16 percent since 1986. A similar decline and rise was also shown in confidence in the military (4.4). Public confidence in the executive branch has generally fallen between that of the judiciary and the legislature (4.1). The unravelling of Watergate in 1974 created the equivalent of the 1929 stock-market crash; the proportion with a great deal of confidence fell from 29 percent to 14 percent, while the share with hardly any confidence more than doubled from 18 percent to 42 percent (Dunham and Mauss, 1976). Jimmy Carter's election in 1976 temporarily restored confidence to pre-Watergate levels during the honeymoon period in early 1977, but the marriage soon became troubled (Smith, Taylor, and Mathiowetz, 1980; on the inaugural honeymoon, see Mueller, 1973). While the percent with hardly any confidence did not quite rise to equal Watergate highs, those with a great deal of confidence fell even lower than Watergate levels in both 1978 and 1980. It appears that Ronald Reagan's election in 1980 led to a similar pattern, although the lack of an observation during the 1981 honeymoon makes this uncertain. In 1982, at least, confidence was above the Carter lows, but by 1983 it had almost fallen to Carter's nadir in 1980. Confidence in the Executive rebounded to 1982 levels in 1984-1987, but in 1988 some slippage had occurred.

Confidence in economic institutions has generally followed the business cycle. Trust in major companies and in banks and financial institutions was low during the recessions of 1975 and 1982/1983 and higher in the immediate recovery years (Tables 4.5-4.6). Lows were also reached in 1986. Confidence in organized labor does not follow economic conditions the way business confidence does, nor does it show a counter-cycle tendency of rising when business confidence falls (4.7). In general, confidence in organized labor fell from the early 1970s to historic lows in 1983-1986 before showing modest recovery since 1986.

Reflecting its often adversarial relationship with government, confidence in the press has tended to move in an opposite direction to governmental confidence (4.8).   For example, in 1974 when the percent with a great deal of confidence in the executive branch fell 16 percentage points, confidence in the press rose 3 percentage points.   Likewise executive confidence gained 15 percentage points in 1977 while press confidence dropped 3 percentage points.   Overall, the press lost ground in the 1970s to a low point in 1983, before staging a slight recovery.

Confidence in the scientific community and medicine has generally topped all other institutions (4.9).   Confidence in the scientific community has fluctuated within a narrow range and shown no clear trend, except for a decline in the proportion saying "don't know."   This may indicate greater interest in and perhaps even more knowledge about scientific matters. Confidence in medicine has remained high compared to other institutions, but did show some decline in the 1970s (4.10).

Confidence in education and its nemesis television both showed the general confidence decline of the 1970s and neither has come close to reobtaining levels of the early 1970s (4.11-4.12).   Education does, however, show some tentative signs of a rise in the late 1980s, while television remains near the bottom of the confidence scale with no clear evidence of revival.

Finally, confidence in organized religion has shown several large fluctuations that are difficult to interpret (4.13).   It showed sharp drops in 1975 and 1978 and is the only institution to be at its historic low in 1988.

REFERENCES

Caldeira, Gregory A. 1986. Neither the Purse Nor the Sword: Dynamics of Public Confidence in the Supreme Court. *American Political Science Review*, 80:1209-1226.

Citrin, Jack, Donald Green, and Beth Reingold.   1987.   The Soundness of Our Structure: Confidence in the Reagan Years. *Public Opinion*, 10:18-19.

Dunham, Roger G., and Atmand L. Mauss. 1976. Waves from Watergate: Evidence Concerning the Impact of the Watergate Scandal Upon Public Legitimacy and Social Control. *Pacific Sociological Review*, 19:469-490.

Lipset, Seymour Martin, and William Schneider. 1983. *The Confidence Gap: Business, Labor and Government in the Public Mind*.   New York: Free Press.

Miller, Arthur. 1983. Is Confidence Rebounding? *Public Opinion*, 6:16-20.

Mueller, John. 1973. *War, Presidents and Public Opinion*. New York: Wiley.

Smith, Tom W.   1981.   Can We Have Confidence in Confidence? Revisited.   In Denis F. Johnston, ed., *The Measurement of Subjective Phenomena*.   Washington, DC: U.S. Government Printing Office.

Smith, Tom W., and Bruce L. Peterson.   1985.   The Impact of Number of Response Categories on Inter-Item Associations: Experimental and Simulated Results.   Presented at the annual meeting of the American Sociological Association, Washington, DC.

Smith, Tom W., D. Garth Taylor, and Nancy A. Mathiowetz. 1980.   Public Opinion and Public Regard for the Federal Government. In Carol Weiss and Allen Barton, eds., *Making Bureaucracies Work*.   Beverly Hills. CA: Sage.

Turner, Charles F., and Elissa Krauss. 1978. Fallible Indicators of the Subjective State of the Nation.   *American Psychologist*, 33:456-470.

Table 4.1   How Much Confidence Do You Have in the Executive
            Branch of the Federal Government?--1973-1988

CONFED--I am going to name some institutions in this country.   As far as the people running these institutions are
concerned, would you say you have a great deal of confidence, only some confidence, or hardly any confidence at all
in them?

Executive branch of the federal government

	A GREAT DEAL	ONLY SOME	HARDLY ANY	DK	N	
Mar 1973	29	50	18	2	1498	GSS
Jan 1974[a]	14	49	33	4	1483	NORC4179
Mar 1974	14	43	42	2	1482	GSS
Mar 1975	13	55	30	3	1488	GSS
Mar 1976	13	59	25	3	1494	GSS
Mar 1977	28	54	14	3	1525	GSS
Mar 1978	13	59	25	3	1528	GSS
Mar 1980	12	50	34	3	1465	GSS
Mar 1982	19	54	24	2	1502	GSS
Mar 1983	13	54	29	3	1597	GSS
Mar 1984	19	50	29	2	977	GSS
Mar 1986	21	53	24	3	1468	GSS
Mar 1987	18	52	26	3	1463	GSS
Mar 1988	16	53	27	3	994	GSS

[a]"...confidence in them, only some...."

Table 4.2   How Much Confidence Do You Have in the U.S.
Supreme Court?--1973-1988

CONJUDGE--I am going to name some institutions in this country...would you say you have a great deal of confidence,
only some confidence, or hardly any confidence at all in
them?

U.S. Supreme Court

	A GREAT DEAL	ONLY SOME	HARDLY ANY	DK	N	
Mar 1973	31	50	15	3	1497	GSS
Jan 1974[a]	34	44	16	6	1485	NORC4179
Mar 1974	33	48	14	5	1482	GSS
Mar 1975	31	46	19	4	1485	GSS
Mar 1976	35	44	15	6	1491	GSS
Mar 1977	36	49	11	4	1522	GSS
Mar 1978	28	53	15	5	1527	GSS
Mar 1980	25	50	19	6	1468	GSS
Mar 1982	31	53	12	4	1500	GSS
Mar 1983	27	55	14	4	1595	GSS
Mar 1984	33	51	12	4	978	GSS
Mar 1986	30	52	14	4	1460	GSS
Mar 1987	36	50	10	4	1462	GSS
Mar 1988	35	50	11	4	992	GSS

[a]"...confidence in them, only some...."

Table 4.3 How Much Confidence Do You Have in Congress?--
1973-1988

CONLEGIS--I am going to name some institutions in this country...would you say you have a great deal of confidence,
only some confidence, or hardly any confidence at all in
them?

Congress

	A GREAT DEAL	ONLY SOME	HARDLY ANY	DK	N	
Mar 1973	24	59	15	3	1497	GSS
Jan 1974[a]	23	57	16	4	1485	NORC4179
Mar 1974	17	59	21	3	1481	GSS
Mar 1975	13	59	25	3	1487	GSS
Mar 1976	14	58	26	3	1494	GSS
Mar 1977	19	61	17	3	1523	GSS
Mar 1978	13	63	21	3	1527	GSS
Mar 1980	9	53	34	4	1466	GSS
Mar 1982	13	62	22	2	1501	GSS
Mar 1983	10	64	23	3	1592	GSS
Mar 1984	13	64	22	2	976	GSS
Mar 1986	16	61	20	3	1465	GSS
Mar 1987	16	63	18	3	1463	GSS
Mar 1988	15	62	19	3	995	GSS

[a]"...confidence in them, only some...."

Table 4.4 How Much Confidence Do You Have in the Military?
--1973-1988

CONARMY--I am going to name some institutions in this country...would you say you have a great deal of confidence,
only some confidence, or hardly any confidence at all in
them?

Military

	A GREAT DEAL	ONLY SOME	HARDLY ANY	DK	N	
Mar 1973	32	49	16	3	1498	GSS
Mar 1974	40	44	13	3	1483	GSS
Mar 1975	35	46	14	5	1487	GSS
Mar 1976	39	41	13	6	1491	GSS
Mar 1977	36	50	10	3	1526	GSS
Mar 1978	30	54	13	4	1528	GSS
Mar 1980	28	52	16	4	1467	GSS
Mar 1982	31	52	15	2	1502	GSS
Mar 1983	29	55	13	3	1596	GSS
Mar 1984	36	48	13	3	977	GSS
Mar 1986	31	52	14	3	1466	GSS
Mar 1987	34	50	12	3	1461	GSS
Mar 1988	34	49	14	3	995	GSS

Table 4.5   How Much Confidence Do You Have in Major
Companies?--1973-1988

CONBUS--I am going to name some institutions in this country...would you say you have a great deal of confidence,
only some confidence, or hardly any confidence at all in
them?

Major companies

	A GREAT DEAL	ONLY SOME	HARDLY ANY	DK	N	
Mar 1973	29	53	11	7	1500	GSS
Jan 1974[a]	22	52	20	6	1484	NORC4179
Mar 1974	31	51	14	4	1483	GSS
Mar 1975	19	54	21	6	1483	GSS
Mar 1976	22	51	22	5	1491	GSS
Mar 1977	27	56	12	4	1526	GSS
Mar 1978	22	58	16	4	1529	GSS
Mar 1980	27	53	14	5	1466	GSS
Mar 1982	23	58	14	5	1502	GSS
Mar 1983	24	59	13	4	1595	GSS
Mar 1984	31	57	9	3	981	GSS
Mar 1986	24	62	10	4	1466	GSS
Mar 1987	30	58	8	4	1463	GSS
Mar 1988	25	60	11	4	993	GSS

[a]"...confidence in them, only some...."

Table 4.6   How Much Confidence Do You Have in Banks and
Financial Institutions?--1973-1988

CONFINAN--I am going to name some institutions in this country...would you say you have a great deal of confidence,
only some confidence, or hardly any confidence at all in
them?

Banks and financial institutions

	A GREAT DEAL	ONLY SOME	HARDLY ANY	DK	N	
Mar 1975	32	54	11	3	1488	GSS
Mar 1976	40	48	10	2	1492	GSS
Mar 1977	42	47	9	2	1526	GSS
Mar 1978	33	54	12	1	1528	GSS
Mar 1980	32	50	15	3	1463	GSS
Mar 1982	27	55	16	2	1501	GSS
Mar 1983	24	58	16	2	1597	GSS
Mar 1984	32	55	11	2	976	GSS
Mar 1986	21	60	18	2	1466	GSS
Mar 1987	27	57	14	2	1463	GSS
Mar 1988	27	58	13	2	995	GSS

Table 4.7   How Much Confidence Do You Have in Organized
Labor?--1973-1988

CONLABOR--I am going to name some institutions in this country...would you say you have a great deal of confidence,
only some confidence, or hardly any confidence at all in
them?

Organized labor

	A GREAT DEAL	ONLY SOME	HARDLY ANY	DK	N	
Mar 1973	16	55	26	4	1495	GSS
Jan 1974[a]	19	50	27	4	1484	NORC4179
Mar 1974	18	54	25	3	1481	GSS
Mar 1975	10	54	29	6	1488	GSS
Mar 1976	12	48	33	8	1494	GSS
Mar 1977	15	50	32	4	1524	GSS
Mar 1978	11	46	38	5	1528	GSS
Mar 1980	15	50	30	6	1466	GSS
Mar 1982	12	53	30	4	1499	GSS
Mar 1983	8	48	39	4	1597	GSS
Mar 1984	9	53	36	2	978	GSS
Mar 1986	8	47	39	5	1465	GSS
Mar 1987	10	51	33	5	1461	GSS
Mar 1988	10	50	35	5	993	GSS

[a]"...confidence in them, only some...."

Table 4.8   How Much Confidence Do You Have in the Press?--
1973-1988

CONPRESS--I am going to name some institutions in this country...would you say you have a great deal of confidence,
only some confidence, or hardly any confidence at all in
them?

Press

	A GREAT DEAL	ONLY SOME	HARDLY ANY	DK	N	
Mar 1973	23	61	15	2	1500	GSS
Jan 1974[a]	25	51	21	3	1480	NORC4179
Mar 1974	26	55	17	1	1481	GSS
Mar 1975	24	55	18	3	1484	GSS
Mar 1976	28	52	18	2	1490	GSS
Mar 1977	57	15		2	1526	GSS
Mar 1978	20	58	20	2	1528	GSS
Mar 1980	22	58	17	3	1467	GSS
Mar 1982	18	59	21	2	1501	GSS
Mar 1983	13	61	24	2	1595	GSS
Mar 1984	17	59	22	2	978	GSS
Mar 1986	18	54	25	2	1465	GSS
Mar 1987	18	56	24	2	1464	GSS
Mar 1988	18	53	25	3	990	GSS

[a]"...confidence in them, only some...."

Table 4.9   How Much Confidence Do You Have in Scientific
Community?--1973-1988

CONSCI--I am going to name some institutions in this country...would you say you have a great deal of confidence,
only some confidence, or hardly any confidence at all in
them?

Scientific community

	A GREAT DEAL	ONLY SOME	HARDLY ANY	DK	N	
Mar 1973	37	47	6	9	1495	GSS
Mar 1974	45	38	7	11	1481	GSS
Mar 1975	38	45	6	11	1487	GSS
Mar 1976	43	38	8	12	1486	GSS
Mar 1977	41	46	5	8	1522	GSS
Mar 1978	36	48	7	8	1527	GSS
Mar 1980	42	43	6	10	1462	GSS
Mar 1982	39	46	6	9	1498	GSS
Mar 1983	42	47	5	6	1593	GSS
Mar 1984	45	44	6	6	976	GSS
Mar 1986	39	48	8	6	1463	GSS
Mar 1987	45	42	6	6	1459	GSS
Mar 1988	39	48	6	8	992	GSS

Table 4.10   How Much Confidence Do You Have in Medicine?--
1973-1988

CONMEDIC--I am going to name some institutions in this country...would you say you have a great deal of confidence,
only some confidence, or hardly any confidence at all in
them?

Medicine

	A GREAT DEAL	ONLY SOME	HARDLY ANY	DK	N	
Mar 1973	54	39	6	1	1496	GSS
Mar 1974	60	34	4	1	1482	GSS
Mar 1975	51	40	8	1	1487	GSS
Mar 1976	54	35	9	1	1492	GSS
Mar 1977	52	41	6	1	1526	GSS
Mar 1978	46	44	9	1	1527	GSS
Mar 1980	52	39	7	1	1467	GSS
Mar 1982	45	46	7	1	1502	GSS
Mar 1983	52	41	6	1	1596	GSS
Mar 1984	51	42	6	1	977	GSS
Mar 1986	46	45	8	1	1466	GSS
Mar 1987	52	42	5	1	1461	GSS
Mar 1988	51	42	6	1	993	GSS

Table 4.11   How Much Confidence Do You Have in Education?--
1973-1988

CONEDUC--I am going to name some institutions in this country...would you say you have a great deal of confidence,
only some confidence, or hardly any confidence at all in
them?

Education

	A GREAT DEAL	ONLY SOME	HARDLY ANY	DK	N	
Mar 1973	37	53	8	1	1495	GSS
Mar 1974	49	41	8	1	1480	GSS
Mar 1975	31	55	13	2	1488	GSS
Mar 1976	37	45	15	2	1489	GSS
Mar 1977	41	50	9	1	1526	GSS
Mar 1978	28	55	15	1	1528	GSS
Mar 1980	30	56	12	2	1466	GSS
Mar 1982	33	52	13	2	1500	GSS
Mar 1983	29	56	13	2	1594	GSS
Mar 1984	28	59	10	2	976	GSS
Mar 1986	28	60	11	1	1465	GSS
Mar 1987	35	55	8	1	1462	GSS
Mar 1988	30	60	9	2	994	GSS

Table 4.12   How Much Confidence Do You Have in TV?--
1973-1988

CONTV--I am going to name some institutions in this country...would you say you have a great deal of confidence,
only some confidence, or hardly any confidence at all in
them?

TV

	A GREAT DEAL	ONLY SOME	HARDLY ANY	DK	N	
Mar 1973	19	58	22	1	1497	GSS
Mar 1974	23	58	17	1	1481	GSS
Mar 1975	18	57	22	2	1486	GSS
Mar 1976	19	52	27	2	1490	GSS
Mar 1977	17	56	25	2	1525	GSS
Mar 1978	14	53	31	2	1526	GSS
Mar 1980	16	55	28	2	1467	GSS
Mar 1982	14	57	27	1	1501	GSS
Mar 1983	12	58	28	2	1596	GSS
Mar 1984	13	57	28	1	978	GSS
Mar 1986	15	56	28	2	1464	GSS
Mar 1987	12	58	29	2	1461	GSS
Mar 1988	14	58	26	1	988	GSS

Table 4.13   How Much Confidence Do You Have in Organized
Religion?--1973-1988

CONCLERG--I am going to name some institutions in this country...would you say you have a great deal of confidence,
only some confidence, or hardly any confidence at all in
them?

Organized religion

	A GREAT DEAL	ONLY SOME	HARDLY ANY	DK	N	
Mar 1973	35	46	16	4	1495	GSS
Jan 1974[a]	32	44	19	5	1485	NORC4179
Mar 1974	44	43	11	2	1481	GSS
Mar 1975	24	48	21	6	1485	GSS
Mar 1976	31	45	18	6	1491	GSS
Mar 1977	40	45	12	3	1526	GSS
Mar 1978	31	47	18	4	1526	GSS
Mar 1980	35	43	18	4	1465	GSS
Mar 1982	32	50	15	3	1503	GSS
Mar 1983	28	51	17	4	1593	GSS
Mar 1984	31	47	19	3	979	GSS
Mar 1986	25	50	21	3	1467	GSS
Mar 1987	29	50	19	3	1459	GSS
Mar 1988	20	46	31	3	995	GSS

[a]"...confidence in them, only some...."

5

Political Tolerance

The benchmark study of political tolerance is Samuel Stouffer's classic *Communism, Conformity, and Civil Liberties*, published in 1955 and based on a large survey conducted in 1954 at the height (or depth) of the McCarthy era. At the center of the Stouffer survey was a series of questions about Communists, Socialists, and anti-religionists that sought to assess the public's willingness to allow such people to speak and to hold various kinds of jobs.

Twenty years later, comparative data became available. In 1973 Stouffer's survey was substantially replicated (Nunn, Crockett, and Williams 1978) and, beginning in 1972, a battery of Stouffer questions was included on the General Social Survey. On the next pages, much of this material is arrayed.

Analyses of these data have generally concluded that there has been a very substantial, broadly based, increase in tolerance since 1954 in the American public (Cutler and Kaufman, 1975; Davis, 1975; Erskine and Siegel, 1975; Nunn, Crockett, and Williams, 1978; McClosky and Brill, 1983, pp. 434-438; Mueller, 1988; see, however, Sullivan, Piereson, and Marcus, 1979, and Sullivan and Marcus, 1988). This is particularly notable in questions about Socialists, antireligionists, and admitted Communists (Tables 5.1-5.6 and 5.10-5.17). For questions about people who have been accused of being Communists but have denied this under oath, however, there has been little change: Americans were comparatively tolerant of these people in 1954 and were little more so in the 1970s (5.18-5.25).

Exactly when what might be called the "Stouffer shift" took place is not clear because the questions were not replicated between 1954 and 1972. Data from a related question, however (Table 5.36), suggest that intolerance lingered on at the levels found during the McCarthy era until 1963 at least. At the end of the 1960s concern about machinations of the

American Communists diminished markedly (suggested in Tables 5.40, 5.41, 5.42), and tolerance levels rose not only for Communists but also for groups seen to be similar. Rather surprisingly, to a substantial degree there has been little further change since 1972 in most of the tolerance measures --not only for left-wing groups but also for racists (5.7-5.9) and militarists (5.26-5.28). However, there may have been an increase of tolerance for the rights of homosexuals (5.29-5.31). Other questions (5.33, 5.35, 5.36) allow one to extra-polate back a bit from 1954, with the suggestion that toler-ance levels were probably higher in the 1940s (see also Glazer and Lipset, 1955).

In summary, the pattern seems to be as follows:

1.   In 1940 and 1941, when there were perceived inter-national subversive threats from right- as well as left-wing extremists, fragmentary evidence suggests that tolerance levels were probably quite low--almost as low as those regis-tered during the McCarthy period (5.36, 5.39).

2.   During World War II, the number of those who said they would tolerate Communist speech-making during peacetime rose as the international entity to which the domestic party was linked became allied with the United States in a total war against a common enemy (5.36). (Presumably tolerance of Nazi or pro-Japanese speech at the time would have been found to be spectacularly less magnanimous had anybody bothered to ask about it.)

3.   After the war international Communism again became a perceived threat as Cold War hostilities emerged and as var-ious dramatic and highly publicized cases of Communist subver-sion, or alleged subversion, came to light. During this pe-riod, tolerance for Communists eroded (5.36, 5.39). Declining with it was tolerance for Socialist publications and possibly willingness to allow newspapers to "criticize our form of government" (5.33, 5.35).

4.   These trends hit bottom in the early 1950s, and the issue was extensively exploited by various politicians of whom Joseph McCarthy is the best remembered (5.1-5.6, 5.10-5.25, 5.33, 5.35, 5.36).

5.   Tolerance of free speech for Communists generally remained at this level at least until the end of 1963 (5.36).

6.   By 1972, tolerance for the civil liberties of Commu-nists, Socialists, and anti-religionists had risen sharply (5.1-5.6, 5.10-5.25).

7.   For the next sixteen years tolerance for these groups and for other divergent groups has mostly remained quite steady at this comparatively high level (5.1-5.31).

There is a problem in assessing attitudes toward atheists because Stouffer asked about "people whose ideas are consider-ed bad or dangerous by other people. For instance, somebody who is against all churches and religion" (for an interesting dissection of this question, see Schuman and Presser, 1981, pp. 289-292). Stouffer, therefore, was not asking so much about an atheist as about a religion-threatener, and accordingly they are labelled "anti-religionists," not atheists, in Tables 5.1-5.3. (Stouffer furnishes data for a question that actually uses the word "atheist," and people are found to be more tolerant of those sorts of people than they are of religion-threateners.)

The importance of question wording in dealing with these issues is vividly suggested in Table 5.32. Replications in 1970 reinforced a finding from 1940: people are far more willing to "not allow" speeches against democracy than they are to "forbid" them. (For an able discussion of this phenomenon, see Schuman and Presser 1981, pp. 276-283.)

Two final tables (5.43, 5.44) record that while political tolerance may have soared between 1954 and 1973, questions designed to tap "authoritarianism" experienced little parallel change.

REFERENCES

Cutler, Stephen J., and Robert L. Kaufman. 1975. Cohort Changes in Political Attitudes: Tolerance of Ideological Nonconformity. *Public Opinion Quarterly*, 39:69-81.

Davis, James A. 1975. Communism, Conformity, Cohorts, and Categories: American Tolerance in 1954 and 1972-73. *American Journal of Sociology*, 81:491-513.

Erskine, Hazel, and Richard L. Siegel. 1975. Civil Liberties and the American Public. *Journal of Social Issues*, 31(2): 13-29.

Glazer, Nathan, and Seymour Martin Lipset. 1955. The Polls on Communism and Conformity. In Daniel Bell, ed., *The New American Right*. New York: Criterion Books.

McClosky, Herbert, and Alida Brill. 1983. *Dimensions in Tolerance*. New York: Russell Sage.

Mueller, John. 1988. Trends in Political Tolerance. *Public Opinion Quarterly*, 52:1-25.

Nunn, Clyde Z., Harry J. Crockett, and J. Allen Williams. 1978. *Tolerance for Nonconformity*. San Francisco: Jossey-Bass.

Rugg, Donald. 1941. Experiments in Wording Questions: II. *Public Opinion Quarterly*, 5:91-92.

Schuman, Howard, and Stanley Presser. 1981. *Questions and Answers in Attitude Surveys*. New York: Academic Press.

Stouffer, Samuel A. 1955. *Communism, Conformity, and Civil Liberties*. Garden City, NY: Doubleday.

Sullivan, John L., James Piereson, and George E. Marcus. 1979.
    An Alternative Conceptualization of Political Tolerance:
    Illusory Increases, 1950's-1970's. *American Political Science Review*, 73:781-794.

Sullivan, John L., and George E. Marcus.   1988.   A Note on
    "Trends in Political Tolerance." *Public Opinion Quarterly*, 52:26-32.

Table 5.1   Should an Anti-Religionist Be Allowed to Speak?--
1954-1988

SPKATH--There are some people whose ideas are considered bad
or dangerous by other people. For instance somebody who is
against all churches and religion.

If such a person wanted to make a speech in your (city/town/
community) against churches and religion, should he be
allowed to speak, or not?

	ALLOWED	NOT ALLOWED	DK	N	
Jun 1954	37	60	3	4933	STOUFFER
Mar 1972	65	33	2	1613	GSS
Mar 1973	65	34	1	1503	GSS
Apr 1973	62	36	2	3540	NUNN
Mar 1974	62	37	1	1482	GSS
Mar 1976	64	35	1	1499	GSS
Mar 1977	62	37	1	1527	GSS
Apr 1978	63	34	3	1509	NORC4269
Mar 1980	66	33	1	1468	GSS
Mar 1982	64	34	1	1506	GSS
Mar 1984	68	31	1	1469	GSS
Mar 1985	65	34	1	1532	GSS
Mar 1987	69	30	0	1461	GSS
Mar 1988	70	29	2	976	GSS

Table 5.2   Should An Anti-Religionist Be Allowed to Teach
College?--1954-1988

COLATH--Should such a person [somebody who is against all
churches and religion] be allowed to teach in a college or
university, or not?

	ALLOWED	NOT ALLOWED	DK	N	
Jun 1954	12	84	4	4933	STOUFFER
Mar 1972	40	56	4	1610	GSS
Mar 1973	41	56	3	1499	GSS
Apr 1973	39	56	5	3540	NUNN
Mar 1974	42	55	4	1482	GSS
Mar 1976	41	57	2	1499	GSS
Mar 1977	39	59	2	1527	GSS
Mar 1980	45	52	3	1464	GSS
Mar 1982	46	51	3	1505	GSS
Mar 1984	46	51	3	1469	GSS
Mar 1985	45	52	3	1529	GSS
Mar 1987	47	49	3	1460	GSS
Mar 1988	45	52	3	975	GSS

Table 5.3   Should an Anti-Religionist's Book Be Allowed in a Public Library?--1954-1988

LIBATH--If some people in your community suggested that a book he [somebody who is against all churches and religion] wrote against churches and religion should be taken out of your public library, would you favor removing this book, or not?

	REMOVE	NOT REMOVE	DK	N	
Jun 1954	60	35	5	4933	STOUFFER
Oct 1964[a]	33	61	6	1973	SRS760
Mar 1972	36	61	3	1607	GSS
Mar 1973	37	61	2	1501	GSS
Apr 1973	40	57	4	3540	NUNN
Mar 1974	38	60	2	1482	GSS
Mar 1976	38	60	2	1497	GSS
Mar 1977	40	59	2	1525	GSS
Mar 1978	36	60	4	1508	NORC4269
Mar 1980	35	62	3	1468	GSS
Mar 1982	36	61	3	1506	GSS
Mar 1984	34	64	2	1470	GSS
Mar 1985	37	61	3	1532	GSS
Mar 1987	32	66	2	1457	GSS
Mar 1988	34	64	2	972	GSS

[a]Suppose a man admitted in public that he did not believe in God. Do you think that a book he wrote should be removed from a public library?

Table 5.4   Should a Socialist Be Allowed to Speak?--1954-1974

SPKSOC--Or consider a person who favored government ownership of all the railroads and all big industries.

If such a (this) person wanted to make a speech in your community favoring government ownership of all the railroads and big industries, should he be allowed to speak, or not?

	ALLOWED	NOT ALLOWED	DK	N	
Jun 1954	59	31	11	4933	STOUFFER
Mar 1972	77	18	5	1612	GSS
Mar 1973	77	20	3	1504	GSS
Apr 1973	72	21	7	3540	NUNN
Mar 1974	76	21	4	1483	GSS

Table 5.5   Should a Socialist Be Allowed to Teach College?--
1954-1974

COLSOC--Should such a person [who favored government ownership of all the railroads and all big industries] be allowed
to teach in a college or university, or not?

	ALLOWED	NOT ALLOWED	DK	N	
Jun 1954	33	54	13	4933	STOUFFER
Mar 1972	56	37	7	1608	GSS
Mar 1973	58	37	5	1499	GSS
Apr 1973	53	38	9	3540	NUNN
Mar 1974	57	37	5	1480	GSS

Table 5.6   Should a Socialist's Book Be Allowed in a Public
Library?--1954-1974

LIBSOC--If some people in your community suggested a book he
[a person who favored government ownership of all the railroads and all big industries] wrote favoring government ownership should be taken out of your public library, would you
favor removing this (the) book, or not?

	REMOVE	NOT REMOVE	DK	N	
Jun 1954	35	52	13	4933	STOUFFER
Mar 1972	26	68	7	1602	GSS
Mar 1973	25	71	4	1501	GSS
Apr 1973	26	66	8	3540	NUNN
Mar 1974	26	69	5	1479	GSS

Table 5.7   Should a Racist Be Allowed to Speak?--1943-1988

SPKRAC--Or consider a person who believes that blacks are
genetically inferior.   If such a person wanted to make a
speech in your community claiming that blacks are inferior,
should he be allowed to speak, or not?

	ALLOWED	NOT ALLOWED	DK	N	
Mar 1976	61	37	2	1495	GSS
Mar 1977	59	40	2	1525	GSS
Apr 1978	62	34	5	1508	NORC4269
Mar 1980	62	36	3	1464	GSS
Mar 1982	59	38	3	1503	GSS
Mar 1984	57	40	2	1469	GSS
Mar 1985	55	42	2	1531	GSS
Mar 1987	61	38	2	1457	GSS
Mar 1988	61	37	2	934	GSS

In peacetime, do you think anyone in the United States
should be allowed to make speeches against certain races in
this country?

	ALLOWED	NOT ALLOWED	DK	N	
Nov 1943	17	77	6	2558	NORC217

Table 5.8   Should a Racist Be Allowed to Teach College?--
1976-1988

COLRAC--Should such a person [who believes that blacks are
genetically inferior] be allowed to teach in a college or
university, or not?

	ALLOWED	NOT ALLOWED	DK	N	
Mar 1976	41	56	4	1495	GSS
Mar 1977	41	57	3	1526	GSS
Mar 1980	43	53	4	1462	GSS
Mar 1982	43	53	4	1504	GSS
Mar 1984	41	56	3	1468	GSS
Mar 1985	42	55	3	1530	GSS
Mar 1987	44	53	3	1460	GSS
Mar 1988	42	55	4	974	GSS

Table 5.9 Should a Racist's Book Be Allowed in a Public
Library?--1976-1988

LIBRAC--If some people in your community suggested that a
book he [a person who believes that blacks are genetically
inferior] wrote which said blacks are inferior should be
taken out of your public library, would you favor removing
this book, or not?

	REMOVE	NOT REMOVE	DK	N	
Mar 1976	37	60	4	1492	GSS
Mar 1977	36	61	3	1525	GSS
Apr 1978	30	65	6	1508	NORC4269
Mar 1980	33	64	4	1463	GSS
Mar 1982	36	60	4	1505	GSS
Mar 1984	34	63	3	1470	GSS
Mar 1985	37	60	3	1530	GSS
Mar 1987	34	64	2	1457	GSS
Mar 1988	35	62	3	975	GSS

Table 5.10 Should an Admitted Communist Be Allowed to
Speak?--1954-1988

SPKCOM--Now, I should (would) like to ask you some questions
about a man who admits he is a Communist.

Suppose this admitted Communist wanted (wants) to make a
speech in your community. Should he be allowed to speak, or
not?

	ALLOWED	NOT ALLOWED	DK	N	
Jun 1954	27	68	5	4933	STOUFFER
Mar 1972	52	45	3	1610	GSS
Mar 1973	60	38	2	1503	GSS
Apr 1973	53	42	6	3540	NUNN
Mar 1974	58	39	3	1481	GSS
Mar 1976	55	43	2	1497	GSS
Mar 1977	55	42	2	1525	GSS
Apr 1978	60	36	4	1508	NORC4269
Mar 1980	55	42	3	1467	GSS
Mar 1982	56	41	3	1502	GSS
Mar 1984	59	38	2	1468	GSS
Mar 1985	57	40	3	1529	GSS
Mar 1987	60	39	2	1462	GSS
Mar 1988	60	37	2	976	GSS

Table 5.11   Should an Admitted Communist Be Allowed to Teach College?--1954-1988

COLCOM--Suppose he [a man who admits he is a Communist] is teaching in a college.   Should he be fired, or not?

	FIRED	NOT FIRED	DK	N	
Jun 1954	89	6	5	4933	STOUFFER
Mar 1972	61	32	7	1607	GSS
Mar 1973	55	39	6	1496	GSS
Apr 1973	63	30	7	3540	NUNN
Mar 1974	52	42	6	1479	GSS
Mar 1976	54	41	5	1496	GSS
Mar 1977	57	39	4	1523	GSS
Mar 1980	53	41	6	1465	GSS
Mar 1982	50	43	6	1500	GSS
Mar 1984	49	46	5	1465	GSS
Mar 1985	51	44	4	1527	GSS
Mar 1987	49	46	5	1459	GSS
Mar 1988	47	48	5	973	GSS

Table 5.12   Should an Admitted Communist's Books Be Allowed in a Public Library?--1954-1988

LIBCOM--Suppose he [a man who admits he is a Communist] wrote a book which is in your public library.   Somebody in your community suggests that the book should be removed from the library.   Would you favor removing it, or not?

	REMOVE	NOT REMOVE	DK	N	
Jun 1954	66	27	7	4932	STOUFFER
Mar 1972	42	53	5	1608	GSS
Mar 1973	39	58	2	1498	GSS
Apr 1973	40	54	6	3540	NUNN
Mar 1974	38	59	3	1478	GSS
Mar 1976	40	56	4	1494	GSS
Mar 1977	42	55	3	1523	GSS
Apr 1978	34	61	5	1504	NORC4269
Mar 1980	39	57	4	1465	GSS
Mar 1982	39	57	4	1497	GSS
Mar 1984	37	60	3	1467	GSS
Mar 1985	39	57	4	1528	GSS
Mar 1987	36	61	3	1456	GSS
Mar 1988	38	59	3	974	GSS

Table 5.13   Should an Admitted Communist Be Allowed to Teach High School?--1954-1973

Suppose he [a man who admits he is a Communist] is a high school teacher. Should he be fired, or not?

	FIRED	NOT FIRED	DK	N	
Jun 1954	91	5	4	4933	STOUFFER
Apr 1973	67	25	7	3540	NUNN

Table 5.14   Should an Admitted Communist Be Allowed to Work in a Defense Plant?--1954-1973

Now I should (would) like to ask you some questions about a man who admits he is a communist.

Suppose he has been working in a defense (defense-related) plant. Should he be fired, or not?

	FIRED	NOT FIRED	DK	N	
Jun 1954	90	6	4	4933	STOUFFER
Apr 1973	70	21	9	3540	NUNN

Table 5.15   Should an Admitted Communist Be Allowed to Clerk in a Store?--1954-1973

Suppose he [a man who admits he is a communist] is a clerk in a store. Should he be fired, or not?

	FIRED	NOT FIRED	DK	N	
Jun 1954	68	26	6	4933	STOUFFER
Apr 1973	36	57	7	3540	NUNN

Table 5.16   Should an Admitted Communist Be Allowed to
Entertain on Radio or TV?--1954-1973

Suppose this admitted Communist is a radio singer (TV entertainer).   Should he be fired, or not?

	FIRED	NOT FIRED	DK	N	
Jun 1954	63	29	8	4933	STOUFFER
Apr 1973	39	52	9	3540	NUNN

Table 5.17   Should an Admitted Communist's Advertising Be
Boycotted?--1954-1973

Now, suppose the radio (TV) program he [a man who admits he
is a Communist] is on advertises a brand of soap.   Somebody
in your community suggests that you stop buying that soap.
Would you stop, or not?

	WOULD STOP	WOULD NOT STOP	DK	N	
Jun 1954	36	56	8	4933	STOUFFER
Apr 1973	23	70	8	3540	NUNN

Table 5.18   Should an Accused Communist Be Allowed to
Speak?--1954-1973

Now I would like you to think of another person: a man whose
loyalty has been questioned before a Congressional committee, but who swears he had never been a Communist.

Should he be allowed to make a speech in your community, or
not?

	ALLOWED	NOT ALLOWED	DK	N	
Jun 1954	70	21	9	4933	STOUFFER
Apr 1973	71	21	8	3540	NUNN

Table 5.19   Should an Accused Communist Be Allowed to Teach
                 College?--1954-1973

Suppose he [a man who is accused of being a Communist] is
teaching in a college or university. Should he be fired, or
not?

	FIRED	NOT FIRED	DK	N	
Jun 1954	22	69	9	4933	STOUFFER
Apr 1973	20	72	9	3540	NUNN

Table 5.20   Should an Accused Communist's Books Be Allowed
                 in a Public Library?--1954-1973

Suppose he [a man who is accused of being a Communist] wrote
a book which is in your public library. Somebody in your
community suggests that the book should be removed from the
library. Would you favor removing it, or not?

	REMOVE	NOT REMOVE	DK	N	
Jun 1954	17	71	12	4932	STOUFFER
Apr 1973	15	76	9	3540	NUNN

Table 5.21   Should an Accused Communist Be Allowed to Teach
                 High School--1954-1973

Suppose this man [a man is accused of being a Communist] is
a high school teacher. Should he be fired or not?

	FIRED	NOT FIRED	DK	N	
Jun 1954	22	69	9	4933	STOUFFER
Apr 1973	23	69	9	3540	NUNN

Table 5.22   Should an Accused Communist Be Allowed to Work
in a Defense Plant?--1954-1973

Now I would like you to think of another person. A man
whose loyalty has been questioned before a Congressional
Committee, but who swears under oath he has never been a
Communist.

Suppose he has been working in a defense (defense-related)
plant. Should he be fired, or not?

	FIRED	NOT FIRED	DK	N	
Jun 1954	18	72	10	4933	STOUFFER
Apr 1973	20	70	11	3540	NUNN

Table 5.23   Should an Accused Communist Be Allowed to Clerk
in a Store?--1954-1973

Suppose he [a man is accused of being a Communist] is a
clerk in a store. Should he be fired, or not?

	FIRED	NOT FIRED	DK	N	
Jun 1954	11	81	8	4933	STOUFFER
Apr 1973	9	84	7	3540	NUNN

Table 5.24   Should an Accused Communist Be Allowed to
Entertain on Radio or TV?--1954-1973

Suppose this man who swears he has never been a Communist,
but who has been criticized by a Congressional Committee is
a radio singer (TV entertainer). Should he be fired, or
not?

	FIRED	NOT FIRED	DK	N	
Jun 1954	12	80	8	4933	STOUFFER
Apr 1973	12	80	9	3540	NUNN

Table 5.25   Should an Accused Communist's Advertising Be
                Boycotted?--1954-1973

Now, suppose the radio (TV) program he [a man who is accused
of being a Communist] is on advertises a brand of soap.
Somebody in your community suggest that you stop buying that
soap.   Would you stop, or not?

	WOULD STOP	WOULD NOT STOP	DK	N	
Jun 1954	9	83	8	4933	STOUFFER
Apr 1973	9	84	8	3540	NUNN

Table 5.26   Should a Militarist Be Allowed to Speak?--
                1976-1988

SPKMIL--Consider a person who advocates doing away with
elections and letting the military run the country.   If such
a person wanted to make a speech in your community, should
he be allowed to speak, or not?

	ALLOWED	NOT ALLOWED	DK	N	
Mar 1976	54	44	2	1495	GSS
Mar 1977	50	48	2	1529	GSS
Apr 1978	55	42	3	1508	NORC4269
Mar 1980	57	41	2	1466	GSS
Mar 1982	54	43	3	1505	GSS
Mar 1984	57	42	1	1467	GSS
Mar 1985	55	43	2	1529	GSS
Mar 1987	56	41	3	1461	GSS
Mar 1988	56	41	3	972	GSS

Table 5.27   Should a Militarist Be Allowed to Teach
College?--1976-1988

COLMIL--Should such a person [a person who advocates doing
away with elections and letting the military run the coun-
try] be allowed to teach in a college or university, or not?

	ALLOWED	NOT ALLOWED	DK	N	
Mar 1976	37	59	4	1494	GSS
Mar 1977	34	63	3	1526	GSS
Mar 1980	39	56	4	1464	GSS
Mar 1982	39	56	5	1499	GSS
Mar 1984	41	56	3	1467	GSS
Mar 1985	40	57	3	1528	GSS
Mar 1987	40	56	4	1460	GSS
Mar 1988	37	59	4	971	GSS

Table 5.28   Should a Militarist's Book Be Allowed in a
Public Library?--1954-1988

LIBMIL--Suppose he [a person who advocates doing away with
elections and letting the military run the country] wrote a
book advocating doing away with elections and letting the
military run the country. Somebody in your community
suggests that the book be removed from the public library.
Would you favor removing it, or not?

	REMOVE	NOT REMOVE	DK	N	
Mar 1976	40	56	3	1493	GSS
Mar 1977	43	55	3	1526	GSS
Apr 1978	35	60	5	1499	NORC4269
Mar 1980	39	58	3	1466	GSS
Mar 1982	40	56	4	1503	GSS
Mar 1984	39	59	2	1468	GSS
Mar 1985	41	56	2	1529	GSS
Mar 1987	38	59	3	1458	GSS
Mar 1988	40	57	4	970	GSS

Table 5.29   Should a Homosexual Be Allowed to Speak?--
                1973-1988

SPKHOMO--What about a man who admits that he is a homosexual? Suppose this admitted homosexual wanted to make a
speech in your community. Should he be allowed to speak, or
not?

	ALLOWED	NOT ALLOWED	DK	N	
Mar 1973	61	35	4	1501	GSS
Mar 1974	62	33	5	1483	GSS
Mar 1976	62	35	3	1496	GSS
Mar 1977	62	35	4	1528	GSS
Mar 1980	66	31	3	1468	GSS
Mar 1982	65	31	4	1500	GSS
Mar 1984	68	28	4	1468	GSS
Mar 1985	67	30	3	1530	GSS
Mar 1987	68	30	2	1461	GSS
Mar 1988	70	26	4	975	GSS

Table 5.30   Should a Homosexual Be Allowed to Teach
                College?--1973-1988

COLHOMO--Should such a person [a man who admits that he is a
homosexual] be allowed to teach in a college or university,
or not?

	ALLOWED	NOT ALLOWED	DK	N	
Mar 1973	47	48	4	1502	GSS
Mar 1974	50	45	5	1481	GSS
Mar 1976	52	45	3	1496	GSS
Mar 1977	49	47	4	1526	GSS
Mar 1980	55	42	4	1466	GSS
Mar 1982	55	41	4	1500	GSS
Mar 1984	59	37	4	1468	GSS
Mar 1985	58	39	3	1529	GSS
Mar 1987	57	40	4	1461	GSS
Mar 1988	57	39	5	972	GSS

Table 5.31   Should a Homosexual's Book Be Allowed in a
              Public Library?--1973-1988

LIBHOMO--If some people in your community suggested that a
book he [a man who admits that he is a homosexual] wrote in
favor of homosexuality should be taken out of your public
library, would you favor removing this book, or not?

	REMOVE	NOT REMOVE	DK	N	
Mar 1973	44	54	3	1502	GSS
Mar 1974	41	55	4	1479	GSS
Mar 1976	41	55	4	1497	GSS
Mar 1977	41	55	3	1526	GSS
Mar 1980	40	58	2	1466	GSS
Mar 1982	41	56	3	1500	GSS
Mar 1984	38	59	3	1468	GSS
Mar 1985	42	55	3	1529	GSS
Mar 1987	40	58	2	1460	GSS
Mar 1988	36	60	4	974	GSS

Table 5.32   Should Speeches Against Democracy Be
              Forbidden/Not Allowed?--1940-1976

Do you think the United States should forbid speeches
against democracy?

		FORBID	NOT FORBID	DK	N	
	1940	39	46	15	c1300	Rugg
Fall	1974	67	26	6	995	SRC-74
Feb	1976	75	19	6	623	SRC-76
Mar	1976	69	19	12	1676	SRC-76

Do you think the United States should allow speeches against
democracy?

		NOT ALLOW	ALLOW	DK	N	
	1940	62	21	17	c1300	Rugg
Fall	1974	42	53	5	520	SRC-74
Feb	1976	42	50	8	642	SRC-76
Mar	1976	42	46	12	1563	SRC-76

Table 5.33   Should Newspapers Be Allowed to Criticize Our
Form of Government?--1943-1953

In peacetime, do you think newspapers should be allowed to
criticize our form of government?

	YES	NO	DK	N	
Nov 1943	66	30	4	2560	NORC217
Nov 1945	64	31	5	1272	NORC239
Apr 1948	70	27	3	1280	NORC157
May 1953[a]	61	35	4	1265	NORC340

[a]Seven percent are "Yes, qualified": "if fair," "if not
Communist," "if not favoring violence," "if not treasonable," "if not libelous."

Table 5.34   How Free Do You Feel to Speak Your Mind?--
1954-1973

Which of these three views is closest to your own?   All
people in this country feel as free to say what they think
as they used to.   Some people do not feel as free to say
what they think as they used to.   Hardly anybody feels as
free to say what they think as they used to.

	ALL FEEL AS FREE	SOME FEEL AS FREE	HARDLY ANY FEELS AS FREE	DK	N	
Jun 1954	56	31	10	4	4933	STOUFFER
Apr 1973	55	11	10	2	3540	NUNN

What about you personally?   Do you or don't you feel as free
to speak your mind as you used to?

	AS FREE	LESS FREE	DK	N	
Jun 1954	85	13	2	4933	STOUFFER
Apr 1973	78	20	2	3540	NUNN

Table 5.35   Should the Socialist Party Be Allowed to Publish
              Newspapers?--1943-1957

Do you think the Socialist Party should be allowed to publish newspapers in this country?

	YES	YES QUALIFIED	NO	DK	N	
Nov 1943[a]	57		25	18	2552	NORC217
Nov 1945[a]	58		28	15	2540	NORC239
May 1953[a]	45	5	34	16	1265	NORC340
Jan 1954[a]	41	6	39	14	1250	NORC351
Jan 1956	41	6	40	13	1238	NORC382
Jan 1957	47	5	38	10	1232	NORC401
Apr 1957	43	5	39	13	1279	NORC404

[a]"In peacetime,...."

NOTE--"Yes, qualified": "if fair," "if not Communist," "if
not favoring violence," "if not treasonable," "if not libelous," etc.

Table 5.36   Should Communists Be Allowed to Speak on the
              Radio?--1943-1963

Do you think members of the Communist Party in this country
should be allowed to speak on the radio?

	YES	YES QUALIFIED	UNDECIDED	NO	N	
Nov 1943[a]	48		12	40	2534	NORC217
Nov 1945[a]	48		13	39	2540	NORC239
Mar 1946	45		11	44	1293	NORC141
Apr 1948[a]	36		7	57	1280	NORC157
Nov 1953	19	9	4	68	1233	NORC34
Jan 1954	14	8	5	73	1250	NORC351
Jan 1956	16	6	3	76	1238	NORC382
Dec 1956	20	4	4	72	1231	NORC401
Apr 1957	17	5	3	75	1279	NORC404
Nov 1963	18	10	5	67	1384	SRS350

[a]"In peacetime,...."

Do you think Communist Party candidates should be allowed
any time on the radio?

	YES	NO	DK	N	
Sep 1940	37	57	6	2964	AIPO211

Table 5.37   Should an Admitted Communist Be Jailed?--
1954-1973

Should an admitted Communist be put in jail, or not?

	JAILED	NOT JAILED	DK	N	
Jun 1954	51	34	15	4933	STOUFFER
Apr 1973	24	62	14	3540	NUNN

Table 5.38   Should an Admitted Communist's Citizenship Be
Taken Away?--1954-1973

Should he [an admitted Communist] have his American citizenship taken away from him, or not?

	TAKEN AWAY	NOT TAKEN AWAY	DK	N	
Jun 1954	77	13	10	4933	STOUFFER
Apr 1973	52	37	11	3540	NUNN

Table 5.39   Should Membership in the Communist Party Be
Forbidden?--1941-1950

Do you think membership in the Communist Party in this
country should be forbidden by law?

	FORBIDDEN	NOT FORBIDDEN	DK	N	
May 1941	70	21	9	1489	AIPO237
Mar 1946	49	36	15	1649	AIPO367
Jun 1946	44	38	17	1511	AIPO373T
Mar 1947	61	26	13	c1500	AIPO393
Oct 1947	61	27	12	1430	PO406K
May 1949	70	22	8	1579	AIPO438
Nov 1949	68	21	11	c1500	AIPO449
Jul 1950[a]	70	24	6	1419	AIPO458
Dec 1950	80	16	5	1305	AIPO469

[a]"...or not?"

Table 5.40   How Great a Danger Are American Communists?--
1954-1976

How great a danger do you feel American Communists are to
this country at the present time--a very great danger, a
great danger, some danger, hardly any danger, or no danger?

	VERY GREAT	GREAT	SOME	HARDLY ANY	NO DANGER	DK	N	
Jun 1964	19	24	38	9	2	8	4933	STOUFFER

How much danger do you think the Communists right here in
America are to this country at the present time?

	VERY GREAT DEAL	GOOD DEAL	NOT VERY MUCH	NONE AT ALL	DK	N	
Sep 1964	14	63	19	1	3		AIPO

How great a danger do you feel American Communists are to
this country at the present time--a great danger, some danger, hardly any danger, or no danger at all?

	GREAT	SOME	HARDLY ANY	NO DANGER	DK	N	
Mar 1974	29	36	20	12	4		Yankelovich
Sep 1974	29	37	18	11	5		Yankelovich
May 1975	30	32	20	14	5		Yankelovich
Jan 1976	30	38	18	9	5		Yankelovich
Apr 1976[a]	27	41	20	13	-		Yankelovich

[a]Registered voters only.

Table 5.41 How Much Danger Are American Communists?--1954-1973

Do you think there might be any Communists within the American government now, or not? [If yes] How much danger is there that these Communists within the government can hurt the country?

	A GREAT DANGER	SOME DANGER	NOT MUCH DANGER	NO DANGER	DK DANGER	AREN'T ANY	DK	N	
Jun 1954	33	32	11	1	1	7	14	4933	STOUFFER
Apr 1973	20	30	13	4	1	11	22	3540	NUNN

Do you think there are any Communists working in key defense (defense-related) plants now, or not? [If yes] How much danger is there that these Communists in defense (defense-related) plants can hurt the country?

	A GREAT DANGER	SOME DANGER	NOT MUCH DANGER	NO DANGER	DK DANGER	AREN'T ANY	DK	N	
Jun 1954	39	32	8	1	1	5	14	4933	STOUFFER
Apr 1973	21	29	9	2	1	11	27	3540	NUNN

Do you think there are any Communists teaching in American colleges and universities now, or not? [If yes] How much danger is there that these Communists in colleges and universities can hurt the country?

	A GREAT DANGER	SOME DANGER	NOT MUCH DANGER	NO DANGER	DK DANGER	AREN'T ANY	DK	N	
Jun 1954	32	29	12	2	1	7	17	4933	STOUFFER
Apr 1973	26	32	14	6	1	5	17	3540	NUNN

Table 5.42   Is It More Important to Find Communists or to Protect the Innocent?--1954-1973

In your opinion, which one of these two is more important: To find out all the Communists even if some innocent people should be hurt, or to protect the rights of innocent people even if some Communists are not found out?

	FIND COMMUNISTS	PROTECT RIGHTS	DK	N	
Jun 1954	58	32	10	4933	STOUFFER
Apr 1973	23	70	7	3540	NUNN

Table 5.43 Should a Leader Be Strict with People Under Him? --1954-1973

Any leader should be strict with people under him in order to gain their respect.

	AGREE STRONGLY	AGREE	DIS- AGREE	DISAGREE STRONGLY	DK	N	
Jun 1954	16	45	29	5	5	4933	STOUFFER
Jun 1973	11	47	33	5	4	3540	NUNN

Table 5.44   Can People Be Divided into the Weak and the Strong?--1954-1973

People can be divided into two classes--the weak and the strong.

	AGREE STRONGLY	AGREE	DIS- AGREE	DISAGREE STRONGLY	DK	N	
Jun 1954	11	52	26	4	6	4933	STOUFFER
Jun 1973	8	47	35	7	3	3540	NUNN

6

Crime and Violence

The United States has been a politically stable but violent nation. American levels of violent crime in general and of murder in particular greatly exceed those of any other industrial country (United Nations, 1987). Even by America's high standard of violence the situation worsened notably during the 1960s and 1970s with the per capita homicide rate rising from 4.5 in 1963 to a peak of 10.7 in 1980. Since then the crime rate in general has levelled off and even fallen a bit, and the homicide rate in particular dropped back to 8.3 in 1985.

While the number of Americans personally experiencing crimes such as robberies and burglaries in a given year is fairly small (Tables 6.1-6.2), the impact of these personal victimizations and those suffered by friends and neighbors is large and widespread.

In response to swings in the crime rate, the American people became more afraid to walk alone at night in their own neighborhood, with fear rising from about a third in the 1960s to 47 percent in 1982 (Table 6.3). Since then street fear has receded slightly. Fear in one's own home did not change much over this period, however (6.4).

Similarly, the rising crime rate has made Americans more punitive (Stinchcombe, Adams, Heimer, Smith, and Taylor, 1980). In 1965 only 48 percent thought that courts should be harsher on criminals, but this rose to 85-86 percent favoring harsher punishments in 1978-1986 (Tables 6.5-6.6). Since 1986 the clamor for getting tough with crime has moderated a bit. Attitudes toward wiretapping appear to follow a similar path (6.7).

Perhaps the clearest connection between crime and punitiveness is found in the area of capital punishment (Smith, 1976; Rankin, 1979). The homicide rate fell from 7.1 in 1936 to 4.5 in 1963 and then rose to 10.7 in 1980 before falling

to 8.3 in 1985.   Support for capital punishment fell from 62
percent in 1936 to 42 percent in 1966 and then grew to 76
percent in 1985 before dropping to 70-71 percent in 1986-1988
(6.8).   Given a slight lag for the public to learn about the
changes in homicide rates, public attitudes on capital punishment have closely followed swings in the level of murders.

Violence, of course, is not restricted to clearly criminal
activities. Violence permeates our popular entertainment from
the sports of boxing and football to R-rated slasher movies
to cops-and-robbers shows on television and mars our personal
relations.   Typically since the late 1960s a little over a
third of adult Americans report having been "punched or beaten
up" sometime during their life and about a fifth say they have
been "threatened with a gun or shot" (6.9-6.14).   While firearm assaults usually happen to adults (in part because they
include military experiences), physical assaults are more
common among children than adults.

Americans believe in the selective use of force to resolve
some but not all types of interpersonal confrontations (Tables
6.15-6.20).   Hitting as a means of expressing political opposition is approved of by less than 5 percent of the public,
and less than 10 percent feel that clumsy drunks should be
hit.   On the other hand, majorities approve of hitting in
retaliation for a man having hit your child, to defend a women
being beaten up, and to stop a home invader.   There has been
very little change in levels of support for these uses of
hitting since the late 1960s.

Similarly, people grant selective approval to hitting by
police (6.21-6.25).   Hitting a murder suspect to force a
confession in opposed by 90 percent, and about 80 percent
opposed a police officer hitting someone who had said "vulgar and obscene things to the policeman." Over 80 percent,
however, support such force to stop an escape, and nearly
every one grants police officers the right of self-defense.
As with interpersonal hitting there has not much change over
the years in level of approval of police hitting.   The one
exception is a decline in approval of hitting when verbally
attacked.   Approval was relatively high (20 percent plus) in
the late 1960s and early 1970s when such attacks were associated with radicalism, but approval has fallen to around 12-
13 percent as the connection with anti-radicalism has
diminished over time.

At first one might assume that gun ownership and gun control would be closely associated with crime and punishment
issues.   Guns, however, are not so much acquired to either
fight or commit crimes, but inherited as part of a hunting
culture (see Table 15.35 for hunting trends; Smith, 1980;
Wright, Rossi, and Daly, 1983).   Support for a police permit
before a firearm could be purchased has been favored by about

70-75 percent of the public since at least as far back as 1959 (Table 6.30). The rising crime rate and corresponding shifts in fear and punitiveness have had no impact on support for gun control because attitudes toward gun control are not primarily shaped by attitudes toward crime. Similarly the drop in gun ownership reflects a decline of the hunting culture as urban and suburban life-styles replace rural ways of life, and is not a reaction to crime (6.26-29).

In sum, public policy preferences on crime have been shaped largely by objective shifts in the level of criminal activity. Items such as gun control and approval of interpersonal hitting that do not follow a similar pattern are actually not closely linked to criminal matters. These attitudes are shaped by different cultural and personality factors than those that form attitudes about crime.

REFERENCES

Rankin, Joseph H. 1979. Changing Attitudes Toward Capital Punishment. *Social Forces*, 58:194-211.

Smith, Tom W. 1976. Trend Analysis of Attitudes Toward Capital Punishment, 1936-1974. In James A. Davis, ed., *Studies of Social Change Since 1948*, Vol. II. NORC report 127B. Chicago: National Opinion Research Center.

Smith, Tom W. 1980. The 75% Solution: An Analysis of the Structure of Attitudes on Gun Control, 1959-1977. *Journal of Criminal Law and Criminology*, 71:300-316.

Stinchcombe, Arthur L., Rebecca Adams, Carol A. Heimer, Kem Lane Scheppele, Tom W. Smith, and D. Garth Taylor. 1980. *Crime and Punishment: Changing Attitudes in America*. San Francisco: Jossey-Bass.

United Nations. 1987. *Demographic Yearbook*, 1985. New York: United Nations.

Wright, James D., Peter H. Rossi, and Kathleen Daly. 1983. *Under the Gun: Weapons, Crime, and Violence in America*. New York: Aldin

Table 6.1   Did Anyone Break into Your Home in the Last
             Year?--1973-1988

BURGLR--During the last year--that is, between March and now
--did anyone break into or somehow illegally get into your
(apartment/home)?

	YES	NO	N	
Mar 1973	8	92	1504	GSS
Mar 1974	8	92	1481	GSS
Mar 1976	7	93	1496	GSS
Mar 1977	7	93	1527	GSS
Mar 1980	8	92	1465	GSS
Mar 1982	8	92	1504	GSS
Mar 1984	7	93	1471	GSS
Mar 1985	7	93	1531	GSS
Mar 1987	7	93	1462	GSS
Mar 1988	7	93	977	GSS

Table 6.2   Were You Forcefully Robbed during the Last Year?
             --1973-1987

ROBBRY--During the last year, did anyone take something directly from you by using force--such as a stickup, mugging,
or threat?

	YES	NO	N	
Mar 1973	2	98	1500	GSS
Mar 1974	4	96	1473	GSS
Mar 1976	2	98	1491	GSS
Mar 1977	2	98	1525	GSS
Mar 1980	2	98	1466	GSS
Mar 1982	2	98	1504	GSS
Mar 1984	2	98	1471	GSS
Mar 1985	2	98	1531	GSS
Mar 1987	2	98	1462	GSS
Mar 1987	2	98	976	GSS

Table 6.3   Is There a Nearby Area Where You Would Be Afraid to Walk at Night?--1965-1988

FEAR--Is there any area right around here--that is, within a mile--where you would be afraid to walk alone at night?

	YES	NO	DK	N	
Mar 1965	34	63	3	3520	AIPO709
Aug 1967	31	67	3	3527	AIPO749
Sep 1968	34	63	2	1504	AIPO768
Mar 1972	39	61	-	1511	AIPO847
Dec 1972	42	57	1	1504	AIPO861
Mar 1973	41	59	1	1496	GSS
Mar 1974	45	55	1	1480	GSS
Jun 1975	44	55	1	1558	AIPO931
Mar 1976	44	56	0	1497	GSS
Mar 1977	45	55	1	1529	GSS
Nov 1977	44	55	2	1506	AIPO989
Nov 1979	42	58	0	1526	AIPO142G
Mar 1980	43	56	1	1466	GSS
Jan 1981	45	54	1	1540	AIPO167G
Jun 1981[a]	46	54	-	1433	CBS/NYT
Jul 1981[b]	41	58	1	1599	NBC/AP
Jan 1982	48	52	-	1500	AIPO189G
Mar 1982	47	53	0	1505	GSS
Jan 1983	45	55	-	1555	AIPO
Jul 1983	37	62	1	1207	AUDITS
Mar 1984	42	57	1	1468	GSS
Feb 1985[b]	41	58	1	1598	NBC
Mar 1985	40	59	1	1531	GSS
Mar 1987	38	61	0	1462	GSS
Mar 1988	40	59	1	975	GSS

[a]"...around your home...."

[b]Is there an area within a mile of your home where you would be afraid to walk around at night?

Table 6.4   Do You Feel Safe at Home?--1972-1983

FEARHOME--How about at home at night--do you feel safe and secure, or not?

	YES	NO	DK	N	
Dec 1972	84	16	0	1504	AIPO861
Jun 1975	81	18	1	1558	AIPO931
Nov 1977	84	15	1	1491	AIPO989
Jan 1981	85	15	0	1534	AIPO167G
Jun 1981	85	15	0	1433	CBS/NYT
Mar 1982	86	14	0	1494	GSS
Jan 1983	84	16	0	1555	AIPO

Table 6.5 Do the Courts Deal Harshly Enough with
Criminals?--1965-1988

COURTS--In general, do you think the courts in this area
deal too harshly or not harshly enough with criminals?

	TOO HARSH	ABOUT RIGHT	NOT HARSH ENOUGH	DK	N	
Apr 1965	2	34	48	16	3521	AIPO709
Aug 1965	2	27	60	12	3522	AIPO716
Feb 1968	2	19	63	16	1500	AIPO757
Jan 1969	2	13	74	10	1460	AIPO773
Mar 1972	7	16	66	11	1609	GSS
Dec 1972	4	13	74	8	1504	AIPO861
Mar 1973	5	13	73	9	1494	GSS
Mar 1974	6	10	78	7	745	GSS
Mar 1975	4	10	79	7	1483	GSS
Mar 1976	3	10	81	6	1494	GSS
Mar 1977	3	8	83	6	1527	GSS
Mar 1978	3	7	85	5	1528	GSS
Mar 1980	3	8	83	6	1465	GSS
Jan 1981	3	13	77	7	1042	LAT39
Mar 1982	3	8	86	4	744	GSS
Mar 1983	4	6	85	4	1595	GSS
Mar 1984	3	11	82	4	1460	GSS
Mar 1985	3	9	84	3	1525	GSS
Mar 1986	3	8	85	4	1467	GSS
Mar 1987	3	12	79	6	1463	GSS
Mar 1988	4	10	82	5	1477	GSS

Table 6.6 Do the Courts Deal Harshly Enough with Criminals,
Filtered Version?--1974-1982

COURTSY--In general, do you think the courts in this area
deal too harshly, or not harshly enough with criminals, or
don't you have enough information about the courts to say?

	TOO HARSH	ABOUT RIGHT	NOT HARSH ENOUGH	CAN'T SAY	N	
Mar 1974	5	6	60	29	723	GSS
Mar 1982	4	5	76	14	752	GSS

Table 6.7   Do you Approve of Wiretapping?--1974-1988

WIRTAP--Everything considered, would you say that, in
      general, you approve or disapprove of wiretapping?

	APPROVE	DISAP-PROVE	DK	N	
Mar 1974	17	80	4	1481	GSS
Mar 1975	16	80	4	1487	GSS
Mar 1977	18	78	3	1528	GSS
Mar 1978	19	78	3	1529	GSS
Mar 1982	19	77	4	1502	GSS
Mar 1983	19	78	4	1596	GSS
Mar 1985	23	74	3	1527	GSS
Mar 1986	22	74	4	1466	GSS
Mar 1988	20	74	6	983	GSS

Do you happen to know what is meant by wiretapping?

	YES	NO	N
Jul 1969	86	14	1482

[Of those who said YES]: Everything considered, would you
say that, in general, you approve or disapprove of
wiretapping?

APPROVE	DISAP-PROVE	DK	N
46	46	8	1273

Table 6.8 Do You Favor the Death Penalty?--1936-1988

CAPPUN--Do you favor or oppose the death penalty for persons convicted of murder?

	FAVOR	OPPOSE	DK	N	
Apr 1936[a]	62	33	5	NA	AIPO
Dec 1936[a]	59	38	3	2201	AIPO59
Nov 1937[a]	61	33	7	2807	AIPO105
Oct 1953[b,c]	68	26	6	1496	AIPO522
Apr 1956[b]	53	34	13	1985	AIPO562
Sep 1957[b]	47	34	18	150	AIPO588
Mar 1960[b]	53	36	11	293	AIPO625
Jan 1965[b]	45	43	12	392	AIPO704
May 1966[b]	42	47	11	518	AIPO729
Jun 1967[b]	54	38	8	3383	AIPO746
Jan 1969[b]	51	40	9	1503	AIPO774
Oct 1971[b]	48	41	11	1558	APO839
Feb 1972[b]	51	41	8	1509	AIPO846
Nov 1972[b]	60	30	10	1462	AIPO860
Mar 1972[b]	53	39	8	1609	GSS
Mar 1973[b]	60	35	5	1492	GSS
Mar 1974	63	32	5	1480	GSS
Mar 1975	60	33	7	1483	GSS
Mar 1976	66	30	5	1496	GSS
Apr 1976[b]	67	27	7	1540	AIPO949
Mar 1977	67	26	6	1520	GSS
Mar 1978	62	26	11	1560	AIPO995
Mar 1978	66	28	6	1532	GSS
Jul 1979	65	27	8	1599	NBC
Mar 1980	67	27	6	1461	GSS
Jan 1981[b]	66	25	9	1609	AIPO168G
Mar 1982	74	21	6	1504	GSS
Jun 1982	71	20	9	1597	NBC
Mar 1983	73	22	5	1597	GSS
Mar 1984	70	24	6	1462	GSS
Mar 1985	76	19	5	1526	GSS
Jan 1985[b]	72	20	8	1523	AIPO
Nov 1985[b]	75	17	8	1008	AIPOTEL
Mar 1986	71	23	5	1466	GSS
Mar 1987	70	24	6	1454	GSS
Mar 1988	71	22	7	1475	GSS

[a]Are you in favor of the death penalty for murder?

[b]Are you in favor of the death penalty for persons convicted of murder?

[c]"Yes" includes qualified yes; "No" includes qualified no.

Table 6.9   Have You Ever Been Punched or Beaten by Another
Person?--1968-1988

HIT--Have you ever been punched or beaten by another person?

	YES	NO	DK	N	
Oct 1968	34	66	-	1607	HARRISVS
Mar 1971	46	54	0	1491	NORC4119
Mar 1973	27	72	0	1504	GSS
Mar 1975	32	68	-	1489	GSS
Mar 1976	28	72	-	1499	GSS
Mar 1978	35	65	0	1532	GSS
Mar 1980	33	67	-	1467	GSS
Mar 1983	46	54	0	1598	GSS
Mar 1984	40	60	0	1471	GSS
Mar 1986	36	64	-	1470	GSS
Mar 1987	36	64	-	1464	GSS
Mar 1988	35	64	0	997	GSS

Table 6.10   Were You Punched or Beaten as a Child or as an
Adult?--1973-1988

IF YOU HAVE EVER BEEN PUNCHED OR BEATEN (see Table 6.9)--
Base for the percentages is those who have ever been punched
or beaten.

HITAGE--Did this happen to you as a child or as an adult?

	CHILD	ADULT	BOTH	DK	N	
Mar 1973	43	30	26	-	412	GSS
Mar 1975	46	33	21	0	470	GSS
Mar 1976	42	36	23	0	424	GSS
Mar 1978	44	33	23	-	537	GSS
Mar 1980	43	37	20	-	489	GSS
Mar 1983	43	33	25	-	727	GSS
Mar 1984	44	33	22	0	585	GSS
Mar 1986	40	37	23	-	532	GSS
Mar 1987	41	36	22	-	523	GSS
Mar 1988	41	40	19	-	349	GSS

Table 6.11   How Many Times Have You Been Punched or Beaten?
--1973-1984

IF YOU HAVE EVER BEEN PUNCHED OR BEATEN (see Table 6.9)--
Base for the percentages is those who have ever been punched
or beaten.

HITNUM--How many times would you guess this has happened to
you?

	ONCE	2-3 TIMES	4+ TIMES	NOT SURE	N	
Mar 1973	20	28	45	7	410	GSS
Mar 1975	20	31	39	9	469	GSS
Mar 1976	24	33	39	4	421	GSS
Mar 1978	23	31	41	5	531	GSS
Mar 1980	24	31	38	6	489	GSS
Mar 1983	17	40	40	3	721	GSS
Mar 1984	22	36	39	3	585	GSS

Table 6.12   Have You Ever Been Threatened with a Gun, or
Shot At?--1968-1988

GUN--Have you ever been threatened with a gun, or shot at?

	YES	NO	DK	N	
Oct 1968	10	90	-	1581	HARRISVS
Mar 1973	16	84	-	1502	GSS
Mar 1975	17	83	0	1487	GSS
Mar 1976	17	83	0	1498	GSS
Mar 1978	20	80	0	1532	GSS
Mar 1980	21	79	0	1465	GSS
Mar 1983	20	79	0	1598	GSS
Mar 1984	20	80	0	1471	GSS
Mar 1986	20	80	0	1470	GSS
Mar 1987	20	80	-	1465	GSS
Mar 1988	22	78	0	997	GSS

Table 6.13   Were You Threatened or Shot At as a Child or as
an Adult?--1973-1988

IF YOU HAVE EVEN BEEN THREATENED WITH A GUN OR SHOT AT (see
Table 6.12)--Base for the percentages is those who have ever
been threatened with a gun or shot at.

GUNAGE--Did this happen to you as a child or as an adult?

	CHILD	ADULT	BOTH	DK	N	
Mar 1973	12	85	2	0	243	GSS
Mar 1975	13	85	3	-	253	GSS
Mar 1976	14	80	5	0	256	GSS
Mar 1978	14	80	5	0	311	GSS
Mar 1980	12	83	4	-	308	GSS
Mar 1983	13	82	5	0	324	GSS
Mar 1984	16	80	3	-	290	GSS
Mar 1986	12	84	4	-	292	GSS
Mar 1987	13	83	3	-	293	GSS
Mar 1988	15	81	4	-	214	GSS

Table 6.14   How Many Times Have You Been Threatened or
Shot At?--1973-1984

IF YOU HAVE EVER BEEN THREATENED WITH A GUN OR SHOT AT (see
Table 6.12)--Base for the percentages is those who have ever
been threatened with a gun or shot at.

GUNNUM--How many times would you guess this has happened to
you?

	ONCE	2-3 TIMES	4+ TIMES	NOT SURE	N	
Mar 1973	60	20	16	5	240	GSS
Mar 1975	57	25	14	5	251	GSS
Mar 1976	53	25	20	2	255	GSS
Mar 1978	61	23	13	4	309	GSS
Mar 1980	56	24	16	3	308	GSS
Mar 1983	56	27	16	2	324	GSS
Mar 1984	59	21	18	2	290	GSS

Table 6.15   Are There Any Situations in Which It Is OK to Punch an Adult Stranger?--1968-1988

HITOK--Are there any situations that you can imagine in which you would approve of a man punching an adult male stranger?

	YES	NO	DK	N	
Oct 1968	51	44	4	1671	HARRISVS
Mar 1973	65	33	2	1504	GSS
Mar 1975	69	28	3	1479	GSS
Mar 1976	66	29	4	1491	GSS
Mar 1978	63	32	5	1524	GSS
Mar 1980	63	34	3	1451	GSS
Mar 1983	68	28	4	1597	GSS
Mar 1984	60	37	4	1460	GSS
Mar 1986	64	32	4	1449	GSS
Mar 1987	63	32	6	1455	GSS
Mar 1988	63	33	5	984	GSS

NOTE--In GSS since 1976, all respondents were asked the follow-up questions shown in Tables 6.16-6.20. The percentages responding YES out of the total sample differ little from the percentages shown in those tables.

Table 6.16   Is It OK to Punch a Stranger Who Is in a Protest March--1968-1988

IF HITTING IN ANY SITUATION IS OK (see Table 6.15)--Base for the percentages is those who approve of hitting in some situation.

HITMARCH--Would you approve [of a man punching an adult male stranger] if the stranger was in a protest march showing opposition to the other man's views?

	YES	NO	DK	N	
Oct 1968	2	96	2	915	HARRISVS
Mar 1973	6	93	1	1012	GSS
Mar 1975	3	95	2	1070	GSS
Mar 1976	3	96	1	1048	GSS
Mar 1978	3	94	2	1030	GSS
Mar 1980	4	94	2	952	GSS
Mar 1983	3	95	2	1149	GSS
Mar 1984	4	95	2	925	GSS
Mar 1986	3	96	1	984	GSS
Mar 1987	4	94	2	1189	GSS
Mar 1988	2	97	1	661	GSS

Table 6.17 Is It OK to Punch a Stranger Who Was Drunk and
Bumped into a Man and His Wife?--1973-1988

IF HITTING IN ANY SITUATION IS OK (see Table 6.15)--Base for
the percentages is those who approve of hitting in some situation.

HITDRUNK--[Would you approve of a man punching an adult male
stranger if the stranger] Was drunk and bumped into the man
and his wife on the street?

	YES	NO	DK	N	
Oct 1968	9	88	3	916	HARRISVS
Mar 1973	10	88	2	1006	GSS
Mar 1975	7	90	2	1072	GSS
Mar 1976	9	88	3	1049	GSS
Mar 1978	8	88	3	1030	GSS
Mar 1980	9	88	3	954	GSS
Mar 1983	10	88	3	1148	GSS
Mar 1984	8	90	3	920	GSS
Mar 1986	8	90	2	984	GSS
Mar 1987	7	90	3	1190	GSS
Mar 1988	10	88	2	660	GSS

Table 6.18 Is It OK to Punch a Stranger Who Had Hit the
Man's Child?--1973-1988

IF HITTING IN ANY SITUATION IS OK (see Table 6.15)--Base for
the percentages is those who approve of hitting in some situation.

HITCHILD--Would you approve of a man punching a stranger who
had hit the man's child after the child accidentally damaged
the stranger's car?

	YES	NO	DK	N	
Oct 1968	60	33	6	924	HARRISVS
Mar 1973	51	47	3	1008	GSS
Mar 1975	51	46	4	1070	GSS
Mar 1976	55	41	4	1046	GSS
Mar 1978	59	38	3	1030	GSS
Mar 1980	56	39	4	953	GSS
Mar 1983	63	33	4	1148	GSS
Mar 1984	61	36	3	918	GSS
Mar 1986	63	34	3	983	GSS
Mar 1987	62	34	4	1189	GSS
Mar 1988	65	32	4	661	GSS

Table 6.19   Is It OK to Punch a Stranger Who Is Beating Up a Woman?--1968-1988

IF HITTING IN ANY SITUATION IS OK (see Table 6.15)--Base for the percentages is those who approve of hitting in some situation.

HITBEATR--[Would you approve of a man punching a stranger who] Was beating up a woman and the man saw it?

	YES	NO	DK	N	
Oct 1968	84	10	6	925	HARRISVS
Mar 1973	85	13	2	1005	GSS
Mar 1975	80	14	6	1072	GSS
Mar 1976	84	12	4	1048	GSS
Mar 1978	87	10	3	1031	GSS
Mar 1980	87	10	3	954	GSS
Mar 1983	88	9	3	1149	GSS
Mar 1984	88	8	4	920	GSS
Mar 1986	88	9	2	982	GSS
Mar 1987	84	11	5	1189	GSS
Mar 1988	87	8	4	661	GSS

Table 6.20   Is It OK to Punch a Stranger Who Broke into Your Home?--1968-1988

IF HITTING IN ANY SITUATION IS OK (see Table 6.15)--Base for the percentages is those who approve of hitting in some situation.

HITROBBR--[Would you approve of a man punching a stranger who] Had broken into the man's house?

	YES	NO	DK	N	
Oct 1968	92	6	2	923	HARRISVS
Mar 1973	85	13	2	1014	GSS
Mar 1975	90	9	2	1072	GSS
Mar 1976	89	9	2	1049	GSS
Mar 1978	88	10	2	1031	GSS
Mar 1980	88	11	2	954	GSS
Mar 1983	88	10	2	1149	GSS
Mar 1984	86	11	3	926	GSS
Mar 1986	89	9	1	981	GSS
Mar 1987	87	11	2	1189	GSS
Mar 1988	89	10	1	661	GSS

Table 6.21 Are There Any Situations in Which It Is OK for a
Policeman to Strike an Adult Citizen?--1968-1988

POLHITOK--Are there any situations you can imagine in which
you would approve of a policeman striking an adult male citizen?

	YES	NO	DK	N	
Oct 1968	72	23	5	1662	HARRISVS
Mar 1973	73	25	2	1502	GSS
Mar 1975	73	23	4	1475	GSS
Mar 1976	76	20	4	1495	GSS
Mar 1978	76	20	3	1527	GSS
Mar 1980	73	24	3	1457	GSS
Mar 1983	78	20	3	1580	GSS
Mar 1984	69	28	3	1466	GSS
Mar 1986	72	25	3	1453	GSS
Mar 1987	73	23	4	1452	GSS
Mar 1988	73	23	4	987	GSS

NOTE--In GSS since 1976, all respondents were asked the
follow-up questions shown in Tables 6.22-6.25. The percentages responding YES out of the total sample differ little
from the percentages shown in those tables.

Table 6.22 Is It OK for a Policeman to Strike a Citizen Who
Said Vulgar Things to Him?--1968-1988

IF POLICE STRIKING CITIZEN IN ANY SITUATION IS OK (see Table
6.21)--Base for the percentages is those who approve of police striking citizen in some situation.

POLABUSE--Would you approve of a policeman striking a citizen who had said vulgar and obscene things to the policeman?

	YES	NO	DK	N	
Oct 1968	25	70	4	1268	HARRISVS
Mar 1973	22	76	2	1123	GSS
Mar 1975	19	77	4	1131	GSS
Mar 1976	22	75	3	1192	GSS
Mar 1978	19	79	2	1218	GSS
Mar 1980	15	83	2	1101	GSS
Mar 1983	15	83	2	1270	GSS
Mar 1984	13	85	3	1051	GSS
Mar 1986	15	83	2	1084	GSS
Mar 1987	12	86	2	1327	GSS
Mar 1988	13	85	2	761	GSS

Table 6.23   Is It OK for a Policeman to Strike a Citizen Who
Is a Suspect in a Murder Case?--1968-1988

IF POLICE STRIKING CITIZEN IN ANY SITUATION IS OK (see Table
6.21)--Base for the percentages is those who approve of police striking citizen in some situation.

POLMURDR--[Would you approve of a policeman striking a citizen who] Was being questioned as a suspect in a murder case?

	YES	NO	DK	N	
Oct 1968	9	88	4	1267	HARRISVS
Mar 1973	8	91	1	1119	GSS
Mar 1975	8	90	2	1129	GSS
Mar 1976	8	90	2	1191	GSS
Mar 1978	8	88	4	1218	GSS
Mar 1980	8	91	2	1101	GSS
Mar 1983	9	90	2	1269	GSS
Mar 1984	8	90	2	1043	GSS
Mar 1986	8	91	2	1082	GSS
Mar 1987	8	88	3	1327	GSS
Mar 1988	8	90	2	760	GSS

Table 6.24   Is It OK for a Policeman to Strike a Citizen Who
Is Attempting to Escape?--1968-1988

IF POLICE STRIKING CITIZEN IN ANY SITUATION IS OK (see Table
6.21)--Base for the percentages is those who approve of police striking citizen in some situation.

POLESCAP--[Would you approve of a policeman striking a citizen who] Was attempting to escape from custody?

	YES	NO	DK	N	
Oct 1968	83	13	4	1273	HARRISVS
Mar 1973	87	12	2	1120	GSS
Mar 1975	86	11	3	1128	GSS
Mar 1976	84	12	4	1192	GSS
Mar 1978	81	15	4	1218	GSS
Mar 1980	82	14	4	1101	GSS
Mar 1983	81	15	4	1269	GSS
Mar 1984	82	16	2	1043	GSS
Mar 1986	79	16	4	1085	GSS
Mar 1987	81	13	6	1327	GSS
Mar 1988	84	12	4	760	GSS

Table 6.25   Is It OK for a Policeman to Strike a Citizen Who
Is Attacking Him?--1968-1988

IF POLICE STRIKING CITIZEN IN ANY SITUATION IS OK (see Table
6.21)--Base for the percentages is those who approve of police striking citizen in some situation.

POLATTAK--[Would you approve of a policeman striking a citizen who] Was attacking the policeman with his fists?

	YES	NO	DK	N	
Oct 1968	97	2	1	1287	HARRISVS
Mar 1973	97	3	0	1122	GSS
Mar 1975	98	1	1	1130	GSS
Mar 1976	97	2	1	1192	GSS
Mar 1978	96	3	1	1218	GSS
Mar 1980	98	2	1	1101	GSS
Mar 1983	95	4	1	1270	GSS
Mar 1984	96	3	1	1050	GSS
Mar 1986	97	2	1	1085	GSS
Mar 1987	96	3	1	1328	GSS
Mar 1988	96	3	1	762	GSS

Table 6.26 Do You Have Any Guns in Your Home?--1959-1988

OWNGUN--Do you happen to have in your home (IF HOUSE: or garage) any guns or revolvers?

	YES	NO	REFUSED TO ANSWER	DK	N	
Jul 1959[a]	49	51	-	-	1538	AIPO616
Jan 1965[a]	48	52	-	-	1689	AIPO704
Aug 1966[a]	47	53	-	-	1509	AIPO733
Apr 1968[b]	51	48	-	1	1577	HARRIS1813
Jan 1971[c]	51	47	-	2	3085	HARRIS2055
Oct 1971[d]	45	53	-	2	1789	HARRIS2137
May 1972[a]	43	57	-	-	1513	AIPO852
Mar 1973	47	52	1	-	1495	GSS
Mar 1974	46	53	1	0	1480	GSS
Mar 1975[e]	46	54	-	-	1512	AIPO925
Mar 1975[e]	45	55	-	-	1536	AIPO926
Oct 1975[e]	47	51	-	2	1558	AIPO937
Oct 1975[f]	48	51	-	1	1503	HARRIS7586
Nov 1975[g]	47	52	-	1	1463	HARRIS7587
Feb 1976[f]	46	53	-	1	1492	HARRIS2521
Mar 1976	47	52	1	-	1493	GSS
Mar 1977	51	49	0	0	1523	GSS
Jun 1979	47	53	-	-	1495	HARRIS7921
Oct 1979[e]	47	53	-	-	1525	AIPO142G
Mar 1980	48	52	0	0	1458	GSS
Nov 1980	44	56	-	-	1606	AIPO146G
Mar 1982	45	53	1	0	1501	GSS
Mar 1984	45	54	1	0	1467	GSS
Mar 1985	44	55	1	-	1530	GSS
Mar 1987	46	53	0	-	1464	GSS
Mar 1988	40	59	1	-	970	GSS

[a]Omits "or garage."

[b]Do you own or does anyone in your house own a gun?

[c]Do you have a gun in your house or not?

[d]Is there a gun in your home, or not?

[e]Do you have any guns in your home?

[f]Do you or anyone in your house own a gun?

[g]Do you or does anyone in this household own a gun, or not?

Table 6.27   Do You Have a Pistol in Your Home?--1959-1988

IF YOU HAVE ANY GUNS IN YOUR HOME (see Table 6.26)--Base for
the percentages is the entire sample.

PISTOL--Is it a pistol, shotgun, rifle, or what?

	YES	NO	REFUSED TO ANSWER	N	
Jul 1959	17	83	-	1501	AIPO616
Jan 1965	15	85	-	1667	AIPO704
Aug 1966	20	80	-	1484	AIPO733
Apr 1972	23	77	-	1560	AIPO852
Mar 1973	20	79	1	1497	GSS
Mar 1974	20	80	1	1479	GSS
Mar 1975	25	75		1512	AIP925
Mar 1975	19	81	-	1536	AIPO926
Mar 1975	19	81	-	1541	AIPO937
Mar 1976	22	77	1	1489	GSS
Mar 1977	21	79	0	1519	GSS
Oct 1979	22	78		1541	AIPO142G
Mar 1980	23	76	1	1458	GSS
Mar 1982	21	77	2	1501	GSS
Mar 1984	21	78	1	1467	GSS
Mar 1985	23	76	1	1530	GSS
Mar 1987	25	74	0	1464	GSS
Mar 1988	23	76	1	970	GSS

Table 6.28   Do You Have a Shotgun in Your Home?--1973-1988

IF YOU HAVE ANY GUNS IN YOUR HOME (see Table 6.26)--Base for
the percentages is the entire sample.

SHOTGUN--Is it a pistol, shotgun, rifle, or what?

	YES	NO	REFUSED TO ANSWER	N	
Mar 1973	28	71	1	1497	GSS
Mar 1974	28	71	1	1479	GSS
Mar 1975	29	71	-	1512	AIPO925
Mar 1975	26	74	-	1536	AIPO926
Mar 1976	28	71	1	1489	GSS
Mar 1977	31	69	0	1519	GSS
Oct 1979	30	70	-	1541	AIPO142G
Mar 1980	30	70	0	1458	GSS
Mar 1982	29	70	2	1501	GSS
Mar 1984	28	72	1	1467	GSS
Mar 1985	27	72	1	1530	GSS
Mar 1987	29	70	0	1464	GSS
Mar 1988	24	73	1	970	GSS

Table 6.29 Do You Have a Rifle in Your Home?--1973-1988

IF YOU HAVE ANY GUNS IN YOUR HOME (see Table 6.26)--Base for the percentages is the entire sample.

RIFLE--Is it a pistol, shotgun, rifle, or what?

	YES	NO	REFUSED TO ANSWER	N	
Mar 1973	29	70	1	1497	GSS
Mar 1974	27	73	1	1479	GSS
Mar 1975	28	72	-	1512	AIPO925
Mar 1975	26	74	-	1536	AIPO926
Mar 1976	28	71	1	1489	GSS
Mar 1977	30	70	0	1519	GSS
Oct 1979	30	70	-	1541	AIPO142G
Mar 1980	29	70	0	1458	GSS
Mar 1982	28	70	2	1501	GSS
Mar 1984	27	72	1	1467	GSS
Mar 1985	28	71	1	1530	GSS
Mar 1987	28	70	0	1464	GSS
Mar 1988	24	75	1	970	GSS

Table 6.30 Do You Favor Requiring a Gun Permit?--1959-1988

GUNLAW--Would you favor or oppose a law which would require a person to obtain a police permit before he could buy a gun?

	FAVOR	OPPOSE	DK	N	
Jul 1959	75	21	4	1529	AIPO616
Dec 1963	79	17	4	4419	AIPO681
Jan 1965	73	23	4	3492	AIPO704
Sep 1965	70	25	5	3555	AIPO717
Aug 1966	67	29	3	3541	AIPO733
Aug 1967	73	24	4	3527	AIPO749
Oct 1971	72	24	4	1502	AIPO838
Mar 1972	70	27	3	1610	GSS
May 1972	72	24	4	1540	AIPO852
Mar 1973	74	25	2	1495	GSS
Mar 1974	75	23	1	1477	GSS
Feb 1975[a]	71	28	1	448	SRC(TEL)
Mar 1975	74	24	3	1488	GSS
Feb 1976[a]	73	24	4	638	SRC(TEL)
Mar 1976	72	27	1	1493	GSS
Mar 1977	72	27	2	1528	GSS
Mar 1980	69	29	2	1467	GSS
Mar 1982	72	26	2	1503	GSS
Mar 1984	70	27	3	1467	GSS
Mar 1985	72	27	1	1530	GSS
Mar 1987	70	28	2	1464	GSS
Mar 1988	74	24	3	973	GSS

[a]"...before he or she...."

Table 6.31 Have You Ever Received a Traffic Ticket?--
1973-1984

TICKET--Have you ever received a ticket, or been charged by
the police, for a traffic violation--other than for illegal
parking?

	YES	NO	REFUSED TO ANSWER	DK	N	
Mar 1973	42	58	0	–	1503	GSS
Mar 1974	41	59	–	–	1483	GSS
Mar 1976	41	59	–	0	1499	GSS
Mar 1977	43	57	–	–	1528	GSS
Mar 1980	52	48	–	0	1463	GSS
Mar 1982	48	52	0	0	1505	GSS
Mar 1984	54	45	–	0	1469	GSS

Table 6.32 Have You Ever Been Picked Up or Charged by the
Police?--1973-1984

ARREST--Were you ever picked up, or charged, by the police,
for any (other) reason [than a traffic violation] whether or
not you were guilty?

	YES	NO	REFUSED TO ANSWER	DK	N	
Mar 1973	11	89	0	–	1445	GSS
Mar 1974	10	90	–	–	1476	GSS
Mar 1976	9	91	–	0	1466	GSS
Mar 1977	10	90	–	–	1497	GSS
Mar 1980	12	87	0	0	1426	GSS
Mar 1982	13	87	0	0	1493	GSS
Mar 1984	13	87	–	0	1452	GSS

7

Tobacco, Alcohol, and Drugs

Drinking and smoking are age-old concerns, so it is hardly
surprising that questions about these topics have been asked
since the 1930s. What is more surprising from the vantage
point of 1989 is that only the most basic questions were
asked: "Do you drink?" and "Do you smoke?" Only in the last
few years have the polls inquired about alcohol abuse, driv-
ing while intoxicated, knowledge about the effects of alcohol
and smoking, smoking in public places, and so on (Gallup,
1987).

Trends since the 1930s show long periods of relative stability in behavior. The proportion of the population saying
it used alcohol hovered around 60-65 percent until the early
1960s (Table 7.1).[1] Since then it has been 65-70 percent. A
reason for the rise in the proportion of those who drink is
apparent in the separate distributions for males and females.
In all surveys, fewer women than men have reported that they
drink. The difference is declining, however, and the rise in
drinking among women is enough to account for most of the
overall increase since the 1960s.

It is more difficult to determine whether there has been
a change in the number of people who think they drink too much
(Table 7.2). GSS data since 1977 show no pattern. Gallup
data go back only three years earlier, and while they show a
lower percentage who overindulge, comparisons of surveys a-
cross organizations suggest that the difference may be arti-
factual.[2] Gallup (1987, No. 258:8) reports an increase since

---

[1]The high numbers for 1945 and 1946 may be overestimates.
See our Introduction on the nature of early Gallup surveys.
Gallup (1987, No. 258:9) reports a 67 percent figure for these
two years.

[2]In the several comparisons possible, Gallup consistently
reports a smaller percentage who say they sometimes drink too

the 1950s in the proportion of people who say that drinking
has created problems in their families. It may be, however,
that increased public concern about drinking has stimulated
greater awareness of and a greater willingness to acknowledge
such problems.

The percentage of the population who smoke showed considerable stability from the 1930s through the 1960s; the percentage never dropped below 40 percent for cigarettes (7.5)
and was apparently over 50 percent overall (7.3).[3] In the two
decades since, smoking has declined significantly but not
dramatically. The decline was more notable among men than
among women, especially if all smoking rather than cigarette
smoking only is considered. Increases in smoking by young
women account for the rather fuzzy patterns of smoking by the
various age groups.[4] Not surprisingly, as smoking declines,
more people report that they have tried to give up smoking
(7.4).

Legalization of marijuana is an instance in which survey
designers "got in on the ground floor" and were thus able to
capture the complex change that has characterized attitudes
on this subject (Table 7.7). When the legalization question
was first asked, barely one person in ten was in favor. Since
then we have seen a rapid increase, so that 30 percent were
favorable in 1978, and a rapid decline over the past decade,
so that current attitudes are not all that different from
those observed in the early 1970s. Men and women differ fairly sharply in their attitudes; men have consistently been more
in favor of legalization.

Large and variable differences in attitudes toward legalization are observed by age (Johnston, Bachman, and O'Malley,
1980, pp. 314-322; Duncan, 1985). Young people have always
been more favorable. But in the 1970s the difference between
the youngest and oldest age groups was on the order of 35-40
percent; in one survey over half of those 18-24 favored legalization whereas no more than 15 percent of the oldest group
ever supported that policy. With the overall decline in

---

much. For example, in 1978 GSS and Gallup recorded almost
identical proportions drinking at least occasionally. Yet GSS
found 25 percent of the entire sample reporting overindulging
(Table 7.2) while Gallup (1987, No. 258:9-10) reported a
figure of 16 percent.

[3]We do not entirely discount the very high percentage in
1939 (7.3), but the multiple surveys from the 1940s (7.5) are
a more reliable guide.

[4]An additional source of time-series data, since 1965, is
the National Health Interview Survey and the Current
Population Survey. See United States Surgeon General (1988).

approval, age differences have narrowed, now showing about a 15 percent difference between youngest and oldest. These age differences heighten the significance of the general decline since 1978. If the only process of change had been the replacement of older generations by new cohorts of adults, there would have been a large, steady increase in favorability. What has happened instead is that those who were young in the 1970s began to rethink their positions, and those entering adulthood, though more favorable than the oldest cohorts, were less positive than those coming of age in the 1970s.

REFERENCES

Duncan, Beverly. 1985. Legalization of Marijuana and Year of Birth: Public Opinion 1969 to 1980. In Leon Brill and Charles Winick, eds., *The Yearbook of Substance Use and Abuse*, Vol. 3. New York: Human Sciences Press.

Gallup. 1987. *Gallup Report*, No. 258, 265. Princeton, NJ: Gallup Poll.

Johnston, Lloyd D., Jerald G. Bachman, and Patrick M. O'Malley. 1980. Drug Use among American High School Students. In Leon Brill and Charles Winick, eds., *The Yearbook of Substance Use and Abuse*, Vol. 2. New York: Human Sciences Press, 1985.

United States Surgeon General. 1988. *The Health Consequences of Smoking: Nicotine Addiction* (1987 Surgeon General's Report on the health consequences of smoking). Washington, DC: U.S. Government Printing Office.

Table 7.1   Do You Ever Drink Alcoholic Beverages?--1939-1988

DRINK--Do you ever have occasion to use any alcoholic beverages such as liquor, wine, or beer, or are you a total abstainer?

	YES	NO	N	
Jun 1939[a]	60	40	3075	AIPO160
Nov 1945	82	18	3066	AIPO360
Jul 1946	78	22	3115	AIPO375
Oct 1947	63	37	2777	AIPO405
Nov 1949	57	43	1352	AIPO450T
Jun 1950	65	35	1335	AIPO456
Aug 1951	61	39	1288	AIPO479TPS
Dec 1952	63	37	1424	AIPO509
Jan 1954[b]	63	37	1441	AIPO526
Feb 1955[c]	61	39	1576	AIPO543
Jan 1956[d]	60	40	1385	AIPO558
Mar 1956[d]	59	41	1992	AIPO562
Mar 1957[d]	58	42	1615	AIPO580
Jan 1958[d]	56	44	1542	AIPO594
Dec 1959[d]	61	39	1517	AIPO622
May 1963	71	29	1509	NORC160
Jan 1966[e]	65	35	1444	AIPO723
Feb 1968[e]	65	35	1467	AIPO758
Jan 1969[e]	65	35	1460	AIPO773
May 1974[f]	69	31	1529	AIPO903
Jan 1977[e]	71	29	1505	AIPO966
Mar 1977	72	28	1520	GSS
Mar 1978	72	28	1526	GSS
Apr 1978[e]	70	30	1503	AIPO100G
May 1979[e]	70	30	1505	AIPO128G
Mar 1980	73	27	1462	GSS
Jan 1981[e]	71	29	1534	AIPO167G
Aug 1982[e]	65	35	1533	AIPO200G
Mar 1983	74	26	1593	GSS
Mar 1983[e]	65	35	1558	AIPO211G
Mar 1984	73	27	1459	GSS
Jul 1984[e]	64	36	1518	A237G
Sep 1984[e]	64	36	1523	AIPO
Feb 1985[e]	67	33	1557	AIPO250G
Mar 1986	68	32	1468	GSS
Mar 1987	73	27	1461	GSS
Mar 1987[e]	66	34	1015	AIPOAI852
Jul 1987	65	35	1607	AIPO278G
Mar 1988	69	31	995	GSS

WOMEN

	YES	NO		
1939	45	55		AIPO
1945	60	40		AIPO
1947	54	46		AIPO
1949	49	51		AIPO
1951	46	54		AIPO
1952	53	47		AIPO
1957	50	50		AIPO

Table 7.1 (Continued)

	YES	NO	N	
1958	45	55		AIPO
1966	61	39		AIPO
1974	61	39		AIPO
Mar 1977	66	34	835	GSS
Mar 1978	68	32	888	GSS
Mar 1980	66	34	826	GSS
Mar 1983	69	31	907	GSS
Mar 1984	68	32	870	GSS
Mar 1986	62	38	848	GSS
Mar 1987	67	33	820	GSS
Mar 1988	65	35	558	GSS

MEN

	YES	NO	N	
1939	70	30		AIPO
1945	75	25		AIPO
1947	72	28		AIPO
1949	66	34		AIPO
1951	70	30		AIPO
1952	68	32		AIPO
1957	67	33		AIPO
1958	66	34		AIPO
1966	70	30		AIPO
1974	77	23		AIPO
Mar 1977	79	21	690	GSS
Mar 1978	79	21	641	GSS
Mar 1980	82	18	639	GSS
Mar 1983	81	19	689	GSS
Mar 1984	79	21	596	GSS
Mar 1986	75	25	620	GSS
Mar 1987	80	20	641	GSS
Mar 1988	74	26	437	GSS

[a]Do you ever drink alcoholic beverages such as wine, beer, cocktails, highballs?

[b]Do you ever have occasion to use beverages like beer, wine, or liquor, or are you a total abstainer?

[c]Do you ever drink any alcoholic beverages like beer, wine, or liquor, or are you a total abstainer?

[d]The word "any" was not in the question.

[e]Do you have occasion to use alcoholic beverages such as liquor, wine, or beer or are you a total abstainer?

[f]Do you have occasion to use alcoholic beverages...?

NOTE--Distributions by sex for AIPO surveys are taken from Gallup (1987, No. 265:7). In some cases they will not yield the overall result shown above.

Table 7.2   Do You Sometimes Drink Too Much?--1974-1988

IF YOU EVER DRINK ALCOHOLIC BEVERAGES (see Table 7.1)--Base
for the percentages is the entire sample.

DRUNK--Do you sometimes drink more than you think you
should?

	YES	NO	DK	N	
May 1974	18	82	–	1529	AIPO903
Mar 1977	27	73	–	1525	GSS
Mar 1978	25	75	0	1526	GSS
Mar 1980	28	72	0	1462	GSS
Mar 1983	27	73	–	1596	GSS
Mar 1984	31	69	0	1463	GSS
Mar 1986	22	78	0	1466	GSS
Mar 1987	29	71	–	1461	GSS
Mar 1987	19	81	0	1015	AIPOAI852
Mar 1988	26	74	–	995	GSS

Table 7.3   Do You Smoke?--1939-1988

SMOKE--Do you smoke?

	YES	NO	N	
Jun 1939	64	36	3080	AIPO160
Jun 1957	48	52	1510	AIPO585
Nov 1957	55	45	1657	AIPO592
Apr 1960	50	50	2407	NORC428
Mar 1977	42	58	1524	GSS
Mar 1978	39	61	1531	GSS
Mar 1980	41	59	1467	GSS
Mar 1983	37	63	1597	GSS
Mar 1984	37	63	1467	GSS
Mar 1986	33	67	1466	GSS
Mar 1987	31	69	1461	GSS
Mar 1988	34	66	995	GSS

WOMEN

	YES	NO	N	
Mar 1977	35	65	834	GSS
Mar 1978	35	65	888	GSS
Mar 1980	35	65	827	GSS
Mar 1983	33	67	908	GSS
Mar 1984	32	68	871	GSS
Mar 1986	29	71	847	GSS
Mar 1987	27	73	820	GSS
Mar 1988	31	69	559	GSS

MEN

	YES	NO	N	
Mar 1977	51	49	690	GSS
Mar 1978	46	54	643	GSS
Mar 1980	48	52	640	GSS
Mar 1983	42	58	689	GSS
Mar 1984	44	56	596	GSS
Mar 1986	38	62	619	GSS
Mar 1987	36	64	641	GSS
Mar 1988	38	62	436	GSS

AGE:18-24

	YES	NO	N	
Mar 1977	48	52	192	GSS
Mar 1978	43	57	204	GSS
Mar 1980	45	55	194	GSS
Mar 1983	38	62	164	GSS
Mar 1984	41	59	208	GSS
Mar 1986	29	71	136	GSS
Mar 1987	34	66	155	GSS
Mar 1988	39	61	110	GSS

Table 7.3 (Continued)

	YES	NO	N	
AGE:25-29				
Mar 1977	45	55	176	GSS
Mar 1978	41	59	203	GSS
Mar 1980	41	59	163	GSS
Mar 1983	41	59	251	GSS
Mar 1984	43	57	185	GSS
Mar 1986	35	64	190	GSS
Mar 1987	27	73	164	GSS
Mar 1988	41	59	128	GSS
AGE:30-49				
Mar 1977	48	52	556	GSS
Mar 1978	42	58	551	GSS
Mar 1980	48	52	529	GSS
Mar 1983	41	59	590	GSS
Mar 1984	42	58	554	GSS
Mar 1986	39	61	584	GSS
Mar 1987	36	64	606	GSS
Mar 1988	39	61	377	GSS
AGE:50-64				
Mar 1977	41	59	364	GSS
Mar 1978	45	55	312	GSS
Mar 1980	42	58	304	GSS
Mar 1983	39	61	319	GSS
Mar 1984	36	64	265	GSS
Mar 1986	34	66	264	GSS
Mar 1987	33	67	262	GSS
Mar 1988	35	65	172	GSS
AGE:65+				
Mar 1977	24	76	229	GSS
Mar 1978	24	76	254	GSS
Mar 1980	25	75	268	GSS
Mar 1983	21	79	266	GSS
Mar 1984	21	79	250	GSS
Mar 1986	18	82	285	GSS
Mar 1987	18	82	270	GSS
Mar 1988	18	82	204	GSS

Table 7.4   Have You Ever Tried to Quit Smoking?--1960-1988

IF YOU SMOKE (see Table 7.3)--Base for the percentages is smokers only.

QUITSMK--Have you ever tried to give up smoking?

	YES	NO	N	
Apr 1960	52	48	1128	NORC428
Mar 1978	69	31	599	GSS
Mar 1980	69	31	595	GSS
Mar 1983	75	25	591	GSS
Mar 1984	74	26	541	GSS
Mar 1986	73	27	474	GSS
Mar 1987	70	30	452	GSS
Mar 1988	78	22	336	GSS

Table 7.5   Do You Smoke Cigarettes?--1939-1984

IF YOU SMOKE (see Table 7.3)--Base for the percentages is
the entire sample.

SMOKECIG--Do you smoke cigarettes?

	YES	NO	N	
Jul 1939	41	59	5223	RFOR7
1944[a]	41	58		AIPO
1949[a]	44	56		AIPO
1954[a]	45	55		AIPO
1957[a]	42	58		AIPO
1958[a]	45	55		AIPO
Jul 1969[a]	41	59	1486	AIPO785
Mar 1977	38	62	1524	GSS
Mar 1978	36	64	1531	GSS
Mar 1980	38	62	1467	GSS
Mar 1983	35	65	1597	GSS
Mar 1984	35	65	1467	GSS

WOMEN

	YES	NO	N	
1944[a]	36	64		AIPO
1949[a]	33	67		AIPO
1954[a]	32	68		AIPO
1957[a]	34	66		AIPO
Mar 1977	34	66	834	GSS
Mar 1978	34	66	888	GSS
Mar 1980	34	66	827	GSS
Mar 1983	33	67	908	GSS
Mar 1984	32	68	871	GSS

MEN

	YES	NO	N	
1944[a]	48	52		AIPO
1949[a]	54	46		AIPO
1954[a]	57	43		AIPO
1957[a]	57	43		AIPO
Mar 1977	43	57	690	GSS
Mar 1978	38	62	643	GSS
Mar 1980	42	58	640	GSS
Mar 1983	38	62	689	GSS
Mar 1984	40	60	596	GSS

[a]Have you, yourself, smoked any cigarettes in the past week?

NOTE--1944-1958 data for AIPO surveys are taken from Gallup
(1987, No. 258:4).

Table 7.6   Have You Ever Smoked Regularly?--1960-1988

IF YOU DO NOT SMOKE (see Table 7.3)--Base for the percentages is those who do not currently smoke.

EVSMOKE--Have you ever smoked regularly?

	YES	NO	N	
Mar 1978	34	66	873	GSS
Mar 1980	35	65	850	GSS
Mar 1983	33	67	996	GSS
Mar 1984	31	69	908	GSS
Mar 1986	32	68	949	GSS
Mar 1987	35	65	964	GSS
Mar 1988	33	67	608	GSS

Table 7.7   Should Marijuana Be Made Legal?--1969-1988

GRASS--Do you think the use of marijuana should be made legal or not?

	LEGAL	NOT LEGAL	DK	N	
Oct 1969	12	84	4	1540	AIPO789
Feb 1972	15	81	4	1513	AIPO846
Jan 1973	16	78	6	1508	AIPO863
Mar 1973	18	80	2	1501	GSS
Mar 1975	20	75	5	1486	GSS
Mar 1976	28	69	3	1497	GSS
Mar 1977	28	66	6	1521	AIPO972
Mar 1978	30	67	3	1509	GSS
May 1979	25	70	5	1514	AIPO129G
Mar 1980	25	72	3	1465	GSS
Jun 1980	25	70	5	1569	AIPO158G
Oct 1982	20	74	6	785	AIPO
Mar 1983	20	76	3	1598	GSS
Mar 1984	23	73	4	1465	GSS
May 1985[a]	23	73	4	1528	AIPOTEL
Mar 1986	18	80	2	1463	GSS
Mar 1987	16	81	3	1465	GSS
Mar 1988	17	79	4	993	GSS

WOMEN

	LEGAL	NOT LEGAL	DK	N	
Mar 1973	15	83	2	802	GSS
Mar 1975	16	80	4	819	GSS
Mar 1976	24	73	2	830	GSS
Mar 1978	26	71	3	871	GSS
Mar 1980	21	76	3	826	GSS
Mar 1983	16	80	3	908	GSS
Mar 1984	19	77	4	869	GSS
Mar 1986	14	84	2	846	GSS
Mar 1987	14	83	3	825	GSS
Mar 1988	14	82	3	558	GSS

MEN

	LEGAL	NOT LEGAL	DK	N	
Mar 1973	22	75	3	699	GSS
Mar 1975	25	69	6	667	GSS
Mar 1976	32	64	4	667	GSS
Mar 1978	34	63	3	638	GSS
Mar 1980	30	67	3	639	GSS
Mar 1983	25	71	3	690	GSS
Mar 1984	28	68	4	596	GSS
Mar 1986	23	75	2	617	GSS
Mar 1987	19	78	3	640	GSS
Mar 1988	21	74	4	435	GSS

Table 7.7 (Continued)

	LEGAL	NOT LEGAL	DK	N	
AGE:18-24					
Mar 1973	44	55	1	214	GSS
Mar 1975	42	50	7	214	GSS
Mar 1976	53	44	3	203	GSS
Mar 1978	50	48	2	201	GSS
Mar 1980	43	54	3	194	GSS
Mar 1983	33	66	1	164	GSS
Mar 1984	31	65	4	208	GSS
Mar 1986	25	73	2	133	GSS
Mar 1987	22	73	5	155	GSS
Mar 1988	24	68	8	111	GSS
AGE:25-29					
Mar 1973	32	65	3	168	GSS
Mar 1975	35	59	6	190	GSS
Mar 1976	47	48	4	184	GSS
Mar 1978	48	49	2	202	GSS
Mar 1980	42	56	2	163	GSS
Mar 1983	28	69	4	598	GSS
Mar 1984	38	58	4	465	GSS
Mar 1986	27	72	2	463	GSS
Mar 1987	27	68	5	465	GSS
Mar 1988	21	73	6	993	GSS
AGE:30-49					
Mar 1973	14	84	2	541	GSS
Mar 1975	18	79	3	510	GSS
Mar 1976	25	72	3	498	GSS
Mar 1978	29	69	2	543	GSS
Mar 1980	27	71	2	528	GSS
Mar 1983	21	76	3	591	GSS
Mar 1984	27	68	4	553	GSS
Mar 1986	20	79	2	585	GSS
Mar 1987	19	79	2	607	GSS
Mar 1988	19	78	3	378	GSS
AGE:50-64					
Mar 1973	11	87	2	358	GSS
Mar 1975	11	85	4	316	GSS
Mar 1976	17	80	4	340	GSS
Mar 1978	17	79	4	307	GSS
Mar 1980	14	83	3	305	GSS
Mar 1983	17	80	3	319	GSS
Mar 1984	11	86	3	266	GSS
Mar 1986	12	86	2	264	GSS
Mar 1987	10	89	1	262	GSS
Mar 1988	15	84	2	170	GSS

Table 7.7 (Continued)

	LEGAL	NOT LEGAL	DK	N	
AGE:65+					
Mar 1973	6	91	3	216	GSS
Mar 1975	7	87	6	251	GSS
Mar 1976	14	83	3	266	GSS
Mar 1978	15	80	5	249	GSS
Mar 1980	10	85	4	266	GSS
Mar 1983	9	86	5	266	GSS
Mar 1984	7	89	4	248	GSS
Mar 1986	12	87	1	284	GSS
Mar 1987	6	90	4	272	GSS
Mar 1988	10	87	3	202	GSS

[a]"Or not" was left off.

8

Race Relations

The American Dilemma, as Gunnar Myrdal so adeptly phrased it
in his classic study of race relations, is the contradiction
between the ideal of equality ("liberty and justice for all,"
"equal protection under the law," "all men are created equal")
and the reality of racism. For a century the American repub-
lic lived "half-slave and half-free." Then for another century we lived with blacks half freed, emancipated from slavery
but enchained by Jim Crow laws, institutionalized segregation,
and white prejudice.

In the 1940s the legal system of segregation in the South
and the informal racism that pervaded all regions seemed to
be as entrenched and vital as any long-established American
institution. But while the foundations of segregation and
racism were sunk deeply in America's history, they were con-
tinually being eroded by the fundamental and transcendent
American ideals of freedom and equality. Pressured by an
invigorated civil rights movement, the repudiation of the
racial ideology of Nazism, critical Supreme Court decisions
undermining the "separate, but equal" pillar of segregation,
and other developments, institutionalized racism began to
crumble after World War II (Burstein, 1985; Schuman, Steeh,
and Bobo, 1985).

Perhaps even more amazing than legal changes were the
changes that occurred in the sphere of "folkways", which
William Graham Sumner had warned were almost impervious to
adaptation. But the racial attitudes that underpinned
segregation and racial discrimination did begin to change
(Smith and Sheatsley, 1984; Schaefer,1986; Schuman, Steeh,
and Bobo, 1985; Smith, 1982, 1985). The shifts in the area
of education illustrate the general process (Tables 8.15-
8.18). In 1942 de jure school segregation was the rule in
all southern and many other states, and over 60 percent of
whites agreed that whites and blacks should attend separate

schools.   By 1985 support for the dual school system had
fallen to just 7 percent.   As *de jure* school segregation fell
both before the courts of law and public opinion, it was often
replaced by *de facto* segregation.   Busing was the most commonly implemented device to combat this form of segregation, and
initially it was uniformly and often vigorous opposed by
whites (Taylor and Stinchcombe, 1977; Smith and Sheastley,
1984).   But even on this issue, attitudes have been changing
(Table 8.19).   Opposition to busing stood at up to 81-82
percent in 1970-1977 but has since fallen to 63 percent.

Attitudes on racial intermarriage (8.1), open housing
(8.9-8.10), interracial socializing (8.4, 8.6), and equal
employment opportunity (8.3) have all followed a similar
course.[1]   In each of these areas support for segregation has
slowly but steadily declined.   Discredited stereotypes of
blacks also changed dramatically (8.20).   Seen from the perspective of Atlanta in 1942 or even Selma in 1965, the overall change in white attitudes has been revolutionary.

But it is still an incomplete revolution.   Stereotypes
have not disappeared (8.21-8.24).   Opposition to racial equality remains strong in certain areas (for example, in remnants
of the old plantation South and urban neighborhoods such as
Cicero and Howard Beach).   Likewise a majority or close to a
majority of whites still oppose busing (8.19), open housing
(8.9), and sending whites to schools with a majority of black
students (8.18).   In particular, affirmative action is re-
jected by most whites, and unlike almost all other racial
items, there is no trend toward acceptance (Kluegel and Smith,
1986; Smith and Sheatsley, 1984).[2]   In fact, some students of
American race relations have concluded that racial tolerance
may not expand further and that newer forms of racism (for
example, attitudes connecting crime with blacks) have merely
replaced traditional forms (Miller and Sears, 1986; Schuman,
Steeh, and Bobo, 1985).

Without ignoring real signs of enduring racism, it is
still fair to conclude that America has been successfully
struggling to resolve its Dilemma and that equality has been
gaining ascendency over racism.

---

[1] See also the series about willingness to vote for a
black presidential candidate (1.5).

[2] Nor has spending or other aid to help blacks been especially popular.   See Tables 1.22 and 3.16-3.17.

REFERENCES

Burstein, Paul.   1985.   *Discrimination, Jobs, and Politics*. Chicago: University of Chicago Press.

Kluegel, James R., and Eliot R. Smith.   1986.   *Beliefs About Inequality*. New York: Aldine.

Miller, Steven D., and David O Sears.   1986.   Stability and Change in Social Tolerance: A Test of the Persistence Hypothesis.   *American Journal of Political Science*, 30: 214-236.

Schaefer, Richard T. 1986. Racial Prejudice in a Capitalist State: What Has Happened to the American Creed?   *Phylon*, 47:192-198.

Schuman, Howard, Charlotte Steeh and Lawrence Bobo.   1985. *Racial Attitudes in America*. Cambridge: Harvard University Press.

Smith, A. Wade. 1985. Cohorts, Education, and the Evolution of Tolerance.   *Social Science Research*, 14:205-225.

_____.   1982.   White Attitudes Toward School Desegregation, 1954-1980: An Update on Continuing Trends. *Pacific Sociological Review*, 25:3-25.

Smith, Tom W., and Paul B. Sheatsley.   1984.   American Attitudes Toward Race Relations.   *Public Opinion*, 7(5):14-15, 50-53.

Taylor, D. Garth, and Artur L. Stinchcombe. 1977. The Boston School Desegregation Controversy. Project Report, National Institute of Education.

Table 8.1   Should There Be Laws against Interracial
Marriages?--1963-1988

WHITES ONLY

RACMAR--Do you think there should be laws against marriages
between (Negroes/blacks) and whites?

	YES	NO	DK	N	
Dec 1963	59	37	3	1351	SRS330
Oct 1964	58	39	3	1724	SRS760
Jan 1965[a]	48	46	6	3500	AIPO705
Apr 1968	53	43	3	1258	SRS4050
Apr 1970	48	48	4	1258	SRS4100
Aug 1970[a]	35	57	8	1506	AIPO812
Mar 1972	38	59	3	1352	GSS
Mar 1973	37	61	2	1309	GSS
Mar 1974	34	64	2	1309	GSS
Mar 1975	38	60	2	1321	GSS
Mar 1976	32	66	2	1363	GSS
Mar 1977	28	71	2	1348	GSS
Mar 1980	30	67	3	1326	GSS
Mar 1982	32	65	3	1347	GSS
Mar 1984	26	71	3	1274	GSS
Mar 1985	27	70	2	1374	GSS
Mar 1988	25	72	3	843	GSS

[a]Some states have laws making it a crime for a white person
to marry a Negro. Do you approve or disapprove of such
laws?

NOTE--Many of the questions in this chapter were asked of
all respondents after 1978; shown are responses from whites
only.

Table 8.2 Does Your Church Have Both Blacks and Whites?--
1978-1988

ALL RESPONDENTS

RACCHURH--Do (Negroes/blacks)/whites) attend the church that
you, yourself, attend most often, or not?

	YES	NO	NO CHURCH	DK	N	
Mar 1978	29	54	17	0	1529	GSS
Mar 1980	36	49	15	0	1464	GSS
Mar 1983	30	54	15	0	1591	GSS
Mar 1984	39	47	14	-	1459	GSS
Mar 1986	31	54	14	0	1466	GSS
Mar 1987	38	50	12	-	1440	GSS
Mar 1988	41	44	15	0	993	GSS

Table 8.3 Should Blacks and Whites Have an Equal Chance at
Jobs?--1944-1972

WHITES ONLY

RACJOB--Do you think (Negroes/blacks) should have as good a
chance as white people to get any kind of a job, or do you
think white people should have the first chance at any kind
of job?

	AS GOOD A CHANCE	WHITE PEOPLE FIRST	DK	N	
May 1944	42	52	6	2523	NORC225
May 1946[a]	47	49	5	2360	NORC241
Dec 1963	83	14	2	1348	NORC330
Jun 1966	87	10	3	1325	NORC889A
Mar 1972	96	3	1	1348	GSS

[a]Question asked of blacks as well. The distribution was:
92% (as good a chance), 5% (whites first), 3% (DK) (N=229).

Table 8.4   Would You Try to Integrate a Social Club You
Belonged To?--1977-1988

WHITES ONLY

RACCHNG--If you and your friends belonged to a social club
that would not let (Negroes/blacks) join, would you try to
change the rules so that (Negroes/blacks) could join?

	YES	NO	WOULDN'T BELONG	DK	N	
Mar 1977	39	54	1	7	1349	GSS
Mar 1985	50	44	-	6	1381	GSS
Mar 1986	60	35	-	5	1276	GSS
Mar 1988	54	37	-	9	854	GSS

Table 8.5   Should Blacks Push Themselves Where They Are Not
Wanted?--1963-1985

WHITES ONLY

RACPUSH--Negroes/Blacks shouldn't push themselves where
they're not wanted.

	AGREE STRONGLY	AGREE SLIGHTLY	DISAGREE SLIGHTLY	DISAGREE STRONGLY	DK	N	
Dec 1963	46	25	15	13	1	1348	SRS330
Jan 1966	49	25	15	7	4	1327	SRS889A
Apr 1968	47	30	13	8	2	1258	SRS4050
Mar 1972	42	29	13	10	7	1346	GSS
Mar 1973	44	29	15	11	1	1313	GSS
Mar 1975	45	28	15	10	2	1321	GSS
Mar 1976	42	28	16	12	2	1363	GSS
Mar 1977	43	28	17	9	2	1349	GSS
Mar 1980	35	32	19	12	2	1324	GSS
Mar 1982	28	31	22	16	3	1347	GSS
Mar 1984	27	31	21	19	2	1296	GSS
Mar 1985	26	33	22	16	2	672	GSS

Table 8.6   Would You Object to Having a Black Person Home
for Dinner?--1963-1985

WHITES ONLY

RACDIN--How strongly would you object if a member of your
family wanted to bring a (Negro/black) friend home to
dinner?   Would you object strongly, mildly, or not at all?

	STRONGLY OBJECT	MILDLY OBJECT	NOT OBJECT	DK	N	
Dec 1963	29	16	50	5	1351	SRS330
Jan 1966	23	20	52	5	1304	SRS889A
Apr 1970	17	16	63	4	1261	SRS4100
Nov 1972	15	15	68	3	1273	NORC5046
Mar 1972	13	15	70	2	1348	GSS
Mar 1973	15	15	68	2	1313	GSS
Mar 1974	11	16	72	2	1310	GSS
Mar 1976	13	14	71	2	1365	GSS
Mar 1977	11	16	71	1	1349	GSS
Mar 1980	11	14	73	2	1325	GSS
Mar 1982	10	12	77	1	1345	GSS
Mar 1984	7	12	80	1	1299	GSS
Mar 1985	11	12	77	0	672	GSS

Table 8.7   Have You Had a Black Person Home for Dinner
Recently?--1973-1985

WHITES ONLY

RACHOME--During the last few years, has anyone in your
family brought a friend who was a (Negro/black) home for
dinner?

	YES	NO	DK	N	
Mar 1973	20	80	-	1310	GSS
Mar 1974	23	77	0	1305	GSS
Mar 1976	23	77	0	1362	GSS
Mar 1977	23	77	0	1349	GSS
Mar 1980	26	73	0	1326	GSS
Mar 1982	27	72	0	1344	GSS
Mar 1984	27	73	0	1296	GSS
Mar 1985	28	72	0	1376	GSS

Table 8.8 Do Whites Have a Right to Keep Blacks Out of Their Neighborhoods?--1963-1988

WHITES ONLY

RACSEG--White people have a right to keep (Negroes/blacks) out of their neighborhoods if they want to, and (Negroes/blacks) should respect that right.

	AGREE STRONGLY	AGREE SLIGHTLY	DISAGREE SLIGHTLY	DISAGREE STRONGLY	DK	N	
Dec 1963	35	19	20	25	1	1547	SRS330
Apr 1968	31	24	24	19	2	1253	NORC4050
Mar 1972	21	17	23	33	7	1349	GSS
Mar 1976	21	17	25	34	2	1363	GSS
Mar 1977	21	20	28	28	3	1349	GSS
Mar 1980	16	16	28	37	3	1324	GSS
Mar 1982	14	14	30	38	3	1348	GSS
Mar 1984	11	15	26	45	2	1297	GSS
Mar 1985	10	15	30	43	2	1376	GSS
Mar 1988	8	16	26	48	3	845	GSS

174

Table 8.9   Would You Favor a Community Open-Housing Law?--
1973-1988

WHITES ONLY

RACOPEN--Suppose there is a community-wide vote on the general housing issue. There are two possible laws to vote on.
Which law would you vote for? One law says that a homeowner can decide for himself whom to sell his house to, even
if he prefers not to sell to (Negros/blacks). The second
law says that a homeowner cannot refuse to sell to someone
because of their race or color.

	OWNER DECIDES	CAN'T DISCRIM- INATE	NEITHER	DK	N	
Mar 1973	63	34	2	1	1314	GSS
Mar 1975	64	34	1	2	1325	GSS
Mar 1976	62	35	2	1	1363	GSS
Mar 1978	56	40	1	2	1529	GSS
Mar 1980	58	39	1	2	1326	GSS
Mar 1983	52	44	2	2	1427	GSS
Mar 1984	48	49	2	1	1295	GSS
Mar 1986	50	47	1	1	1285	GSS
Mar 1988	43	52	3	2	878	GSS

Table 8.10   Would You Mind if a Black with Equal Income and
Education Moved into Your Block?--1942-1972

WHITES ONLY

RACOBJCT--If a (Negro/black) with the same income and education as you have, moved into your block, would it make any
difference to you?

	YES, WOULD LIKE	YES, WOULD NOT LIKE	NO DIFFERENCE	DK	N	
Jun 1942[a]		62	35	3	3587	NORC113
Jun 1956[a]		46	52	2	1275	NORC390
May 1963	5	36	57	3	1345	SRS160
Dec 1963	6	33	59	2	1347	SRS330
May 1964	5	33	59	3	1317	SRS630
Jun 1965	2	30	66	2	1286	SRS857
Oct 1965	2	22	72	3	1311	SRS868
Jun 1966[b]	1	28	68	3	1319	SRS889A
Apr 1970	4	21	72	3	1259	SRS4050
Mar 1972	1	14	83	2	1349	GSS

[a]No differentiations coded among "Yes" responses.

[b]"...same education and income...."

Table 8.11   Are There Any Blacks in Your Neighborhood?--
             1966-1988

WHITES ONLY

RACLIVE--Are there any (Negroes/blacks) living in this
neighborhood now?

	YES	NO	DK	N	
Jun 1966[a]	20	80		1322	SRS889A
Apr 1970[a]	29	71		1258	SRS4100
Mar 1972	29	67	4	1351	GSS
Mar 1973	40	56	4	1320	GSS
Apr 1973[a]	29	71		723	CNS1
May 1973[a]	29	71		647	CNS2
Jun 1973[a]	28	72		644	CNS3
Jul 1973[a]	30	70		616	CNS4
Aug 1973[a]	37	63		644	CNS5
Sep 1973[a]	38	62		631	CNS6
Oct 1973[a]	39	61		688	CNS7
Nov 1973[a]	31	69		700	CNS8
Jan 1974[a]	32	68		697	CNS9
Feb 1974[a]	32	68		696	CNS10
Mar 1974	42	54	3	1310	GSS
May 1974[a]	30	70		658	CNS12
Mar 1975	33	63	4	1326	GSS
Mar 1976	42	54	4	1367	GSS
Mar 1977	39	58	3	1350	GSS
Mar 1978	45	51	4	1372	GSS
Mar 1980	43	53	4	1326	GSS
Mar 1982	44	52	4	1348	GSS
Mar 1983	43	54	3	1431	GSS
Mar 1984	47	49	4	1296	GSS
Mar 1985	44	51	5	1377	GSS
Mar 1986	44	53	3	1285	GSS
Mar 1988	49	46	5	1290	GSS

[a]DK not coded separately.   "Now" omitted.

Table 8.12   Are There Any Black Families Living Close to You?--1972-1988

WHITES ONLY

RACCLOS--Are there any (Negro/black) families living close to you?

	YES	NO	DK	N	
Mar 1972	74	26	-	383	GSS
Mar 1973	71	29	-	517	GSS
Mar 1974	68	31	0	551	GSS
Mar 1975	71	29	-	432	GSS
Mar 1976	72	27	0	576	GSS
Mar 1977	71	29	-	524	GSS
Mar 1978	70	30	-	624	GSS
Mar 1980	71	29	0	569	GSS
Mar 1982	72	28	0	595	GSS
Mar 1983	67	33	-	619	GSS
Mar 1984	75	25	-	602	GSS
Mar 1985	71	29	-	599	GSS
Mar 1986	70	29	1	561	GSS
Mar 1988	76	23	0	627	GSS

NOTE--Asked only of those who said that (Negroes/blacks) were living in their neighborhood.

Table 8.13   How Far Away Are the Closest Black Neighbors?--
1972-1988

WHITES ONLY

RACDIS--How many blocks (or miles) away do they (the [Negro/
black] families who live closest to you) live?

	SAME BLOCK	1-3 BLKS AWAY	4-8 BLKS AWAY	OVER 8 BLKS	DK	N	
Mar 1972	41	39	14	6	-	380	GSS
Mar 1973	38	40	15	6	0	519	GSS
Mar 1974	42	35	16	7	0	547	GSS
Mar 1975	41	35	15	9	1	433	GSS
Mar 1976	42	32	17	9	-	575	GSS
Mar 1977	39	34	19	8	0	527	GSS
Mar 1978	40	39	14	7	-	617	GSS
Mar 1980	43	35	17	4	1	564	GSS
Mar 1982	43	36	13	8	0	590	GSS
Mar 1983	42	33	14	10	1	617	GSS
Mar 1984	51	33	10	6	0	596	GSS
Mar 1985	46	31	16	7	0	598	GSS
Mar 1986	47	32	12	8	1	560	GSS
Mar 1988	50	35	9	5	0	627	GSS

NOTE--Asked only of those who said that (Negroes/blacks)
were living in their neighborhood.

Table 8.14   Will Your Neighborhood Become All Black?--
1972-1988

WHITES ONLY

RACINTEG--Do you think this neighborhood will become all
(Negro/black) in the next few years, or will it remain
integrated?

	ALL BLACK	STAY INTE-GRATED	DK	N	
Mar 1972	10	83	7	378	GSS
Mar 1973	5	90	4	516	GSS
Mar 1974	5	90	5	549	GSS
Mar 1975	6	88	5	431	GSS
Mar 1976	6	91	3	575	GSS
Mar 1977	5	92	3	524	GSS
Mar 1978	3	94	3	609	GSS
Mar 1980	4	92	3	561	GSS
Mar 1982	4	93	4	588	GSS
Mar 1983	3	43	5	617	GSS
Mar 1984	4	95	1	593	GSS
Mar 1985	3	95	2	596	GSS
Mar 1986	6	91	3	565	GSS
Mar 1988	3	94	3	627	GSS

NOTE--Asked only of those who said that (Negroes/blacks)
were living in their neighborhood.

Table 8.15   Should Whites and Blacks Go to the Same Schools?
--1942-1985

WHITES ONLY

RACSCHOL--Do you think white students and (Negro/black) students should go to the same schools or to separate schools?

	SAME SCHOOLS	SEPARATE SCHOOLS	DK	N	
Jun 1942	30	66	4	3587	NORC113
Apr 1956	49	47	4	1224	NORC386
Jun 1956	49	49	2	1275	NORC390
Sep 1956	48	49	3	1263	NORC393
May 1963	63	32	5	1340	NORC160
Dec 1963	65	29	6	1219	SRS350
Jun 1964	62	32	5	1314	SRS630
Oct 1964[a]	60	37	2	1726	SRS760
Jun 1965	67	30	3	1288	SRS857
Oct 1965	68	28	4	1309	SRS868
Apr 1970	74	24	3	1255	SRS4100
Mar 1972	85	14	2	1345	GSS
Nov 1972	80	15	5	1459	NORC5046
Mar 1976	83	15	3	1367	GSS
Mar 1977	85	14	2	1345	GSS
Mar 1980	86	12	2	1322	GSS
Mar 1982	88	9	2	1349	GSS
Mar 1984	90	8	2	1294	GSS
Mar 1985	92	7	1	672	GSS

[a]Do you think white children and Negro children should go to the same schools or to separate but equal schools?

Table 8.16   Do You Object to Your Children Going to a School
Where There Are a Few Black Children?--1958-1988

WHITES WITH SCHOOL-AGE CHLDREN ONLY[a]

RACFEW--Would you, yourself, have any objection to sending
your children to a school where

A few of the children are (colored/Negro/black)?

	YES, OBJECT	NO	DK	N	
Sep 1958	24	74	1	629	AIPO604
Feb 1959	19	80	1	634	AIPO610
May 1963	23	75	2	1430	AIPO673
Apr 1965	14	85	2	1205	AIPO710
Jun 1965	18	80	2	1153	AIPO712
May 1966	10	89	1	1237	AIPO728
Jul 1969	11	88	0	550	AIPO784
Mar 1970	7	92	1	529	AIPO801
Apr 1970	9	90	1	566	AIPO804
Mar 1972	5	94	1	535	GSS
Jul 1973	8	92	1	449	AIPO875
Mar 1974	4	96	0	491	GSS
Sep 1975	6	93	1	539	AIPO936
Mar 1975	5	95	1	470	GSS
Mar 1977	7	93	0	474	GSS
Jul 1978	5	92	2	420	AIPO106G
Mar 1978	4	96	-	472	GSS
Dec 1980	5	94	1	464	AIPO166G
Mar 1982	4	96	-	359	GSS
Mar 1983	3	96	-	454	GSS
Mar 1985	4	96	-	398	GSS
Mar 1986	4	96	0	366	GSS
Mar 1988	3	97	-	231	GSS

[a]On AIPO surveys a screen asked, "Do you have any children
in grade or high school?" On the GSS, families with
children 6 to 17 were screened.

NOTE--In early AIPO surveys, there is some ambiguity about
whether follow-up questions were asked of those with no
opinion. As was clearly done in later surveys, we have
assumed for all surveys that those answering DK to one
question were not asked the follow-up--i.e., they were
assumed to have expressed some objection. An alternative
approach--deleting "DKs" to one question from later
computations--changes these results by at most two
percentage points.

Table 8.17   Do You Object to Your Children Going to a School
Where Half the Children Are Black?--1958-1988

WHITES WITH SCHOOL-AGE CHILDREN ONLY[a]

IF DON'T OBJECT TO OR DON'T KNOW ABOUT A SCHOOL WITH A FEW
BLACKS (see Table 8.16)--Base for percentages is all whites
with school-age children.

RACHAF--Would you, yourself, have any objection to sending
your children to a school where

Half of the children are (colored/Negro/black)?

	YES, OBJECT	NO	DK	N	
Sep 1958	49	48	4	629	AIPO604
Feb 1959	45	53	2	634	AIPO610
May 1963	47	48	5	1430	AIPO673
Apr 1965	38	58	4	1205	AIPO710
Jun 1965	41	55	3	1153	AIPO712
May 1966	39	58	2	1237	AIPO728
Jul 1969	34	62	4	550	AIPO784
Mar 1970	28	69	4	529	AIPO801
Apr 1970	30	67	4	566	AIPO804
Mar 1972	22	75	3	534	GSS
Jul 1973	31	64	5	449	AIPO875
Mar 1974	30	67	3	490	GSS
Sep 1975	29	65	6	539	AIPO936
Mar 1975	35	62	3	471	GSS
Mar 1977	25	74	1	472	GSS
Jul 1978	30	64	6	420	AIPO106G
Mar 1978	22	76	2	472	GSS
Dec 1980	25	72	3	464	AIPO166G
Mar 1982	19	79	2	359	GSS
Mar 1983	23	75	2	454	GSS
Mar 1985	20	78	2	398	GSS
Mar 1986	22	76	2	364	GSS
Mar 1988	20	79	1	224	GSS

---

[a]See note a, Table 8.16.

NOTE--Those who object to sending their children to a school
with a few black children are assumed to object to schools
where half the children are black.

Table 8.18   Do You Object to Your Children Going to a School
Where More Than Half the Chilren Are Black?--
1958-1988

WHITES WITH SCHOOL-AGE CHILDREN ONLY[a]

IF DON'T OBJECT TO OR DON'T KNOW ABOUT A SCHOOL WHERE HALF
THE STUDENTS ARE BLACKS (see Table 8.16)--Base for percentages is all whites with school-age children.

RACMOST--Would you, yourself, have any objection to sending
your children to a school where

More than half of the children are (colored/Negro/
black)?

	YES, OBJECT	NO	DK	N	
Sep 1958	65	30	5	629	AIPO604
Feb 1959	68	29	3	634	AIPO610
May 1963	70	25	5	1430	AIPO673
Apr 1965	64	33	3	1205	AIPO710
Jun 1965	66	31	2	1153	AIPO712
May 1966	63	33	4	1237	AIPO728
Jul 1969	62	35	4	550	AIPO784
Mar 1970	61	34	5	529	AIPO801
Apr 1970	59	37	4	566	AIPO804
Mar 1972	50	45	5	502	GSS
Jul 1973	62	32	5	449	AIPO875
Mar 1974	63	33	4	488	GSS
Sep 1975	59	38	3	539	AIPO936
Mar 1975	62	34	4	469	GSS
Mar 1977	62	36	2	472	GSS
Jul 1978	63	33	4	420	AIPO106G
Mar 1978	57	39	4	471	GSS
Dec 1980	60	38	2	464	AIPO166G
Mar 1982	51	46	3	356	GSS
Mar 1983	62	35	3	453	GSS
Mar 1985	57	40	3	395	GSS
Mar 1986	62	36	2	364	GSS
Mar 1988	47	48	5	180	GSS

[a]See note a, Table 8.16.

NOTE--Those who object to sending their children to a school
where a few or half the children are black are assumed to
object to schools where more than half of the children are
black.

Table 8.19 Do You Favor or Oppose Busing for Integration?--
1970-1988

ALL RESPONDENTS

BUSING--In general, do you favor or oppose the busing of
(Negro/black) and white school children from one district to
another?

	FAVOR	OPPOSE	DK	N	
Mar 1970[a,b]	14	81	5	1434	AIPO801
Aug 1971[a]	18	74	8	1516	AIPO836
Oct 1971[a,c]	17	78	5	1436	AIPO838
Mar 1972	19	77	4	1606	GSS
Mar 1974	20	76	4	1481	GSS
Mar 1975	17	78	5	1486	GSS
Mar 1976	16	82	3	1498	GSS
Mar 1977	16	81	3	1522	GSS
Mar 1978	20	76	4	1516	GSS
Mar 1982	19	78	3	1504	GSS
Mar 1983	23	71	6	1578	GSS
Mar 1985	22	75	3	1525	GSS
Mar 1986	29	68	3	1464	GSS
Mar 1988	32	63	4	985	GSS

[a]In general, do...one school district....

[b]Asked of 94% who "heard or read about the busing of Negro
and white school children from one school district to another."

[c]Asked of 96% as in note b.

Table 8.20 Are Blacks as Smart as Whites?--1942-1968

WHITES ONLY

In general, do you think Negroes are as intelligent as white
people--that is, can they learn things just as well if they
are given the same education and training?

	YES	NO	DK	N	
1942	42	48	10	3587	NORC
May 1944	44	48	8	2523	NORC225
May 1946	53	40	7	2360	NORC241
Jan 1956	78	19	3	1238	NORC382
Apr 1956	77	20	3	1224	NORC386
May 1963	77	17	6	1348	SRS160
Dec 1963	74	22	3	1347	SRS330
Oct 1964	81	16	2	1972	SRS760
Jan 1966	78	19	3	1328	NORC889
Apr 1968	73	22	5	1249	NORC4050

Table 8.21   Are Racial Differences Due to Discrimination?--
1981-1988

WHITES ONLY

RACDIF1--On the average (Negroes/blacks) have worse jobs,
income, and housing than white people. Do you think these
differences are

Mainly due to discrimination?

	YES	NO	DK	N	
Feb 1981[a]	38	59	4	1426	WP/ABC
Mar 1977	39	56	4	1347	GSS
Mar 1985	40	56	4	1380	GSS
Mar 1986	40	58	3	1283	GSS
Mar 1988	38	58	5	857	GSS

[a]Most people agree that on average...whites.

Table 8.22   Are Racial Differences Due to Inborn
Disabilities?--1981-1988

WHITES ONLY

RACDIF2--On the average...Do you think these differences are

Because most (Negroes/blacks) have less inborn
ability to learn?

	YES	NO	DK	N	
Feb 1981	23	74	3	1426	WP/ABC
Mar 1977	25	70	5	1347	GSS
Mar 1985	21	75	4	1379	GSS
Mar 1986	20	76	4	1285	GSS
Mar 1988	20	76	4	857	GSS

Table 8.23   Are Racial Differences Due to Lack of Education?
--1981-1988

WHITES ONLY

RACDIF3--On the average...Do you think these differences are

Because most (Negroes/blacks) don't have the chance
for education that it takes to rise out of poverty?

	YES	NO	DK	N	
Feb 1981	54	44	2	1426	WP/ABC
Mar 1977	49	48	4	1346	GSS
Mar 1985	51	47	2	1381	GSS
Mar 1986	50	48	2	1285	GSS
Mar 1988	50	46	4	858	GSS

Table 8.24   Are Racial Differences Due to Lack of
Motivation?--1981-1988

WHITES ONLY

RACDIF4--On the average...Do you think these differences are

Because most (Negroes/Blacks) just don't have the
motivation or will power to pull themselves up out
of poverty?

	YES	NO	DK	N	
Feb 1981[a]	58	37	5	1426	WP/ABC
Mar 1977	62	32	6	1347	GSS
Mar 1985	58	38	5	1381	GSS
Mar 1986	62	34	4	1283	GSS
Mar 1988	58	37	5	857	GSS

[a]Omits "just" and "up."

9

Sexual and Reproductive Morality

Since the mid-1960s the mass media and social commentators
have been chronicling the development of America's "Sexual
Revolution." Stories of the decline of the traditional family
and the rise of alternative life-styles from communes to
single parenthood and on to homosexual marriages have been
widespread. The collapse of traditional sexual and reproductive morality has been heralded as the overthrow of
repressive Puritanism by modernists and condemned as the
triumph of hedonistic sin by Fundamentalists. Then in the
mid-1980s the media and cultural interpreters declared that
the "Sexual Revolution is Over" (*Time*, 4/9/84). Harried by
Falwell's Moral Majority and directly assaulted by fear of
AIDS, the Revolution was deemed to have been crushed.

But when this standard account is subjected to trial by
empirical, survey research, it comes up wanting. Although
many survey time series do not start as early as one would
like (many beginning in the late 1960s or early 1970s after
the Sexual Revolution's inception, rather than before its
start), it is possible in large measure to track the development of our Sexual Revolution. In general, this analysis
indicates that the so-called Sexual Revolution was a complex
social change that neither swept so far, nor receded so much,
as the popular chronicles would have it.

Perhaps the surest sign of the Sexual Revolution was the
related Contraception Revolution, which made inexpensive,
easy-to-use, effective birth control widely available for the
first time. Oral contraceptives and other birth control de-
vices were almost universally adopted by all segments of the
population (including Catholics, Smith, 1985), and public
support for the availability of information on birth control
increased steadily from 73 percent in 1959 to 90 percent plus
by 1974 (Table 9.1). Similarly, support for birth control

information for teenagers also grew to 85 percent plus by 1982 (Table 9.2). Likewise, the public also favored the dissemination of sexual information via sex education in the public schools (9.3). In 1969, 71 percent favored such instruction, and by 1988 this had risen to 85 percent.

In the area of norms of sexual behavior, the Sexual Revolution's impact was more restricted. Approval of premarital sexual intercourse (9.4) did increase, with 26 percent considering it "Not wrong at all" in 1972 and approximately 40 percent from 1982 on (Singh, 1980). Approval of extramarital or homosexual relations, however, showed no permissive trend with about 70-75 percent considering these actions "always wrong" throughout the 1970s and 1980s (9.5-9.6).

The trends on pornographic materials also suggest that the Sexual Revolution's impact on attitudes was limited. There may have been an increased acceptance of sexually explicit material in the early stages of the revolt, as indicated by the sharp increase in approval of topless waitresses, "Playboy center-folds," and nude actors and actresses in legitimate theater between 1969 and 1973 (Table 9.7-9.9), but during the 1970s and 1980s beliefs in the positive and negative consequences of sexual materials changed little, and even shaded a bit toward the conservative (9.11-9.12). Likewise, support for the legal control of pornography remained virtually unchanged from 1973 to 1988 (9.14) (Wood and Hughes, 1984).

Perhaps the most interesting trend in the pornography area is the drop from 1973 to 1978 in the percent viewing an X-rated film in the last year from 25 percent to 15 percent, followed by the rise to 27-28 percent viewing such films in 1987-1988 (9.15). The initial decline is probably the result of the X rating being dropped from mass market films in the early 1970s and being used instead entirely to denote sexually explicit, adult movies. The rebound is almost certainly due to home viewing on VCRs (Smith, 1987).

Overall, the increase in permissive and modern sexual attitudes during the Sexual Revolution was more limited in breadth and more modest in magnitude than commonly pictured. In addition, signs of an AIDS-induced Thermidor are weak. Attitudes towards homosexuality are obviously most closely linked to AIDS, and it is on this topic that on would expect to find a reaction (Schneider and Lewis, 1984). But since approval of homosexuality did not increase during the Revolution (it actually fell marginally), no reaction was strictly possible. In addition, the items on civil liberties toward homosexuals in Tables 5.28-5.30 show no signs of an AIDS-induced anti-homosexuality.

Likewise, evidence of a return to stricter heterosexual standards is limited. Increased approval of premarital sex did level off in 1982-1983, but no reversal has occurred.   In fact, the trends on X-rated movie viewing suggest that in at least one area not even a levelling off has happened.

Attitudes toward abortion are only somewhat related to contraceptive morality and even more remotely to sexual morality (9.16-9.23).   From the start of polling on this issue in 1962 until 1974-1975 approval of legalized abortions under various circumstances rose appreciably (Smith, 1985; Legge, 1983; Benin, 1985).   The liberalizing of state laws in the late 1960s and early 1970s and the Supreme Court decision in 1973 legalizing abortion seem to have aided the growth of approval.   Support then settled on a plateau for almost a decade.   Since then approval has drifted downwards, but still remained well above the levels of the 1960s.

Men and women have shown little difference in their approval of abortion.   Differences between major religious groups have been more notable.   Jews and those without religious affiliation have been most supportive of abortion, followed by Protestants, and then Catholics.   Among Protestants, however, there is considerable disagreement, with Fundamentalists the most opposed and liberal denominations such as Episcopalians and Unitarians much more supportive.

Significant changes in sexual and reproductive morality have occurred over the last twenty-some years.   These alternations of existing attitudes and behaviors about these most intimate of human matters are of great importance.   Yet the changes of the 1960s do not quite amount to an overthrow of an older, sexual order and its replacement with a new one. Nor have AIDS, the New Religious Right, nor other recent events reversed the changes that have occurred.

REFERENCES

Benin, Mary Holland.   1985.   Determinants of Opposition to Abortion: An Analysis of the Hard and Soft Scales. *Sociological Perspectives*, 28:199-216.

Legge, Jerome S., Jr.   1983.   The Determinants of Attitudes Toward Abortion in the American Electorate. *Western Political Quarterly*, 36:479-490.

Schneider, William, and I. A. Lewis. 1984. The Straight Story on Homosexuality and Gay Rights. *Public Opinion*, 7(1): 16-60.

Singh, B. Krishna. 1980. Trends in Attitudes Towards Premarital Sexual Relations. *Journal of Marriage and the Family*, 36:387-393.

Smith, Tom W. 1985. Trends in Attitudes on Sexual and Reproductive Issues.   Presented at the NORC/Allensbach Conference on the Family, Chicago.

Smith, Tom W. 1987. The Use of Public Opinion Data by the At-
torney General's Commission on Pornography. *Public Opinion
Quarterly*, 51:249-267.

Wood, Michael, and Hughes, Michael. 1984. The Moral Basis of
Moral Reform: Status Discontent vs. Culture and Socializa-
tion as Explanations of Anti-Pornography Social Movement
Adherence. *American Sociological Review*, 49:86-99.

Table 9.1   Should Birth Control Information Be Available to
Anyone Who Wants It?--1959-1983

PILL--In some places in the United States, it is not legal
to supply birth control information. How do you feel about
this--do you think birth control information should be
available to anyone who wants it, or not?

	AVAIL- ABLE	NOT AVAIL- ABLE	DK	N	
Dec 1959	73	14	13	1549	AIPO621
Mar 1961	75	15	10	3509	AIPO642
Aug 1962	72	21	7	3350	AIPO662
Apr 1963	74	17	9	3876	AIPO671
Nov 1964	81	11	8	3528	AIPO702
Feb 1965	75	16	9	551	POS655
Mar 1974	91	8	1	1484	GSS
Mar 1975	89	8	2	1488	GSS
Mar 1977	91	7	2	1525	GSS
Mar 1982	90	8	2	1506	GSS
Mar 1983	90	8	2	1597	GSS

Table 9.2   Should Birth Control Information Be Available to
Teenagers?--1974-1983

TEENPILL--Do you think birth control information should be
available to teenagers who want it, or not?

	AVAIL- ABLE	NOT AVAIL- ABLE	DK	N	
Mar 1974	78	19	3	1471	GSS
Mar 1975	79	19	3	1483	GSS
Mar 1977	82	16	2	1523	GSS
Mar 1982	86	12	2	1502	GSS
Mar 1983	85	13	2	1592	GSS

Table 9.3   Are You For Sex Education in the Public Schools?
--1943-1988

SEXEDUC--Would you be for or against sex education in the
public schools?

	FAVOR	DEPENDS	OPPOSE	DK	N	
May 1943[a]	68	-	17	15	3052	AIPO295
Jan 1951[a]	67	-	23	11	1355	AIPO470
Apr 1965[b]	69	-	22	9	3499	AIPO710
May 1970[c]	56	14	23	6	2486	RAC
Mar 1974	79	1	17	3	1481	GSS
Mar 1975	76	-	20	4	1488	GSS
Mar 1977	77	-	21	2	1524	GSS
Dec 1977[d]	77	6	6	6	1518	AIPO990
Mar 1982	82	-	15	3	1504	GSS
Mar 1983	84	-	14	3	1595	GSS
Mar 1985	82	-	15	2	1526	GSS
Mar 1986	82	-	16	3	1468	GSS
Mar 1988	85	-	13	3	984	GSS

WOMEN

	FAVOR	DEPENDS	OPPOSE	DK	N	
Mar 1974	80	16	1	4	792	GSS
Mar 1975	79	18	-	3	819	GSS
Mar 1977	77	20	-	2	835	GSS
Mar 1982	82	14	-	3	866	GSS
Mar 1983	82	15	-	3	907	GSS
Mar 1985	81	16	-	2	842	GSS
Mar 1986	80	17	-	3	848	GSS
Mar 1988	84	14		4	546	GSS

MEN

	FAVOR	DEPENDS	OPPOSE	DK	N	
Mar 1974	78	19	0	3	689	GSS
Mar 1975	73	22	-	4	669	GSS
Mar 1977	77	22	-	2	689	GSS
Mar 1982	81	16	-	3	638	GSS
Mar 1983	86	12	-	2	688	GSS
Mar 1985	83	14	-	2	584	GSS
Mar 1986	84	13	-	3	620	GSS
Mar 1988	86	11		2	438	GSS

[a]It has been suggested that a course in sex education be
given to students in high schools. Do you approve or disapprove of this?

[b]Many schools give courses in sex education. Do you approve
or disapprove of such courses?

[c]"By the way,..."

[d]Do you approve or disapprove of schools giving courses in
sex education?

Table 9.4   Is Premarital Sex Wrong?--1972-1988

PREMARSX--There's been a lot of discussion about the way
morals and attitudes about sex are changing in this country.
If a man and woman have sex relations before marriage, do
you think it is always wrong, almost always wrong, wrong
only sometimes, or not wrong at all?

	ALWAYS WRONG	ALMOST ALWAYS WRONG	SOME-TIMES WRONG	NOT WRONG AT ALL	DK	N	
Mar 1972	35	11	23	26	4	1602	GSS
Nov 1972	37	10	27	22	4	1460	NORC5046
Mar 1974	32	12	23	30	3	1477	GSS
Mar 1975	30	12	23	32	4	1485	GSS
Mar 1977	30	9	22	36	3	1520	GSS
Mar 1978	29	11	20	38	2	1528	GSS
Mar 1982	28	9	21	40	3	1501	GSS
Mar 1983	27	10	24	38	2	1592	GSS
Mar 1985	28	8	19	42	3	1530	GSS
Mar 1986	27	9	22	39	3	1464	GSS
Mar 1988	26	10	22	40	3	982	GSS

WOMEN

	ALWAYS WRONG	ALMOST ALWAYS WRONG	SOME-TIMES WRONG	NOT WRONG AT ALL	DK	N	
Mar 1972	42	12	23	19	5	798	GSS
Mar 1974	35	13	24	25	3	792	GSS
Mar 1975	33	14	23	26	4	817	GSS
Mar 1977	36	10	22	30	2	833	GSS
Mar 1978	33	11	20	33	2	887	GSS
Mar 1982	32	10	21	35	3	865	GSS
Mar 1983	31	11	24	33	2	905	GSS
Mar 1985	33	8	19	37	3	843	GSS
Mar 1986	32	8	22	34	3	845	GSS
Mar 1988	29	12	23	34	2	546	GSS

MEN

	ALWAYS WRONG	ALMOST ALWAYS WRONG	SOME-TIMES WRONG	NOT WRONG AT ALL	DK	N	
Mar 1972	29	11	23	34	3	804	GSS
Mar 1974	29	11	21	36	3	685	GSS
Mar 1975	25	10	23	38	4	668	GSS
Mar 1977	23	8	23	43	3	687	GSS
Mar 1978	22	12	20	44	2	641	GSS
Mar 1982	22	8	21	46	4	636	GSS
Mar 1983	22	8	24	44	2	687	GSS
Mar 1985	21	8	20	48	3	687	GSS
Mar 1986	20	9	22	47	2	619	GSS
Mar 1988	23	8	20	46	3	436	GSS

Table 9.5   Is Extramarital Sex Wrong?--1970-1988

XMARSEX--What is your opinion about a married person having
sexual relations with someone other than the marriage part-
ner--is it always wrong, almost always wrong, wrong only
sometimes, or not wrong at all?

	ALWAYS WRONG	ALMOST ALWAYS WRONG	SOME- TIMES WRONG	NOT WRONG AT ALL	DK	N	
Sep 1970[a]	72	14	11	2	0	3016	NORC4088
Apr 1978	65	16	11	4	4	1523	AIPO1000
Mar 1973	69	15	12	4	1	1500	GSS
Mar 1974	73	12	11	2	1	1482	GSS
Mar 1976	68	15	11	4	1	1494	GSS
Mar 1977	72	14	10	3	1	1523	GSS
Mar 1980	69	16	10	4	2	1467	GSS
Mar 1982	72	13	10	3	1	1499	GSS
Mar 1984	70	18	9	2	1	1465	GSS
Mar 1985	74	14	8	3	1	1530	GSS
Mar 1987	73	16	8	2	1	1458	GSS
Mar 1988	78	13	6	2	1	975	GSS

WOMEN

	ALWAYS WRONG	ALMOST ALWAYS WRONG	SOME- TIMES WRONG	NOT WRONG AT ALL	DK	N	
Mar 1973	74	14	10	2	1	803	GSS
Mar 1974	77	10	9	2	1	791	GSS
Mar 1976	71	14	10	4	2	825	GSS
Mar 1977	76	13	8	2	1	834	GSS
Mar 1980	72	15	8	3	2	826	GSS
Mar 1982	75	12	9	2	1	864	GSS
Mar 1984	74	18	6	1	1	869	GSS
Mar 1985	77	13	7	2	1	842	GSS
Mar 1987	76	14	7	2	1	822	GSS
Mar 1988	82	12	4	1	1	575	GSS

MEN

	ALWAYS WRONG	ALMOST ALWAYS WRONG	SOME- TIMES WRONG	NOT WRONG AT ALL	DK	N	
Mar 1973	63	15	14	6	1	697	GSS
Mar 1974	68	13	14	3	2	691	GSS
Mar 1976	64	18	13	5	1	669	GSS
Mar 1977	68	14	13	4	1	689	GSS
Mar 1980	66	16	12	5	1	641	GSS
Mar 1982	69	14	12	3	2	635	GSS
Mar 1984	64	19	13	4	1	696	GSS
Mar 1985	71	14	10	4	2	688	GSS
Mar 1987	69	18	9	2	1	636	GSS
Mar 1988	73	14	7	4	2	400	GSS

[a]And now, would you look at the card again and tell me which
answer applies if a married person has sexual intercourse
with someone other than the marriage partner?

Table 9.6   Is Homosexuality Wrong?--1973-1988

HOMOSEX--What about sexual relations between two adults of
the same sex--do you think it is always wrong, almost always
wrong, wrong only sometimes, or not wrong at all?

	ALWAYS WRONG	ALMOST ALWAYS WRONG	SOME-TIMES WRONG	NOT WRONG AT ALL	OTHER	DK	N	
Mar 1973	70	6	7	11	2	3	1497	GSS
Mar 1974	67	5	8	12	3	5	1484	GSS
Mar 1976	67	6	8	15	-	4	1488	GSS
Mar 1978	69	6	7	14	-	5	1522	GSS
Mar 1980	70	6	6	14	-	5	1465	GSS
Mar 1982	70	5	6	14	-	4	1497	GSS
Mar 1984	71	5	7	14	-	4	1466	GSS
Mar 1985	73	4	7	13	-	3	1531	GSS
Mar 1987	75	4	6	12	-	3	1450	GSS
Mar 1988	74	4	5	12	-	4	973	GSS

WOMEN

	ALWAYS WRONG	ALMOST ALWAYS WRONG	SOME-TIMES WRONG	NOT WRONG AT ALL		DK	N	
Mar 1973	71	6	7	10		6	799	GSS
Mar 1974	66	5	8	12		9	793	GSS
Mar 1976	67	6	6	16		5	820	GSS
Mar 1977	70	5	7	13		5	835	GSS
Mar 1980	70	6	6	13		5	827	GSS
Mar 1982	68	4	8	15		4	863	GSS
Mar 1984	71	4	8	13		5	870	GSS
Mar 1985	73	4	7	13		3	843	GSS
Mar 1987	75	5	6	12		3	817	GSS
Mar 1988	73	5	6	13		4	573	GSS

MEN

	ALWAYS WRONG	ALMOST ALWAYS WRONG	SOME-TIMES WRONG	NOT WRONG AT ALL		DK	N	
Mar 1973	70	7	8	11		4	698	GSS
Mar 1974	68	7	7	12		8	691	GSS
Mar 1976	67	5	9	14		3	668	GSS
Mar 1977	67	6	7	16		4	687	GSS
Mar 1980	70	6	5	15		4	638	GSS
Mar 1982	73	6	4	13		4	634	GSS
Mar 1984	70	5	6	15		2	596	GSS
Mar 1985	73	4	7	13		3	688	GSS
Mar 1987	75	3	7	12		3	633	GSS
Mar 1988	76	4	5	12		3	400	GSS

NOTE--"Other" combined with DK in distributions by sex.

Table 9.7   Are Topless Nightclub Waitresses Objectionable?--
            1969-1973

Would you find topless nightclub waitresses objectionable?

	YES	NO	N	
May 1969	77	23	1472	AIPO780
Jul 1973	60	40	1509	AIPO874
WOMEN				
May 1969	89	11	752	AIPO780
Jul 1973	74	26	752	AIPO874
MEN				
May 1969	64	36	720	AIPO780
Jul 1973	47	53	757	AIPO874

NOTE: DK not coded separately.

Table 9.8   Are Nude Actors and Actresses Objectionable?--
            1969-1973

Would you find actors and actresses appearing in the nude in
Broadway plays objectionable?

	YES	NO	N	
May 1969	84	16	1467	AIPO780
Jul 1973	66	34	1520	AIPO874

NOTE: DK not coded separately.

Table 9.9   Are Pictures of Nudes in Magazines Objectionable?
--1969-1973

Would you find pictures of nudes in magazines objectionable?

	YES	NO	N	
May 1969	75	25	1474	AIPO780
Jul 1973	56	44	1526	AIPO874

NOTE: DK not coded separately.

Table 9.10   Does Pornography Provide Information about Sex?
--1970-1988

PORNINF--The next questions are about pornography--books, movies, magazines, and photographs that show or describe sex activities. I'm going to read some opinions about the effects of looking at or reading such sexual materials. As I read each one, please tell me if you think sexual materials do or do not have that effect.

Sexual materials provide information about sex.

	YES	NO	DK	N	
Feb 1970[a]	61	27	11	2486	RAC
Mar 1973	62	33	6	1499	GSS
Mar 1975	62	29	9	1486	GSS
Mar 1976	57	36	7	1493	GSS
Mar 1978	61	33	6	1529	GSS
Mar 1980	58	34	7	1465	GSS
Mar 1983	60	35	5	1591	GSS
Mar 1984	58	37	5	1463	GSS
Mar 1986	57	38	5	1466	GSS
Mar 1987	62	32	6	1459	GSS
Mar 1988	58	35	6	993	GSS

[a]On this card are some opinions about the effects of looking at or reading sexual materials. As I read the letter of each one please tell me if you think sexual materials do or do not have these effects. Lets start with the letter a. Sexual materials provide information about sex.

Table 9.11   Does Pornography Lead to a Breakdown of Morals?
              --1970-1988

PORNMORL--The next questions are about pornography...please
tell me if you think sexual materials do or do not have that
effect.

               Sexual materials lead to breakdown of morals.

	YES	NO	DK	N	
Feb 1970[a]	56	30	13	2486	RAC
Mar 1973	53	41	6	1500	GSS
Mar 1975	51	40	9	1487	GSS
Mar 1976	55	38	7	1490	GSS
Mar 1978	57	38	5	1529	GSS
Mar 1980	60	33	7	1461	GSS
Mar 1983	59	36	5	1589	GSS
Mar 1984	62	33	5	1462	GSS
Mar 1986	62	32	5	1463	GSS
Mar 1987	62	32	6	1459	GSS
Mar 1988	62	33	5	992	GSS

[a]See note a, Table 9.10.

Table 9.12   Does Pornography Lead to Rape?--1970-1988

PORNRAPE--The next questions are about pornography...please
tell me if you think sexual materials do or do not have that
effect.

               Sexual materials lead people to commit rape.

	YES	NO	DK	N	
Feb 1970[a]	49	29	21	2486	RAC
Mar 1973	50	43	7	1495	GSS
Mar 1975	52	38	10	1484	GSS
Mar 1976	53	38	9	1492	GSS
Mar 1978	57	36	7	1528	GSS
Mar 1980	54	37	9	1462	GSS
Mar 1983	55	38	7	1589	GSS
Mar 1984	55	37	8	1462	GSS
Mar 1986	57	36	7	1461	GSS
Mar 1987	54	37	9	1458	GSS
Mar 1988	56	35	8	989	GSS

[a]See note a, Table 9.10.

Table 9.13   Does Pornography Provide an Outlet for Bottled-
             Up Impulses?--1970-1988

PORNOUT--The next questions are about pornography...please
tell me if you think sexual materials do or do not have that
effect.

Sexual materials provide an outlet for bottled-
up impulses.

	YES	NO	DK	N	
May 1970[a]	34	46	20	2486	RAC
Mar 1973	55	35	10	1499	GSS
Mar 1975	56	28	16	1485	GSS
Mar 1976	56	29	16	1491	GSS
Mar 1978	59	29	12	1527	GSS
Mar 1980	59	27	14	1462	GSS
Mar 1983	57	32	11	1588	GSS
Mar 1984	61	27	12	1463	GSS
Mar 1986	60	31	10	1462	GSS
Mar 1987	60	27	13	1457	GSS
Mar 1988	56	30	13	992	GSS

[a]See note a, Table 9.10.

Table 9.14   Should There Be Law against the Distribution of
Pornography?--1973-1988

PORNLAW--Which of these statements comes closest to your
feelings about pornography laws?

There should be laws against the distribution of pornography whatever the age.

There should be laws against the distribution of pornography to persons under 18.

There should be no laws forbidding the distribution of
pornography.

	ILLEGAL TO ALL	ILLEGAL UNDER 18	LEGAL	DK	N	
Mar 1973	42	47	9	2	1498	GSS
Mar 1975	40	48	11	1	1489	GSS
Mar 1976	40	50	8	2	1496	GSS
Mar 1978	43	49	7	1	1531	GSS
Mar 1980	40	51	6	2	1468	GSS
Mar 1983	41	53	4	1	1595	GSS
Mar 1984	41	54	4	1	1464	GSS
Mar 1986	43	53	4	1	1469	GSS
Mar 1987	40	55	4	1	1461	GSS
Mar 1988	43	50	5	2	994	GSS

Table 9.15   Have You Seen an X-Rated Movie in the Last Year?
--1973-1988

XMOVIE--Have you seen an X-rated movie in the last year?

	YES	NO	DK	N	
Mar 1973	25	74	1	1500	GSS
Mar 1975	19	81	0	1489	GSS
Mar 1976	18	82	0	1495	GSS
Mar 1978	15	85	1	1532	GSS
Mar 1980	16	84	0	1467	GSS
Mar 1983	19	80	0	1595	GSS
Mar 1984	24	76	0	1466	GSS
Mar 1986	25	75	0	1466	GSS
Mar 1987	28	72	0	1462	GSS
Mar 1988	27	73	0	997	GSS

Table 9.16 Should Abortion Be Possible if There is a Chance of Serious Defect in the Baby?--1962-1988

ABDEFECT--Please tell me whether or not you think it should be possible for a pregnant woman to obtain a legal abortion if

There is a strong chance of serious defect in the baby?

	YES	NO	DK	N	
Aug 1962[a]	55	31	14	1493	AIPO662
Dec 1965[a]	54	32	14	1565	AIPO721
Dec 1965	55	41	4	1482	SRS870
Dec 1968[a]	67	23	10	1517	AIPODEC
May 1968[a]	64	26	10	1611	AIPOMAY
Sep 1969[a]	63	25	12	1560	AIPO788
Nov 1972	78	17	5	1461	NORC5046
Mar 1972	75	20	5	1607	GSS
Mar 1973	82	15	2	1500	GSS
Mar 1974	83	14	3	1484	GSS
Mar 1975	80	16	3	1487	GSS
Mar 1976	82	16	3	1495	GSS
Mar 1977	83	14	2	1524	GSS
Mar 1978	80	18	2	1528	GSS
Mar 1980	80	16	3	1467	GSS
Mar 1982	81	15	4	1502	GSS
Mar 1983	76	20	3	1567	GSS
Mar 1984	78	19	3	1465	GSS
Mar 1985	76	21	3	1531	GSS
Mar 1987	77	20	3	1459	GSS
Mar 1988	76	20	3	975	GSS

WOMEN

	YES	NO	DK	N	
Mar 1972	73	21	6	803	GSS
Mar 1973	82	15	2	802	GSS
Mar 1974	84	13	3	793	GSS
Mar 1975	82	14	3	820	GSS
Mar 1976	82	16	2	828	GSS
Mar 1977	85	13	2	835	GSS
Mar 1978	80	18	2	887	GSS
Mar 1980	79	18	3	826	GSS
Mar 1982	81	16	4	864	GSS
Mar 1983	76	22	3	889	GSS
Mar 1984	77	20	3	868	GSS
Mar 1985	75	22	3	844	GSS
Mar 1987	77	21	2	823	GSS
Mar 1988	75	20	4	575	GSS

MEN

	YES	NO	DK	N	
Mar 1972	76	20	4	804	GSS
Mar 1973	82	15	2	698	GSS
Mar 1974	81	16	3	691	GSS

Table 9.16 (Continued)

	YES	NO	DK	N	
Mar 1975	78	18	3	667	GSS
Mar 1976	81	16	3	667	GSS
Mar 1977	82	16	3	689	GSS
Mar 1978	80	18	2	641	GSS
Mar 1980	82	15	4	641	GSS
Mar 1982	82	14	4	638	GSS
Mar 1983	77	19	4	678	GSS
Mar 1984	79	18	3	597	GSS
Mar 1985	77	20	3	687	GSS
Mar 1987	78	18	4	636	GSS
Mar 1988	78	20	2	400	GSS

PROTESTANT

	YES	NO	DK	N	
Mar 1972	76	20	5	1028	GSS
Mar 1973	84	14	2	938	GSS
Mar 1974	83	14	3	954	GSS
Mar 1975	81	16	4	972	GSS
Mar 1976	83	14	3	948	GSS
Mar 1977	84	14	2	1002	GSS
Mar 1978	81	17	2	977	GSS
Mar 1980	81	16	3	935	GSS
Mar 1982	81	15	4	967	GSS
Mar 1983	75	21	4	950	GSS
Mar 1984	77	20	3	928	GSS
Mar 1985	76	21	3	955	GSS
Mar 1987	75	21	3	950	GSS
Mar 1988	75	22	3	603	GSS

CATHOLIC

	YES	NO	DK	N	
Mar 1972	67	26	6	410	GSS
Mar 1973	77	20	3	386	GSS
Mar 1974	77	20	3	376	GSS
Mar 1975	75	22	3	363	GSS
Mar 1976	75	23	2	389	GSS
Mar 1977	78	19	2	371	GSS
Mar 1978	73	25	2	382	GSS
Mar 1980	75	22	4	362	GSS
Mar 1982	76	22	4	364	GSS
Mar 1983	72	24	3	429	GSS
Mar 1984	74	23	3	373	GSS
Mar 1985	72	26	3	407	GSS
Mar 1987	75	22	3	353	GSS
Mar 1988	76	21	3	262	GSS

JEWISH

	YES	NO	DK	N	
Mar 1972	91	7	2	54	GSS
Mar 1973	100	–	–	42	GSS
Mar 1974	100	–	–	44	GSS

Table 9.16 (Continued)

	YES	NO	DK	N	
Mar 1975	87	4	9	23	GSS
Mar 1976	96	–	4	27	GSS
Mar 1977	100	–	–	34	GSS
Mar 1978	100	–	–	29	GSS
Mar 1980	91	9	–	32	GSS
Mar 1982	95	5	–	37	GSS
Mar 1983	98	2	–	43	GSS
Mar 1984	93	4	4	27	GSS
Mar 1985	91	6	3	32	GSS
Mar 1987	100	–	–	20	GSS
Mar 1988	100	–	–	17	GSS

NONE

	YES	NO	DK	N	
Mar 1972	89	8	2	83	GSS
Mar 1973	90	8	2	96	GSS
Mar 1974	94	4	2	101	GSS
Mar 1975	95	5	–	113	GSS
Mar 1976	91	7	2	114	GSS
Mar 1977	94	4	2	93	GSS
Mar 1978	92	7	1	119	GSS
Mar 1980	89	8	4	105	GSS
Mar 1982	94	4	2	108	GSS
Mar 1983	92	7	1	116	GSS
Mar 1984	88	9	3	106	GSS
Mar 1985	92	8	–	109	GSS
Mar 1987	95	3	2	102	GSS
Mar 1988	84	12	3	64	GSS

[a]Do you think abortion operations should or should not be legal in the following cases: when the child may be born deformed?

Table 9.17   Should Abortion Be Possible if a Woman Wants No
               More Children?--1965-1988

ABNOMORE--Please tell me whether or not you think it should
be possible for a pregnant woman to obtain a legal abortion
if

She is married and does not want any more children?

	YES	NO	DK	N	
Dec 1965	15	82	2	1480	SRS870
Dec 1968[a]	13	81	6	1517	AIPODEC
May 1968[a]	11	85	4	1611	AIPOMAY
Nov 1972	41	53	6	1457	NORC5046
Mar 1972	38	57	5	1608	GSS
Mar 1973	46	51	3	1502	GSS
Mar 1974	45	50	5	1484	GSS
Mar 1975	44	52	4	1488	GSS
Mar 1976	45	52	3	1493	GSS
Mar 1977	45	51	4	1523	GSS
Mar 1978	39	58	3	1529	GSS
Mar 1980	45	51	4	1465	GSS
Mar 1982	46	49	4	1503	GSS
Mar 1983	38	59	3	1569	GSS
Mar 1984	41	56	3	1463	GSS
Mar 1985	39	58	3	1529	GSS
Mar 1987	40	56	3	1459	GSS
Mar 1988	39	58	3	975	GSS

WOMEN

	YES	NO	DK	N	
Mar 1972	35	59	6	805	GSS
Mar 1973	41	55	4	803	GSS
Mar 1974	44	52	4	793	GSS
Mar 1975	43	52	5	820	GSS
Mar 1976	42	54	4	828	GSS
Mar 1977	43	53	4	835	GSS
Mar 1978	38	59	3	888	GSS
Mar 1980	44	52	4	826	GSS
Mar 1982	45	51	4	865	GSS
Mar 1983	34	62	3	890	GSS
Mar 1984	40	58	2	867	GSS
Mar 1985	36	60	3	842	GSS
Mar 1987	37	60	3	822	GSS
Mar 1988	38	60	3	575	GSS

MEN

	YES	NO	DK	N	
Mar 1972	40	55	4	803	GSS
Mar 1973	52	45	3	699	GSS
Mar 1974	45	49	6	691	GSS
Mar 1975	45	52	4	668	GSS
Mar 1976	48	50	2	665	GSS
Mar 1977	47	49	4	688	GSS
Mar 1978	41	56	3	641	GSS

Table 9.17 (Continued)

	YES	NO	DK	N	
Mar 1980	47	50	4	639	GSS
Mar 1982	49	47	5	638	GSS
Mar 1983	42	55	3	679	GSS
Mar 1984	44	53	4	596	GSS
Mar 1985	43	55	2	687	GSS
Mar 1987	44	52	4	637	GSS
Mar 1988	40	57	3	400	GSS

PROTESTANT

	YES	NO	DK	N	
Mar 1972	36	58	5	1028	GSS
Mar 1973	46	50	4	939	GSS
Mar 1974	43	52	5	954	GSS
Mar 1975	42	53	5	973	GSS
Mar 1976	42	54	4	947	GSS
Mar 1977	44	52	4	1001	GSS
Mar 1978	37	60	3	977	GSS
Mar 1980	45	51	4	933	GSS
Mar 1982	42	52	6	968	GSS
Mar 1983	34	62	4	952	GSS
Mar 1984	38	59	3	928	GSS
Mar 1985	37	60	3	955	GSS
Mar 1987	36	61	3	951	GSS
Mar 1988	33	64	2	603	GSS

CATHOLIC

	YES	NO	DK	N	
Mar 1972	29	67	4	411	GSS
Mar 1973	34	63	3	387	GSS
Mar 1974	37	59	4	376	GSS
Mar 1975	37	60	3	363	GSS
Mar 1976	39	59	2	388	GSS
Mar 1977	36	60	4	371	GSS
Mar 1978	31	66	3	383	GSS
Mar 1980	34	63	3	362	GSS
Mar 1982	46	51	2	364	GSS
Mar 1983	30	68	2	429	GSS
Mar 1984	38	58	4	372	GSS
Mar 1985	31	67	2	405	GSS
Mar 1987	40	58	3	352	GSS
Mar 1988	41	56	3	262	GSS

JEWISH

	YES	NO	DK	N	
Mar 1972	70	28	2	54	GSS
Mar 1973	90	10	–	42	GSS
Mar 1974	84	4	11	44	GSS
Mar 1975	78	13	9	23	GSS
Mar 1976	85	15	–	27	GSS
Mar 1977	85	15	–	34	GSS
Mar 1978	79	21	–	29	GSS

Table 9.17 (Continued)

	YES	NO	DK	N	
Mar 1980	75	22	3	32	GSS
Mar 1982	78	19	3	37	GSS
Mar 1983	84	16	–	43	GSS
Mar 1984	78	18	4	27	GSS
Mar 1985	81	19	–	32	GSS
Mar 1987	90	5	5	20	GSS
Mar 1988	88	12	–	17	GSS

NONE

Mar 1972	74	24	2	83	GSS
Mar 1973	76	24	–	96	GSS
Mar 1974	70	21	9	101	GSS
Mar 1975	72	26	3	113	GSS
Mar 1976	74	25	2	114	GSS
Mar 1977	77	19	3	93	GSS
Mar 1978	73	24	3	119	GSS
Mar 1980	73	21	6	105	GSS
Mar 1982	74	23	3	108	GSS
Mar 1983	70	27	3	116	GSS
Mar 1984	66	32	2	106	GSS
Mar 1985	72	24	4	109	GSS
Mar 1987	74	21	5	102	GSS
Mar 1988	59	36	5	64	GSS

[a]Do you think abortion operations should or should not be legal in the following cases: where the parents simply have all the children they want although there would be no major health or financial problems involved in having another child?

Table 9.18   Should Abortion Be Possible if the Mother's
             Health Is Endangered?--1962-1988

ABHLTH--Please tell me whether or not you think it should be
possible for a pregnant woman to obtain a legal abortion if

The woman's own health is seriously endangered by
the pregnancy?

	YES	NO	DK	N	
Aug 1962[a]	77	16	7	3344	AIPO662
Dec 1965[a]	77	16	7	3532	AIPO721
Dec 1965	70	26	3	1480	SRS870
Dec 1968[a]	84	11	5	1517	AIPODEC
May 1968[a]	84	11	5	1611	AIPOMAY
Sep 1969[a]	80	14	6	1560	AIPO788
Mar 1972	83	13	4	1605	GSS
Mar 1973	91	8	2	1502	GSS
Mar 1974	90	7	2	1484	GSS
Mar 1975	88	9	3	1487	GSS
Mar 1976	89	9	2	1492	GSS
Mar 1977	89	9	2	1522	GSS
Mar 1978	88	9	2	1528	GSS
Mar 1980	88	10	3	1466	GSS
Mar 1982	90	8	2	1503	GSS
Mar 1983	87	10	3	1567	GSS
Mar 1984	88	10	2	1462	GSS
Mar 1985	87	10	3	1531	GSS
Mar 1987	86	11	3	1461	GSS
Mar 1988	86	11	3	974	GSS

WOMEN

	YES	NO	DK	N	
Mar 1972	82	13	4	803	GSS
Mar 1973	90	9	2	803	GSS
Mar 1974	90	7	2	793	GSS
Mar 1975	89	9	2	819	GSS
Mar 1976	88	10	2	827	GSS
Mar 1977	88	10	2	835	GSS
Mar 1978	88	9	3	887	GSS
Mar 1980	86	12	2	826	GSS
Mar 1982	88	9	3	865	GSS
Mar 1983	87	10	3	888	GSS
Mar 1984	86	12	2	866	GSS
Mar 1985	85	12	3	844	GSS
Mar 1987	83	13	3	823	GSS
Mar 1988	84	12	4	574	GSS

MEN

	YES	NO	DK	N	
Mar 1972	84	12	4	802	GSS
Mar 1973	92	6	2	699	GSS
Mar 1974	90	8	2	691	GSS
Mar 1975	88	9	3	668	GSS

Table 9.18 (Continued)

	YES	NO	DK	N	
Mar 1976	90	8	1	665	GSS
Mar 1977	89	8	2	687	GSS
Mar 1978	89	10	2	641	GSS
Mar 1980	90	7	3	640	GSS
Mar 1982	92	7	2	638	GSS
Mar 1983	87	9	4	679	GSS
Mar 1984	90	8	2	596	GSS
Mar 1985	90	8	2	687	GSS
Mar 1987	88	9	3	638	GSS
Mar 1988	89	10	2	400	GSS

[a]Do you think abortion operations should or should not be legal in the following cases: where the health of the mother is in danger?

Table 9.19   Should Abortion Be Possible if the Family Cannot Afford More Children?--1962-1988

ABPOOR--Please tell me whether or not you think it should be possible for a pregnant woman to obtain a legal abortion if

The family has a very low income and cannot afford any more children?

	YES	NO	DK	N	
Aug 1962[a]	15	74	11	3341	AIPO662
Dec 1965[a]	18	72	10	3532	AIPO721
Dec 1965	21	76	2	1480	SRS870
Dec 1968[a]	23	69	8	1517	AIPODEC
May 1968[a]	20	72	8	1611	AIPOMAY
Sep 1968[a]	23	67	9	1560	AIPO788
Mar 1972	46	48	6	1605	GSS
Mar 1973	52	45	3	1502	GSS
Mar 1974	52	43	4	1482	GSS
Mar 1975	51	45	5	1485	GSS
Mar 1976	51	45	4	1491	GSS
Mar 1977	52	45	3	1522	GSS
Mar 1978	46	51	4	1528	GSS
Mar 1980	50	46	4	1466	GSS
Mar 1982	50	46	4	1501	GSS
Mar 1983	42	54	4	1568	GSS
Mar 1984	45	52	3	1459	GSS
Mar 1985	42	55	3	1530	GSS
Mar 1987	44	53	4	1460	GSS
Mar 1988	40	56	4	975	GSS

Table 9.19 (Continued)

	YES	NO	DK	N	
WOMEN					
Mar 1972	44	49	7	803	GSS
Mar 1973	49	48	4	803	GSS
Mar 1974	53	43	4	791	GSS
Mar 1975	50	46	4	818	GSS
Mar 1976	49	47	4	825	GSS
Mar 1977	52	45	3	834	GSS
Mar 1978	44	52	4	887	GSS
Mar 1980	48	47	5	826	GSS
Mar 1982	50	46	4	864	GSS
Mar 1983	41	56	4	890	GSS
Mar 1984	44	53	3	866	GSS
Mar 1985	41	56	3	843	GSS
Mar 1987	41	56	3	823	GSS
Mar 1988	40	56	3	575	GSS
MEN					
Mar 1972	47	47	5	802	GSS
Mar 1973	55	42	3	699	GSS
Mar 1974	51	44	5	691	GSS
Mar 1975	52	43	5	667	GSS
Mar 1976	54	43	3	666	GSS
Mar 1977	51	46	3	688	GSS
Mar 1978	48	48	4	641	GSS
Mar 1980	52	45	3	640	GSS
Mar 1982	50	46	4	637	GSS
Mar 1983	44	52	4	678	GSS
Mar 1984	46	51	3	593	GSS
Mar 1985	45	53	2	687	GSS
Mar 1987	46	49	5	637	GSS
Mar 1988	40	56	4	400	GSS

[a]Do you think abortion operations should or should not be legal in the following cases: where the family does not have enough money to support another child?

Table 9.20   Should Abortion Be Possible if The Pregnancy Is
a Result of Rape?--1965-1988

ABRAPE--Please tell me whether or not you think it should be
possible for a pregnant woman to obtain a legal abortion if

She became pregnant as a result of rape?

	YES	NO	DK	N	
Dec 1965	56	38	6	1479	SRS870
Mar 1972	75	20	6	1604	GSS
Mar 1973	81	16	3	1501	GSS
Mar 1974	83	13	4	1482	GSS
Mar 1975	80	16	4	1487	GSS
Mar 1976	81	16	3	1492	GSS
Mar 1977	81	16	3	1521	GSS
Mar 1978	81	16	3	1526	GSS
Mar 1980	80	16	4	1465	GSS
Mar 1982	83	13	4	1500	GSS
Mar 1983	80	16	4	1567	GSS
Mar 1984	77	19	4	1463	GSS
Mar 1985	78	18	4	1531	GSS
Mar 1987	78	18	4	1458	GSS
Mar 1988	77	18	5	974	GSS

WOMEN

	YES	NO	DK	N	
Mar 1972	75	20	5	803	GSS
Mar 1973	80	17	3	802	GSS
Mar 1974	83	12	5	791	GSS
Mar 1975	80	15	4	819	GSS
Mar 1976	81	15	4	826	GSS
Mar 1977	81	16	4	833	GSS
Mar 1978	81	16	3	887	GSS
Mar 1980	78	18	3	825	GSS
Mar 1982	83	13	4	865	GSS
Mar 1983	79	17	4	888	GSS
Mar 1984	75	20	5	868	GSS
Mar 1985	77	19	4	844	GSS
Mar 1987	76	21	3	821	GSS
Mar 1988	75	19	6	575	GSS

MEN

	YES	NO	DK	N	
Mar 1972	74	20	6	801	GSS
Mar 1973	81	15	4	699	GSS
Mar 1974	83	14	3	691	GSS
Mar 1975	80	16	5	668	GSS
Mar 1976	80	17	3	666	GSS
Mar 1977	81	16	3	688	GSS
Mar 1978	81	16	3	639	GSS
Mar 1980	83	13	4	640	GSS
Mar 1982	84	12	4	635	GSS
Mar 1983	80	16	4	679	GSS

Table 9.20 (Continued)

	YES	NO	DK	N	
Mar 1984	80	17	3	595	GSS
Mar 1985	80	17	3	687	GSS
Mar 1987	80	15	5	637	GSS
Mar 1988	79	16	4	399	GSS

Table 9.21   Should Abortion Be Possible if the Woman is
Unmarried and Does Not Wish to Marry?--1965-1988

ABSINGLE--Please tell me whether or not you think it should
be possible for a pregnant woman to obtain a legal abortion
if

She is not married and does not want to marry the
man?

	YES	NO	DK	N	
Dec 1965	17	80	2	1480	SRS870
Mar 1972	41	53	6	1605	GSS
Mar 1973	47	49	3	1499	GSS
Mar 1974	48	48	4	1484	GSS
Mar 1975	46	49	5	1485	GSS
Mar 1976	48	48	4	1494	GSS
Mar 1977	48	48	4	1523	GSS
Mar 1978	40	57	4	1528	GSS
Mar 1980	46	49	4	1466	GSS
Mar 1982	47	49	5	1502	GSS
Mar 1983	38	58	5	1566	GSS
Mar 1984	43	54	3	1462	GSS
Mar 1985	40	57	3	1529	GSS
Mar 1987	40	56	3	1460	GSS
Mar 1988	38	58	4	973	GSS

WOMEN

	YES	NO	DK	N	
Mar 1972	38	55	7	803	GSS
Mar 1973	46	51	3	801	GSS
Mar 1974	48	48	4	793	GSS
Mar 1975	45	50	5	819	GSS
Mar 1976	46	51	3	828	GSS
Mar 1977	46	49	5	835	GSS
Mar 1978	38	58	4	888	GSS
Mar 1980	47	48	5	826	GSS
Mar 1982	46	49	5	865	GSS
Mar 1983	36	59	4	887	GSS

Table 9.21 (Continued)

	YES	NO	DK	N	
Mar 1984	41	56	3	867	GSS
Mar 1985	38	59	3	842	GSS
Mar 1987	38	60	3	823	GSS
Mar 1988	37	59	4	575	GSS

MEN

	YES	NO	DK	N	
Mar 1972	43	51	6	802	GSS
Mar 1973	49	48	3	698	GSS
Mar 1974	48	48	5	691	GSS
Mar 1975	47	48	5	666	GSS
Mar 1976	51	44	4	666	GSS
Mar 1977	49	47	4	688	GSS
Mar 1978	42	55	3	640	GSS
Mar 1980	46	51	4	640	GSS
Mar 1982	47	48	4	637	GSS
Mar 1983	39	56	5	679	GSS
Mar 1984	46	52	3	595	GSS
Mar 1985	42	56	3	687	GSS
Mar 1987	44	52	4	637	GSS
Mar 1988	39	56	4	398	GSS

Table 9.22   Should Abortion Be Possible for Any Reason?--
1977-1988

ABANY--Please tell me whether or not you think it should be
possible for a pregnant woman to obtain a legal abortion if

The woman wants it for any reason?

	YES	NO	DK	N	
Mar 1977	37	60	3	1523	GSS
Mar 1978	32	65	3	1527	GSS
Mar 1980	39	57	4	1465	GSS
Mar 1982	39	56	4	1499	GSS
Mar 1983	33	64	3	1565	GSS
Mar 1984	37	60	3	1462	GSS
Mar 1985	36	59	3	1529	GSS
Mar 1987	38	63	4	1455	GSS
Mar 1988	35	57	4	973	GSS

Table 9.22 (Continued)

	YES	NO	DK	N
WOMEN				
Mar 1977	36	62	2	835 GSS
Mar 1978	31	66	3	888 GSS
Mar 1980	39	56	4	825 GSS
Mar 1982	39	57	4	864 GSS
Mar 1983	32	64	3	889 GSS
Mar 1984	36	61	3	867 GSS
Mar 1985	34	62	3	842 GSS
Mar 1987	35	62	3	821 GSS
Mar 1988	35	62	4	575 GSS
MEN				
Mar 1977	38	59	3	688 GSS
Mar 1978	34	63	3	639 GSS
Mar 1980	40	57	4	640 GSS
Mar 1982	40	55	5	635 GSS
Mar 1983	34	63	3	676 GSS
Mar 1984	39	58	3	595 GSS
Mar 1985	38	59	3	687 GSS
Mar 1987	41	54	5	634 GSS
Mar 1988	34	51	4	398 GSS

Table 9.23 Should Abortions Be Legal at All?--1975-1985

ABLEGAL--Do you think abortions should be legal under any circumstances, legal only under certain circumstances, or illegal in all circumstances?

	ANY	CERTAIN	NEVER	DK	N	
Apr 1975	21	54	22	3	1535	AIPO927
Dec 1977	22	55	18	5	1518	AIPO990
Mar 1977[a]	22	68	9	1	1519	GSS
Feb 1979	22	54	19	5	1534	AIPO123G
Jul 1980	25	53	18	4	1548	AIPO159G
May 1981	24	53	20	3	1519	AIPO173G
Jun 1983	23	58	16	3	1558	AIPO215G
Jan 1985	21	55	21	3	757	AIPONEWSWEEK

[a]...or never legal in any circumstances.

10

Death and Dying

Ethical, medical, legal, and even economic studies of health
care (e.g., Abrams and Buckner, 1983; VanDeVeer and Regan,
1987) have become *de rigueur* in programs of medicine, nurs-
ing, public policy, and philosophy. Attitudinal aspects--in
the sense of informed consent of patients and relatives--play
an important role in these discussions. Yet considered more
broadly, public opinion has been measured and explored very
little--at least in regard to death and dying. (Attitudes
about abortion have been studied more extensively; see chapter
9.)

Fortunately, of the items now available, two were first
asked forty years ago. To be sure, the direction of change
simply verifies what what we might already suspect--that currently there is more sympathy for euthanasia when a patient
has an incurable disease. What is far less obvious is how
prevalent such views were years ago. As far back as 1947,
nearly 40 percent of the population felt that doctors should
be allowed to end a patient's life in the circumstances described in Table 10.1 and nearly 50 percent in the circumstances described in Table 10.2. (See also the response to
a question about "mercy deaths" asked by Gallup in the 1930s;
Ostheimer, 1980.)

As limited as the time series on euthanasia is, it shows
two distinct changes and one unchanging result.[1] First, the
percentage who would allow euthanasia has increased dramatically, with similar degrees of change over the first twenty-
five years and the last fifteen. Second, there is a declining
difference between the percentage who would allow euthansia

---

[1]The apparent crystallization of opinion--the decline in
the proportion of DK responses in Table 10.1--may be a simple
"house effect." NORC surveys tend to record fewer "don't
know" responses.

if the patient and family requested it and the percentage who would allow it under the more stringent conditions of Table 10.2.   The unchanging result is the male-female difference. Over the past ten years, 8 to 9 percent more males have been more permissive about euthanasia.

The suicide time series is considerably shorter, with a clear upward trend in one of the items but virtually no movement in the other three.   Males are more willing to condone suicide; differences for the "incurable disease" item are of the same size as for euthanasia.

Given current interest in medical ethics, it is surprising that very few questions have been asked about death and dying.[2]   In 1984, for example, the *American Public Opinion Index* listed two surveys with one question each under the heading "Euthanasia," one covering Hawaii and one Houston. This was in contrast to the twelve questions in three national surveys about baseball's designated hitter rule.[3]   Considerable change has already occurred in public attitudes on death and dying, but opinion is far from unanimous, as indicated in Table 10.3.   Here, then, is a subject that is ripe for more sustained questioning of the general public.

REFERENCES

Abrams, Natalie, and Michael D. Buckner, eds. 1983. *Medical Ethics*.   Cambridge: MIT Press.

Ostheimer, John M. 1980. The Polls: Changing Attitudes toward Euthanasia. *Public Opinion Quarterly*, 44:123-128.

Sawyer, Darwin O.   1982.   Public Attitudes toward Life and Death.   *Public Opinion Quarterly*, 46:521-533.

VanDeVeer, Donald, and Tom Regan, eds.   1987.   *Health Care Ethics*.   Philadelphia: Temple University Press.

---

[2]In general, there has been little systematic analysis of attitudes toward death and dying except as it relates to abortion and the death penalty. An exception is Sawyer, 1982.

[3]A check of the Roper POLL data base turned up more items mentioning death, but almost all were about the death penalty (see Table 6.8).

Table 10.1   Should Doctors Be Allowed to End a Life if the
             Patient Has an Incurable Disease and the Patient
             and Family Request It?--1947-1988

LETDIE1--When a person has a disease that cannot be cured,
do you think doctors should be allowed by law to end the patient's life by some painless means if the patient and his
family request it?

	YES	NO	DK	N	
Jun 1947	38	54	8	3078	AIPO398
Jan 1950	38	56	7	1495	AIPO451
Jul 1973	52	41	7	1544	AIPO874
Apr 1975	52	33	15	1404	MAP
Jun 1977	52	34	15	1501	MAP
Mar 1977	60	36	4	1519	GSS
Mar 1978	58	38	4	1531	GSS
Mar 1982	61	34	5	1503	GSS
Mar 1983	63	33	4	1594	GSS
Mar 1985	64	33	3	1532	GSS
Mar 1986	66	31	4	1466	GSS
Mar 1988	66	29	5	983	GSS
Jun 1988[a]	63	30	7	2014	NBC/WSJ

WOMEN

	YES	NO	DK	N	
Mar 1977	55	39	6	833	GSS
Mar 1978	55	41	4	888	GSS
Mar 1982	57	37	5	865	GSS
Mar 1983	59	36	5	905	GSS
Mar 1985	60	37	3	844	GSS
Mar 1986	62	35	3	847	GSS
Mar 1988	62	32	5	547	GSS

MEN

	YES	NO	DK	N	
Mar 1977	65	32	3	686	GSS
Mar 1978	62	35	4	643	GSS
Mar 1982	65	30	4	638	GSS
Mar 1983	69	28	4	689	GSS
Mar 1985	69	29	2	688	GSS
Mar 1986	71	25	4	619	GSS
Mar 1988	70	25	5	436	GSS

[a]If someone has a disease that cannot be cured, do you think
there should be a law allowing doctors to end the patient's
life by some painless way if the patient and his family
request it, or don't you think so?

Table 10.2   Should Doctors Be Allowed to End a Life if a
Board of Doctors Agreed that the Patient
Could Not Be Cured?--1950-1983

LETDIE2--Would you approve of ending a patient's life if a
board of doctors appointed by the court agreed that the patient could not be cured?

	YES	NO	DK	N	
Jan 1950	47	47	6	1497	AIPO451
Mar 1977	64	32	4	1514	GSS
Mar 1978	62	35	3	1517	GSS
Mar 1982	64	33	3	1493	GSS
Mar 1983	65	31	3	1590	GSS
WOMEN					
Mar 1977	60	36	4	831	GSS
Mar 1978	60	37	3	882	GSS
Mar 1982	61	36	3	859	GSS
Mar 1983	62	35	3	902	GSS
MEN					
Mar 1977	69	28	3	683	GSS
Mar 1978	66	32	2	635	GSS
Mar 1982	68	29	3	634	GSS
Mar 1983	70	26	3	688	GSS

NOTE--"YES" includes those who said "yes" to LETDIE1 (Table
10.1), and therefore were not asked this question, plus
those who said "YES" to this question.

Table 10.3 Is Suicide Acceptable if a Person Has an
             Incurable Disease?--1977-1988

SUICIDE1--Do you think a person has the right to end his or
her own life if this person

              Has an incurable disease?

	YES	NO	DK	N	
Mar 1977	38	59	3	1524	GSS
Mar 1978	38	58	3	1532	GSS
Mar 1982	45	50	5	1502	GSS
Mar 1983	48	48	4	1591	GSS
Mar 1985	44	53	3	1532	GSS
Mar 1986	52	45	3	1467	GSS
Mar 1988	50	46	4	983	GSS

WOMEN

	YES	NO	DK	N	
Mar 1977	34	62	4	835	GSS
Mar 1978	35	62	3	889	GSS
Mar 1982	41	54	6	863	GSS
Mar 1983	44	51	4	904	GSS
Mar 1985	40	56	3	844	GSS
Mar 1986	46	51	3	848	GSS
Mar 1988	46	49	5	548	GSS

MEN

	YES	NO	DK	N	
Mar 1977	42	55	2	689	GSS
Mar 1978	43	54	3	643	GSS
Mar 1982	51	45	4	639	GSS
Mar 1983	53	44	3	687	GSS
Mar 1985	49	48	4	688	GSS
Mar 1986	60	37	3	619	GSS
Mar 1988	55	42	3	435	GSS

Table 10.4   Is Suicide Acceptable if a Person Has Gone
Bankrupt?--1977-1988

SUICIDE2--Do you think a person has the right to end his or
her own life if this person

Has gone bankrupt?

	YES	NO	DK	N	
Mar 1977	7	92	1	1523	GSS
Mar 1978	5	94	1	1531	GSS
Mar 1982	8	90	2	1502	GSS
Mar 1983	6	92	1	1589	GSS
Mar 1985	8	90	2	1530	GSS
Mar 1986	7	93	1	1467	GSS
Mar 1988	6	93	2	982	GSS
WOMEN					
Mar 1977	6	92	1	835	GSS
Mar 1978	4	95	1	889	GSS
Mar 1982	8	90	2	863	GSS
Mar 1983	5	93	2	902	GSS
Mar 1985	7	91	2	843	GSS
Mar 1986	6	93	1	848	GSS
Mar 1988	5	93	2	546	GSS
MEN					
Mar 1977	8	92	1	688	GSS
Mar 1978	7	92	1	642	GSS
Mar 1982	9	90	1	639	GSS
Mar 1983	8	91	1	687	GSS
Mar 1985	9	89	2	687	GSS
Mar 1986	7	92	1	619	GSS
Mar 1988	6	92	2	436	GSS

Table 10.5 Is Suicide Acceptable if a Person Has Dishonored His/Her Family?--1977-1988

SUICIDE3--Do you think a person has the right to end his or her own life if this person

Has dishonored his or her family?

	YES	NO	DK	N	
Mar 1977	7	91	1	1523	GSS
Mar 1978	6	93	0	1531	GSS
Mar 1982	8	90	2	1501	GSS
Mar 1983	7	92	2	1590	GSS
Mar 1985	8	90	2	1530	GSS
Mar 1986	6	93	1	1467	GSS
Mar 1988	7	91	2	982	GSS

WOMEN

	YES	NO	DK	N	
Mar 1977	7	92	2	835	GSS
Mar 1978	5	95	0	889	GSS
Mar 1982	8	90	2	863	GSS
Mar 1983	6	93	1	903	GSS
Mar 1985	6	91	2	843	GSS
Mar 1986	5	94	1	848	GSS
Mar 1988	6	92	2	546	GSS

MEN

	YES	NO	DK	N	
Mar 1977	9	91	1	688	GSS
Mar 1978	8	91	1	642	GSS
Mar 1982	9	90	1	638	GSS
Mar 1983	8	91	2	687	GSS
Mar 1985	10	88	2	687	GSS
Mar 1986	7	91	2	619	GSS
Mar 1988	8	91	1	436	GSS

Table 10.6   Is Suicide Acceptable if a Person Is Tired of
Living?--1977-1988

SUICIDE4--Do you think a person has the right to end his or
her own life if this person

Is tired of living and ready to die?

	YES	NO	DK	N	
Mar 1977	13	85	2	1523	GSS
Mar 1978	12	87	1	1531	GSS
Mar 1982	14	83	3	1501	GSS
Mar 1983	15	83	3	1590	GSS
Mar 1985	12	85	2	1530	GSS
Mar 1986	15	84	1	1466	GSS
Mar 1988	12	85	3	980	GSS
WOMEN					
Mar 1977	11	87	2	835	GSS
Mar 1978	10	89	2	889	GSS
Mar 1982	12	84	4	862	GSS
Mar 1983	12	84	3	903	GSS
Mar 1985	11	87	2	843	GSS
Mar 1986	14	85	1	848	GSS
Mar 1988	12	86	3	545	GSS
MEN					
Mar 1977	16	82	2	688	GSS
Mar 1978	15	84	1	642	GSS
Mar 1982	16	81	3	639	GSS
Mar 1983	18	81	2	687	GSS
Mar 1985	15	83	2	687	GSS
Mar 1986	16	82	2	618	GSS
Mar 1988	13	84	3	435	GSS

11

Role of Women

Polls document rather clearly that attitudes toward women's role in society have been undergoing quite substantial changes toward acceptance of nontraditional roles. They also demonstrate that these changes are broadly based: they have occurred among men as well as among women, and often to much the same degree.

Long range data are presented in Tables 11.1 and 11.2 (see also Smith, 1976). In part, at least, these questions deal with an issue that may be less an issue of feminism than a relic of the depression when there was a strong feeling that, because jobs were limited, women with husbands who had jobs should not work. This notion survived World War II when working women were strongly encouraged to go back to the home and to give up their jobs to returning soldiers. At any rate, through 1945 little support was generated for the notion that women with a working husband should themselves work. Men were found less likely to support the notion than women according to the question in Table 11.1, but no more so according to 11.2. By 1969, before the current feminist movement really took flight, the notion had become far more popular among both men and women, and it continued to gain support at least through 1985. Since 1969 attitudes on this issue have not differed between men and women.

Tables 11.3-11.9 cover the 1970s and 1980s, a period in which the role of women has been of substantial discussion. In all cases attitudes of both men and of women have clearly moved in a feminist direction.[1] Increasingly, Americans have come to believe that working mothers can establish warm and beneficial relations with their children (11.3, 11.5) and

---

[1]Changes in sex-role attitudes tend to be found across all cohorts and demographic groups (Cherlin and Walters, 1981; Mason and Lu, 1986, 1988).

maintain independent, productive careers (11.4, 11.6).   Men
have been about 10 percentage points less willing to accept
these notions than women.

An increasing willingness to have a women as president
was documented in Table 1.4. Paralleling this change, respondents have come more and more to reject the ideas that women
should leave the running of the country up to men (11.7) and
that women are emotionally less well suited for politics
(11.8, 11.9).   Interestingly, the impact of the 1984 election
campaign, in which the (losing) Democratic ticket sported a
woman in the vice presidential slot, seems to have arrested
this trend a bit (11.7, 11.8), but later it resumed.   For the
most part, the attitudes of men and women on these issues have
not differed substantially.

REFERENCES

Cherlin, Andrew, and Pamela Barnhouse Walters.   1981.   Trends
in United States Men's and Women's Sex Roles Attitudes:
1972 to 1978.   *American Sociological Review*, 46:453-460.

Glenn, Norval D.   1987.   Social Trends in the United States:
Evidence from Sample Surveys.   *Public Opinion Quarterly*,
51:109-126.

Mason, Karen Oppenheim, and Yu-Hsia Lu. 1986. Recent Changes
in Attitudes toward Women's Roles in the United States.
Proceedings of the International Conference on "The USA:
A Decade after the Vietnam War."   Institute of American
Culture, Taipei, 1987.

_____.   1988.   Attitudes toward Women's Familial Roles, 1977-
1985.   *Gender and Society*, 2:39-57.

Smith, Tom W. 1976. A Study of Trends in the Political Role
of Women 1936-1974. In James A. Davis, ed., *Studies of Social Changes since 1948*, Vol. 2.   Chicago: National Opinion
Research Center.

Table 11.1   Should a Married Woman Work?--1936-1988

FEWORK--Do you approve or disapprove of a married woman earning money in business or industry if she has a husband capable of supporting her?

	APPROVE	DISAPPROVE	DK	N	
Aug 1936[a]	18	82	-	c1500	AIPO45
Oct 1938[b]	21	75	4	3042	AIPO136
Oct 1945[c]	18	62	20	1562	AIPO359K
Sep 1969	55	40	5	1500	AIPOSP
Jun 1970[d]	60	35	4	1525	AIPO808
Mar 1972	64	34	2	1611	GSS
Mar 1974	68	30	2	1478	GSS
Mar 1975	70	28	2	1485	GSS
Sep 1975	69	27	3	1592	AIPO936
Mar 1977	65	33	1	1528	GSS
Mar 1978	72	26	1	1530	GSS
Mar 1982	74	24	2	1505	GSS
Mar 1983	75	23	2	1593	GSS
Mar 1985	84	13	2	1524	GSS
Mar 1986	77	22	2	1465	GSS
Mar 1988	79	19	2	981	GSS

WOMEN

Oct 1938[b]	26	71	3	957	AIPO136
Oct 1945[c]	20	60	20	779	AIPO359K
Jun 1970[d]	60	35	4	784	AIPO808
Mar 1972	66	31	3	806	GSS
Mar 1974	71	27	2	790	GSS
Mar 1975	71	27	2	818	GSS
Mar 1977	64	34	1	836	GSS
Mar 1978	74	25	1	887	GSS
Mar 1982	75	23	2	867	GSS
Mar 1983	75	23	2	907	GSS
Mar 1985	84	14	2	842	GSS
Mar 1986	76	22	2	848	GSS
Mar 1988	78	20	2	545	GSS

MEN

Oct 1938[b]	18	77	5	2085	AIPO136
Oct 1945[c]	16	65	20	783	AIPO359K
Jun 1970[d]	60	36	4	741	AIPO808
Mar 1972	62	37	2	805	GSS
Mar 1974	64	34	2	688	GSS
Mar 1975	69	30	1	667	GSS
Mar 1977	67	32	1	692	GSS
Mar 1978	71	28	2	643	GSS
Mar 1982	73	26	2	638	GSS
Mar 1983	75	23	2	686	GSS
Mar 1985	85	12	2	682	GSS
Mar 1986	78	21	1	617	GSS
Mar 1988	80	18	2	436	GSS

Table 11.1 (Continued)

---

aShould a married woman earn money if she has a husband capable of supporting her?

bDo you approve of a married woman earning money in business or industry if she has a husband capable of supporting her?

cDo you approve of a married woman holding a job in business or industry if her husband is able to support her?

dDo you approve of a married woman earning money in business or industry if she has a husband capable of supporting her?

Table 11.2   Should a Married Woman Work if Jobs Are
Limited?--1945-1977

FEWORKIF--If there is a limited number of jobs, do you approve or disapprove of a married woman holding a job in business or industry when her husband is able to support her?

	APPROVE	DISAPPROVE	DK	N	
Oct 1945	10	87	3	1548	AIPO359T
Mar 1977	36	62	2	1526	GSS
WOMEN					
Oct 1945	10	88	2	796	AIPO359T
Mar 1977	34	64	2	835	GSS
MEN					
Oct 1945	10	86	5	741	AIPO359T
Mar 1977	38	60	2	691	GSS

Table 11.3   Can a Working Mother Establish a Warm
Relationship with Her Children?--1977-1988

FECHLD--Now I'm going to read several more statements. As I
read each one, please tell me whether you strongly agree,
agree, disagree, or strongly disagree with it. For example,
here is the statment

A working mother can establish just as warm and
secure a relationship with her children as a mother
who does not work.

	STRONGLY AGREE	AGREE	DISAGREE	STRONGLY DISAGREE	DK	N	
Mar 1977	15	33	33	17	1	1527	GSS
Mar 1985	21	39	29	10	1	1529	GSS
Mar 1986	22	40	30	8	1	1469	GSS
Mar 1988	24	39	27	9	1	986	GSS
WOMEN							
Mar 1977	21	33	28	17	1	835	GSS
Mar 1985	28	39	24	8	1	843	GSS
Mar 1986	27	40	24	8	0	848	GSS
Mar 1988	29	40	22	8	1	548	GSS
MEN							
Mar 1977	9	32	40	18	2	692	GSS
Mar 1985	13	39	34	13	1	686	GSS
Mar 1986	15	40	37	7	1	621	GSS
Mar 1988	17	38	34	10	1	438	GSS

Table 11.4   Should a Wife Help Her Husband's Career First?--
1977-1988

FEHELP--Now I'm going to read...tell me whether you strongly
agree, agree, disagree, or strongly disagree with it [the
statement].

It is more important for a wife to help her
husband's career than to have one herself.

	STRONGLY AGREE	AGREE	DISAGREE	STRONGLY DISAGREE	DK	N	
Mar 1977	13	42	35	6	3	1524	GSS
Mar 1985	6	30	44	16	4	1527	GSS
Mar 1986	6	29	46	16	2	1469	GSS
Mar 1988	5	26	47	20	2	987	GSS
WOMEN							
Mar 1977	15	44	31	7	3	834	GSS
Mar 1985	7	30	41	20	3	842	GSS
Mar 1986	7	30	44	18	1	848	GSS
Mar 1988	4	24	45	24	2	549	GSS
MEN							
Mar 1977	12	39	40	5	4	690	GSS
Mar 1985	6	30	49	11	4	685	GSS
Mar 1986	5	28	50	14	3	621	GSS
Mar 1988	6	27	50	15	2	438	GSS

Table 11.5 Does a Preschool Child Suffer if the Mother
              Works?--1977-1988

FEPRESCH--Now I'm going to read...tell me whether you
strongly agree, agree, disagree, or strongly disagree with
it [the statement].

A preschool child is likely to suffer if his or
her mother works.

	STRONGLY AGREE	AGREE	DISAGREE	STRONGLY DISAGREE	DK	N	
Mar 1977	20	46	28	4	2	1526	GSS
Mar 1985	13	40	36	10	2	1527	GSS
Mar 1986	11	40	39	9	2	1469	GSS
Mar 1988	10	37	40	11	2	984	GSS
WOMEN							
Mar 1977	19	43	31	6	2	834	GSS
Mar 1985	11	35	38	14	2	843	GSS
Mar 1986	11	35	41	11	1	848	GSS
Mar 1988	11	32	43	14	1	546	GSS
MEN							
Mar 1977	22	49	23	3	2	692	GSS
Mar 1985	15	47	32	4	2	684	GSS
Mar 1986	10	46	36	6	2	621	GSS
Mar 1988	10	43	36	7	3	438	GSS

Table 11.6   Is It Better if a Man Works and a Woman Tends
                 the Home?--1977-1988

FEFAM--Now I'm going to read...tell me whether you strongly
agree, agree, disagree, or strongly disagree with it [the
statement].

It is much better for everyone involved if the man is
the achiever outside the home and the woman takes
care of the home and family.

	STRONGLY AGREE	AGREE	DISAGREE	STRONGLY DISAGREE	DK	N	
Mar 1977	18	47	28	6	2	1526	GSS
Mar 1985	10	38	38	13	2	1528	GSS
Mar 1986	9	38	39	12	2	1468	GSS
Mar 1988	9	32	41	16	2	983	GSS
WOMEN							
Mar 1977	17	45	28	8	1	835	GSS
Mar 1985	9	37	35	17	1	843	GSS
Mar 1986	11	36	37	15	1	847	GSS
Mar 1988	8	31	41	19	2	548	GSS
MEN							
Mar 1977	19	49	27	4	2	691	GSS
Mar 1985	10	39	40	8	2	685	GSS
Mar 1986	7	40	42	9	2	621	GSS
Mar 1988	11	34	40	13	2	435	GSS

Table 11.7   Should Women Leave Running the Country up to
Men?--1974-1988

FEHOME--Do you agree or disagree with this statement: Women
should take care of running their homes and leave running
the country up to men.

	AGREE	DISAGREE	NOT SURE	N	
Mar 1974	34	62	4	1484	GSS
Mar 1975	35	63	3	1488	GSS
Mar 1977	37	60	2	1528	GSS
Mar 1978	31	66	3	1530	GSS
Mar 1982	26	71	3	1506	GSS
Mar 1983	22	74	3	1594	GSS
Mar 1985	26	72	2	1529	GSS
Mar 1986	23	74	3	1467	GSS
Mar 1988	20	76	4	984	GSS

WOMEN

	AGREE	DISAGREE	NOT SURE	N	
Mar 1974	34	63	3	793	GSS
Mar 1975	35	62	3	819	GSS
Mar 1977	38	60	2	835	GSS
Mar 1978	32	66	3	888	GSS
Mar 1982	26	72	2	867	GSS
Mar 1983	23	74	3	905	GSS
Mar 1985	27	71	2	843	GSS
Mar 1986	25	71	3	847	GSS
Mar 1988	20	77	3	546	GSS

MEN

	AGREE	DISAGREE	NOT SURE	N	
Mar 1974	35	61	5	691	GSS
Mar 1975	34	63	3	669	GSS
Mar 1977	36	60	3	693	GSS
Mar 1978	30	66	4	642	GSS
Mar 1982	26	71	3	639	GSS
Mar 1983	22	74	4	689	GSS
Mar 1985	24	73	2	686	GSS
Mar 1986	21	77	3	620	GSS
Mar 1988	21	75	4	438	GSS

Table 11.8 Are Men Better Suited Emotionally for Politics?
--1974-1988

FEPOL--Tell me if you agree or disagree with this statement:
Most men are better suited emotionally for politics than are
most women.

	AGREE	DISAGREE	NOT SURE	N	
Aut 1974	44	52	4	1012	SRCOMNI
Mar 1974	44	49	7	752	GSS
Mar 1975	48	48	4	1488	GSS
Mar 1977	47	48	5	1529	GSS
Mar 1978	42	54	4	1530	GSS
Mar 1982	35	59	6	743	GSS
Mar 1983	34	62	4	1589	GSS
Mar 1985	37	59	4	1524	GSS
Mar 1986	36	60	3	1466	GSS
Mar 1988	32	64	4	984	GSS
WOMEN					
Mar 1974	44	51	5	400	GSS
Mar 1975	51	47	2	820	GSS
Mar 1977	48	50	3	836	GSS
Mar 1978	44	53	3	889	GSS
Mar 1982	35	60	5	332	GSS
Mar 1983	33	65	2	901	GSS
Mar 1985	38	59	4	840	GSS
Mar 1986	38	59	3	846	GSS
Mar 1988	30	68	2	547	GSS
MEN					
Mar 1974	43	47	10	352	GSS
Mar 1975	44	50	6	668	GSS
Mar 1977	46	46	8	693	GSS
Mar 1978	39	56	6	641	GSS
Mar 1982	36	57	7	411	GSS
Mar 1983	36	58	6	688	GSS
Mar 1985	36	60	4	684	GSS
Mar 1986	33	62	5	620	GSS
Mar 1988	35	60	6	437	GSS

Table 11.9   Are Men or Women Better Suited Emotionally for
             Politics?--1974-1982

FEPOLY--Would you say that most men are better suited emotionally for politics than are most women, that men and
women are equally suited, or that women are better suited
than men in this area?

	MEN	EQUAL	WOMEN	DK	N	
Mar 1974	33	62	4	2	730	GSS
Aut 1974	38	55	5	2	488	SRCOMNI
Mar 1982	24	69	5	2	755	GSS

12

Work

Work is probably the focus of more interviews than any other topic--at least if one counts the 50,000 plus monthly interviews used to determine the federal unemployment level and other workforce statistics (Bregger, 1984). In addition, occupation is a standard demographic item included in countless surveys on other topics. The time series in this chapter are therefore but a narrow, though significant, slice of the overall material on occupations. In one way or other, most of the items touch on job satisfaction.

The first item (Table 12.1) asks very directly whether respondents are satisfied with their job. If there is any trend toward dissatisfaction in an overall sense, it is not apparent in these figures. The same result, based on a slightly different but equally long time series, is reported elsewhere (Tausky, 1984, p. 97; see also Chelte, Wright, and Tausky, 1982).

It is widely recognized, however, that global questions fail to capture the complex feelings that individuals have about their work (Hall, 1986, pp. 90-91; Rothman, 1987, p. 233), and some other studies show declining satisfaction (e.g., Glenn and Weaver, 1982). Indeed, insofar as one's financial situation is tied closely to one's work, the second item (Table 12.2) suggests a somewhat different interpretation of jobs and rewards in the 1970s and 1980s. When compared with the 1960s, satisfaction with one's financial situation has declined ten to fifteen percentage points, with most of the change occurring by the late 1960s or early 1970s. Ironically, over the same thirty-year period, there is no change in the percentages saying that their financial situations worsened (12.3), and the numbers considering themselves to have above and below average incomes remained steady (12.4).

A major consideration in research on job satisfaction is the matter of worker or occupational characteristics that lead to satisfaction (Rothman, 1987, chap. 10). Job components are often divided into internal and external features. The next six items deal with both kinds of attributes.

Tables 12.5-12.18 inquire about job rewards and related characteristics. The first of these (12.5) is rather indirect, asking about work generally and not necessarily about one's current job. There is little pattern, but if anything, the movement is upward; there is no evidence here of increasing dissatisfaction with the current world of work. Tables 12.6-12.8 suggest that even in the relatively short span of the last fifteen years there have been changes in the way people view their jobs. In the 1970s there was more emphasis on short working hours, though it was a truly important characteristics for few workers. High income shows the opposite pattern--important to many workers and increasing slightly in importance between 1973 and the present. Job security--surprisingly in light of large job layoffs in recent years--has not become more (or less) important.

Characteristics of occupations themselves have long been studied as the assembly line created jobs consisting of narrow, routine tasks (Herzberg, 1966). In the past fifteen years, there has been little change in the perceived importance of chances for improvement or of a feeling of accomplishment (12.9-12.10).

Given the economic upheavals of recent years, it is somewhat surprising that individuals report only small changes in actual employment. There is a very small rise in the percentage citing personal unemployment in the past ten years (12.11) and no trend at all in the percentage reporting that a close relative was unemployed during the past five years (12.12). There is a greater change in the number of relatives cited as unemployed (12.13), but the short time period covered makes it difficult to interpret. Equally significant, however, may be changes in fear of unemployment. There are wide fluctuations in anticipated job losses (12.14), probably as a result of business cycles. While there is no trend since 1973, there was evidently a large drop during the previous four years in the extent to which people felt they could replace their current job with one of equal pay (12.15).

Table 12.16 records the declining membership in labor unions over the past fifteen years.

A recent controversy is whether the middle class in America is shrinking. Relative poverty of single-parent (especially female-headed) families, a felt need for both spouses to work in order to maintain a high standard of living, the rising cost of housing, making it especially difficult for first-time buyers, and what is alleged to be a growing disparity between the wealth of rich and "average" families, are cited as evidence that middle Americans are being squeezed out (*Time*, 8/10/88).

In "objective" terms, such as the proportion of the population that falls within certain "middle" incomes—there is some evidence that the middle class is indeed declining (Horrigan and Haugen, 1988). But if such a phenomenon is occurring, it is not yet apparent in people's self-classifications (Table 12.17). Fluctuations in the results of pre-1950s polls make trend-spotting somewhat difficult; some of the high figures in the 1940s may be the result of polls' biases, but it may also be that optimism in the immediate post-World War II years led an unusual number to call themselves middle or even upper class. In any event, the self-reported middle class seems to have been at its nadir in the late 1940s and early 1950s. The 1960s witnessed a more than 10 percent increase. Since then there has been little change, but the most recent measurements in no way indicate a declining middle class.

The results of an alternative wording (12.17) are too few to draw conclusions about trends, but they do indicate that individuals in the broad middle class do not see themselves as an undifferentiated mass. One can speculate that there will be no rapid decline in the percentage of those calling themselves middle class, but that there may be some changes of feeling about one's place within that broad classification.

REFERENCES

Bregger, John E.   1984.   The Current Population Survey: A Historical Perspective and BLS' Role. *Monthly Labor Review*, 107(6):8-14.

Chelte, Anthony F., James Wright, and Curt Tausky. 1982. Did Job Satisfaction Really Drop during the 1970s? *Monthly Labor Review*, 105 (11):33-36.

Glenn, Norval, and Charles N. Weaver. 1982. Enjoyment of Work by Full-Time Workers in the U.S., 1955 and 1980. *Public Opinion Quarterly*, 46:459-470.

Hall, Richard H. 1986. *Dimensions of Work*. Beverly Hills, CA: Sage.

Herzberg, Frederick. 1966. *Work and the Nature of Man*. Cleveland: World.

Horrigan, Michael W., and Steven E. Haugen. 1988. The Declining Middle-Class Thesis: A Senstivity Analysis. *Monthly Labor Review*, 111(5):3-12.

Rothman, Robert A. 1987. *Working: Sociological Perspectives*. Englewood Cliffs, NJ: Prentice-Hall.

Tausky, Curt. 1984. *Work and Society*. Itasca, IL: Peacock.

Table 12.1 How Satisfied Are You with Your Job?--1962-1988

SATJOB--On the whole, how satisfied are you with the work you do--would you say you are very satisfied, moderately satisfied, a little dissatisfied, or very dissatisfied?

	VERY SATIS- FIED	MODER- ATELY SATIS- FIED	A LITTLE DISSAT- ISFIED	VERY DISSAT- ISFIED	DK	N	
Jun 1962[a]	46	36	12	5	0	1025	NORC447
Mar 1972[b]	48	37	11	3	0	947	GSS
Mar 1973	49	38	8	4	0	1143	GSS
Mar 1974	48	37	10	5	0	1228	GSS
Mar 1975[c]	54	33	9	4	0	1168	GSS
Mar 1976[c]	52	34	9	4	0	1188	GSS
Mar 1977	48	39	10	3	0	1263	GSS
Mar 1978	51	36	8	5	0	1281	GSS
Mar 1980	47	36	13	5	0	1247	GSS
Mar 1982	47	38	10	6	-	1224	GSS
Mar 1983	49	37	9	5	-	1333	GSS
Mar 1984	46	35	12	7	-	1208	GSS
Mar 1985	48	38	10	4	0	1237	GSS
Mar 1986	49	39	9	3	0	1163	GSS
Mar 1987	44	38	13	4	-	1465	GSS
Mar 1988	46	39	10	4	0	1155	GSS

[a]How satisfied are you with your job?

[b]Not asked of those keeping house.

[c]Not asked of those "unemployed, laid off, looking for work."

Table 12.2   How Satisfied Are You with Your Financial
              Situation?--1956-1988

SATFIN--We are interested in how people are getting along
financially these days. So far as you and your family are
concerned, would you say that you are pretty well satisfied
with your present financial situation, more or less satisfied, or not satisfied at all?

	PRETTY WELL SATISFIED	MORE OR LESS SATISFIED	NOT AT ALL SATISFIED	DK	N	
Aut 1956	42	40	19	0	1750	ELEC56
Aut 1958	40	40	20	0	1832	ELEC58
Aut 1960	37	40	23	0	1922	ELEC60
Aut 1964	45	40	15	0	1559	ELEC64
Mar 1972	32	45	23	0	1609	GSS
Mar 1973	31	45	24	0	1502	GSS
Mar 1974	31	46	23	0	1480	GSS
Mar 1975	31	42	27	0	1483	GSS
Mar 1976	31	46	23	0	1496	GSS
Mar 1977	34	44	22	0	1524	GSS
Mar 1978	34	42	24	0	1531	GSS
Mar 1980	28	44	27	0	1466	GSS
Mar 1982	26	46	28	0	1501	GSS
Mar 1983	29	41	30	0	1597	GSS
Mar 1984	28	46	26	0	1467	GSS
Mar 1985	30	44	26	0	1530	GSS
Mar 1986	30	43	27	0	1469	GSS
Mar 1987	30	48	22	0	1463	GSS
Mar 1988	30	45	24	0	1477	GSS

Table 12.3 Has Your Financial Situation Changed?--1956-1988

FINALTER--During the last few years, has your financial situation been getting better, worse, or has it stayed the
same?

	BETTER	STAYED SAME	WORSE	DK	N	
Aut 1956	38	43	18	0	1752	ELEC56
Aut 1958	34	44	21	0	1834	ELEC58
Aut 1960	35	45	19	0	1917	ELEC60
Aut 1964	45	40	15	0	1563	ELEC64
Mar 1972	43	38	18	1	1598	GSS
Mar 1973	42	41	16	0	1463	GSS
Mar 1974	39	39	22	0	1478	GSS
Mar 1975	35	36	28	0	1485	GSS
Mar 1976	36	41	23	0	1496	GSS
Mar 1977	38	40	22	0	1524	GSS
Mar 1978	41	40	19	0	1531	GSS
Mar 1980	34	40	25	0	1464	GSS
Mar 1982	31	39	29	0	1502	GSS
Mar 1983	35	37	27	1	1587	GSS
Mar 1984	39	39	22	0	1465	GSS
Mar 1985	39	40	22	0	1531	GSS
Mar 1986	40	38	21	0	1464	GSS
Mar 1987	40	41	19	0	1461	GSS
Mar 1988	40	41	18	0	1477	GSS

Table 12.4 Is Your Family Income Above or Below Average?--1972-1988

FINRELA--Compared with American families in general, would you say your family income is far below average, below average, average, above average, or far above average?

	FAR BELOW AVERAGE	BELOW AVERAGE	AVERAGE	ABOVE AVERAGE	FAR ABOVE AVERAGE	DK	N	
Mar 1972	4	22	57	16	1	1	1608	GSS
Mar 1973	4	19	58	17	1	1	1504	GSS
Mar 1974	4	21	56	18	1	0	1480	GSS
Mar 1975	4	23	52	18	1	1	1487	GSS
Mar 1976	4	25	55	15	1	1	1496	GSS
Mar 1977	5	24	51	18	2	1	1525	GSS
Mar 1978	5	22	53	18	2	1	1532	GSS
Mar 1980	5	23	52	17	2	1	1465	GSS
Mar 1982	5	26	51	16	1	1	1500	GSS
Mar 1983	6	23	49	18	2	1	1595	GSS
Mar 1984	5	24	51	18	1	1	1469	GSS
Mar 1985	6	23	51	18	2	1	1531	GSS
Mar 1986	6	24	49	18	2	1	1469	GSS
Mar 1987	5	24	49	20	1	1	1462	GSS
Mar 1988	4	23	52	18	2	1	1478	GSS

Table 12.5   If You Were Rich, Would You Continue Working?--
1973-1988

RICHWORK--If you were to get enough money to live as com-
fortably as you would like for the rest of your life, would
you continue to work or would you stop working?

	CONTINUE WORKING	STOP WORKING	DK	N	
Mar 1973	68	30	1	831	GSS
Mar 1974	64	35	2	837	GSS
Mar 1976[a]	68	31	1	757	GSS
Mar 1977	69	30	1	954	GSS
Mar 1980	76	23	1	886	GSS
Mar 1982	72	27	1	946	GSS
Mar 1984	75	24	1	955	GSS
Mar 1985	69	30	1	988	GSS
Mar 1987	74	25	1	967	GSS
Mar 1988	70	29	1	626	GSS

[a]Note asked of those "unemployed, laid off, looking for
work."

Table 12.6   Is High Income an Important Job Characteristic?
--1973-1988

JOBINC--Would you please look at this card and tell me which
one thing on this list you would most prefer in a job?   (b)
Which comes next?   (c)   Which is third most important?   (d)
Which is fourth most important?

High income.

	IMPORTANCE						
	MOST	SECOND	THIRD	FOURTH	FIFTH	N	
Mar 1973	19	24	31	20	7	1462	GSS
Mar 1974	19	21	31	21	9	1454	GSS
Mar 1976	20	22	32	19	5	1449	GSS
Mar 1977	21	24	31	18	6	1480	GSS
Mar 1980	20	27	32	16	5	1436	GSS
Mar 1982	26	25	26	17	5	719	GSS
Mar 1984	19	25	33	19	4	1441	GSS
Mar 1985	19	26	31	20	4	1500	GSS
Mar 1987	22	26	31	15	6	1430	GSS
Mar 1988	21	24	33	17	5	946	GSS

Table 12.7   Is Job Security an Important Job
              Characteristic?--1973-1988

JOBSEC--Would you...<u>fourth</u> most important?

     No danger of being fired.

IMPORTANCE

	MOST	SECOND	THIRD	FOURTH	FIFTH	N	
Mar 1973	7	14	20	30	29	1462	GSS
Mar 1974	8	11	20	29	33	1454	GSS
Mar 1976	8	15	20	32	26	1449	GSS
Mar 1977	8	14	22	32	24	1480	GSS
Mar 1980	6	12	17	34	31	1436	GSS
Mar 1982	10	18	23	29	21	719	GSS
Mar 1984	8	13	20	36	24	1441	GSS
Mar 1985	7	11	21	35	26	1500	GSS
Mar 1987	6	11	20	33	29	1430	GSS
Mar 1988	7	14	20	32	28	946	GSS

Table 12.8   Are Short Working Hours an Important Job
              Characteristic?--1973-1988

JOBHOUR--Would you...<u>fourth</u> most important?

     Working hours are short, lots of free time.

IMPORTANCE

	MOST	SECOND	THIRD	FOURTH	FIFTH	N	
Mar 1973	5	10	13	25	47	1462	GSS
Mar 1974	5	11	14	27	43	1454	GSS
Mar 1976	4	9	12	22	52	1449	GSS
Mar 1977	4	8	11	25	52	1480	GSS
Mar 1980	3	8	11	26	52	1436	GSS
Mar 1982	3	8	15	20	54	719	GSS
Mar 1984	3	7	10	22	59	1441	GSS
Mar 1985	3	7	10	21	59	1500	GSS
Mar 1987	4	8	10	27	52	1430	GSS
Mar 1988	3	8	10	26	52	946	GSS

Table 12.9   Are Chances for Advancement an Important Job Characteristic?--1973-1988

JOBPROMO--Would you...<u>fourth</u> most important?

Chances for advancement.

	IMPORTANCE						
	MOST	SECOND	THIRD	FOURTH	FIFTH	N	
Mar 1973	18	35	23	13	10	1462	GSS
Mar 1974	18	38	23	13	8	1454	GSS
Mar 1976	18	37	21	15	10	1449	GSS
Mar 1977	20	34	23	14	9	1480	GSS
Mar 1980	19	35	25	14	7	1436	GSS
Mar 1982	17	31	21	21	10	719	GSS
Mar 1984	19	36	24	14	7	1441	GSS
Mar 1985	22	36	23	13	6	1500	GSS
Mar 1987	18	36	24	16	7	1430	GSS
Mar 1988	20	34	23	14	8	946	GSS

Table 12.10   Is a Feeling of Accomplishment an Important Job Characteristic?--1973-1988

JOBMEANS--Would you...<u>fourth</u> most important?

Work important and gives a feeling of accomplishment.

	IMPORTANCE						
	MOST	SECOND	THIRD	FOURTH	FIFTH	N	
Mar 1973	52	16	13	12	8	1462	GSS
Mar 1974	51	19	13	10	7	1454	GSS
Mar 1976	50	17	14	12	7	1449	GSS
Mar 1977	47	19	13	12	8	1480	GSS
Mar 1980	52	18	15	10	5	1436	GSS
Mar 1982	43	18	15	14	10	719	GSS
Mar 1984	51	19	14	10	6	1441	GSS
Mar 1985	48	20	16	11	5	1500	GSS
Mar 1987	50	19	15	10	6	1430	GSS
Mar 1988	49	20	13	11	7	946	GSS

Table 12.11   Have You Been Unemployed in the Last Ten
Years?--1973-1988

UNEMP--At any time during the last ten years, have you been
unemployed and looking for work for as long as a month?

	YES	NO	DK	N	
Mar 1973	28	72	-	1503	GSS
Mar 1974	26	74	-	1482	GSS
Mar 1975	28	72	-	1479	GSS
Mar 1976	28	72	0	1499	GSS
Mar 1977	28	72	-	1527	GSS
Mar 1978	29	71	0	1532	GSS
Mar 1980	28	72	-	1468	GSS
Mar 1983	34	66	0	1596	GSS
Mar 1984	33	67	0	1469	GSS
Mar 1986	30	70	0	1467	GSS
Mar 1988	31	68	0	995	GSS

Table 12.12   Have Close Relatives Been Unemployed During the
Past Five Years?--1978-1987

UNEMP5--At any time during the years [last five years], were
any of the people listed on this card unemployed and looking
for work for as long as a month?

	YES	NO	N	
Mar 1978	22	78	1525	GSS
Mar 1980	21	79	1464	GSS
Mar 1983	26	75	1589	GSS
Mar 1984	25	75	1457	GSS
Mar 1986	22	78	1461	GSS
Mar 1987	23	77	1455	GSS

NOTE--Listed on the card were: husband or wife, father,
mother, father- or mother-in-law, child, child's husband or
wife, brother or sister, brother- or sister-in-law.

Table 12.13 How Many of Your Relatives Were Unemployed
During the Last Year?----1978-1984

UNREL1--a. Number of relatives unemployed during last year.

	0	1	2	3	4	5	N	
Mar 1978	72	23	4	0	0	-	1532	GSS
Mar 1980	73	23	4	1	0	-	1468	GSS
Mar 1983	60	30	8	2	1	0	1599	GSS
Mar 1984	65	27	6	1	0	-	1473	GSS

NOTE--Relatives are listed in Table 12.12.

Table 12.14 How Likely Are You to Lose Your Job?--1975-1988

JOBLOSE--Thinking about the next 12 months, how likely do
you think it is that you will lose your job or be laid off--
very likely, fairly likely, not too likely, or not at all
likely?

FOR THOSE WHO ARE EMPLOYED--Base for the percentages is
those currently working full- or part-time or temporarily
not working due to illness, vacation, or strike.

	VERY LIKELY	FAIRLY LIKELY	NOT TOO LIKELY	NOT LIKELY	DK	N	
Jan 1975	6	9	23	59	4	1004	AIPO922
Oct 1976	5	7	20	64	4	841	AIPO960
Mar 1977	4	6	24	64	2	912	GSS
Mar 1978	4	4	20	71	1	889	GSS
Nov 1979	3	8	18	66	4	894	AIPO
May 1980	6	8	24	60	2	800	AIPO
Jan 1982	5	10	25	57	3	798	AIPO
Mar 1982	7	6	26	60	2	879	GSS
Jun 1982	7	7	28	54	4	812	AIPO
Nov 1982	9	9	28	49	4	1540	AIPO
Mar 1983	6	8	25	60	2	940	GSS
Apr 1983	8	8	26	55	4	800	AIPO
Mar 1985	7	4	23	65	1	942	GSS
Mar 1986	4	7	22	66	2	869	GSS
Mar 1988	4	4	25	66	1	617	GSS

Table 12.15   Could You Find a Job Equal to the One You
Have?--1969-1988

FOR THOSE WHO ARE EMPLOYED--Base for the percentages is
those working 20 or more hours a week.

JOBFIND--About how easy would it be for you to find a job
with another employer with approximately the same income and
fringe benefits you now have? Would you say very easy,
somewhat easy, or not easy at all?

	VERY EASY	SOMEWHAT EASY	NOT EASY	DK	N	
Nov 1969[a]	40	29	30		1301	SRCQEMP
Jan 1973[a]	27	36	37		1887	SRCQEMP
Mar 1977	27	30	42	2	909	GSS
Mar 1978	28	32	38	2	888	GSS
Mar 1982	22	26	50	3	876	GSS
Mar 1983	19	29	50	2	940	GSS
Mar 1985	25	31	42	2	940	GSS
Mar 1986	27	32	39	2	870	GSS
Mar 1988	28	36	34	2	615	GSS

[a]DK not reported.

Table 12.16   Do You or Your Spouse Belong to a Labor Union?
--1973-1988

UNION--Do you (or your [spouse]) belong to a labor union?
(Who?)

	RESPOND- ENT BELONGS	SPOUSE BELONGS	R AND SPOUSE BELONG	NEITHER BELONGS	DK	N	
Mar 1973	15	10	3	72	–	1495	GSS
Mar 1975	14	10	2	74	–	1484	GSS
Mar 1976	15	8	2	75	0	1483	GSS
Mar 1978	14	8	2	77	–	1531	GSS
Mar 1980	13	7	1	78	0	1464	GSS
Mar 1983	12	7	2	80	0	1597	GSS
Mar 1984	14	5	2	79	0	1459	GSS
Mar 1985	15	4	1	81	–	663	GSS
Mar 1986	9	6	2	83	–	1465	GSS
Mar 1987	13	5	2	80	–	1456	GSS
Mar 1988	12	5	1	82	–	996	GSS

Table 12.17 Which Social Class Do You Belong To?--1945-1988

CLASS--If you were asked to use one of four names for your social class, which would you say you belong in: the lower class, the working class, the middle class, or the upper class?

	LOWER CLASS	WORKING CLASS	MIDDLE CLASS	UPPER CLASS	NO CLASS	DK	N	
Jul 1945	1	50	45	3	1		1144	OPOR52
Feb 1946a	5	52	36	4	3		2820	AIPO365-C
Mar 1947a	4	43	45	6	3		2930	AIPO393
Feb 1948a	4	52	48	6	0		1583	AIPO412K
Jun 1949	3	60	32	2	-	3	1283	NORC166DU-1
Aug 1949	2	61	32	3	-	2	1232	NORC168DU-1
Mar 1950	1	59	35	3	-	2	1270	NORC276-270
Sep 1952a	6	56	36	3	-	-	3051	AIPO502
Aut 1952	2	59	36	2	0	1	1762	ELEC52
Dec 1963	3	49	45	2	0	1	1526	SRS330
Nov 1963	2	48	44	3	-	2	1345	SRS350
Feb 1966	3	47	44	2	2	2	1495	SRS876
Jun 1969a	3	50	42	2	3	2	1545	AIPO783
Mar 1972	6	47	44	2	-	-	1604	GSS
Mar 1973	4	48	46	3	-	-	748	GSS
Mar 1974	4	47	46	3	-	-	1475	GSS
Mar 1975	5	48	44	3	-	-	1483	GSS
Mar 1976	4	46	48	2	-	0	1493	GSS
Mar 1977	4	49	43	4	0	0	1519	GSS
Mar 1978	4	42	49	3	2	1	1466	NORC4269
Mar 1978	5	47	45	2	-	0	1529	GSS
Mar 1980	5	46	45	3	-	0	1463	GSS
Mar 1982	5	48	44	3	-	0	1499	GSS
Mar 1983	6	47	44	4	-	-	799	GSS
Mar 1984	5	46	46	3	-	-	1462	GSS
Mar 1985	4	45	47	4	-	-	1529	GSS
Mar 1986	6	43	47	3	-	0	1462	GSS
Mar 1987	5	43	47	4	-	1	1460	GSS
Mar 1988	5	45	47	2	-	0	1480	GSS

a"....: the middle class, the lower class, the working class, or upper class?"

Table 12.18 Which Social Class Do You Belong To?--1964-1973

CLASSY--If you had to pick one, which of the five social classes would you say you belong in: upper class, upper-middle class, middle class, working class, or lower class?

	LOWER CLASS	WORKING CLASS	MIDDLE CLASS	UPPER MIDDLE CLASS	UPPER CLASS	NO CLASS	DK	N	
May 1964	2	34	44	17	2	1	0	920	NORC466
Oct 1964	3	37	45	11	2	-	2	1966	SRS760
Jun 1965	2	33	46	14	3	1	1	506	NORC466
Jun 1965	1	36	46	13	3	1	1	1440	SRS857
Dec 1965	3	42	40	9	2	2	2	1433	SRS870
Mar 1973[a]	4	41	41	11	2	0	0	745	GSS

[a]order of classes reversed.

249

13

Religion

Two great, contradictory myths surround religion in contemporary America. The first is that secularization is rapidly and inevitably changing America from a religious nation into a secular state. This myth emerges from early sociological theorizing about how modernization in general and science and education in particular would undermine the superstitious and tribal basis of religion (Hammond, 1985; Hadden, 1987; Wuthnow, 1976). The second holds that America is undergoing a great, religious revival. It is asserted that the televangelists and political preachers like Jerry Falwell and his Moral Majority are not only reviving that old time religion, but also successfully placing the goals of the New Christian Right at the top of the political agenda (Kelley, 1972; Mueller, 1983; Yinger and Cutler, 1982).

Survey data question both of these popular interpretations. Available data cover basic beliefs about God and an afterlife back to the 1940s and religious behaviors such as prayer, church attendance, and religious affiliation over the last two decades. In addition two key items closely related to Fundamentalism and the New Christian Right, belief in Bible inerrancy and attitudes toward school prayers, can be followed from the mid-1960s to the present.

Overall, the main pattern that emerges is not one of major change, but of basic stability. Religious beliefs, behaviors, and preferences have have not undergone striking shifts, but rather have been part of America's bedrock culture (Greeley, forthcoming). Belief in God has been in the mid to upper 90s for the last forty years (Table 13.1) and faith in an afterlife has been around 75 percent in both the 1940s and the 1980s (with a slight dip to the upper 60s in the 1970s) (Table 13.8).

Religious behaviors have also shown basic consistency. During the 1970s and 1980s a little over half reported that they prayed daily (Table 13.5), and around 30 percent attended church weekly (13.3). Similarly, while there has been some slow changes in religious preference (Smith, 1988), the balance of major religions has not undergone any major alteration (13.2).

The Fundamentalization of American politics notion is also on the shaky ground. Support for the Supreme Court's ruling against mandatory school prayers increased moderately from the 1960s to the early 1980s (13.9) while belief in the inerrancy of the Bible fell from the 1960s to the 1980s (13.6). The possible impact of the recent activism of the Fundamentalists appears in the recent levelling off of support for the separation of church and state in the public schools and in belief in Bible inerrancy. In both cases however the levelling off follows a swing away from Fundamentalism and shows no clear sign of a reversal back toward religious conservativism (Smith, 1988).

REFERENCES

Greeley, Andrew. Forthcoming. *Religious Indicators*, 1935–1985. Cambridge: Harvard University Press.

Hadden, Jeffrey K. 1987. Towards Desacralizing Secularization Theory. *Social Forces*, 65:587–611.

Hammond, Phillip E., ed. 1985. *The Sacred in a Secular Age*. Berkeley: University of California Press.

Kelley, Dean M. 1972. *Why Conservative Churches Are Growing: A Study in Sociology of Religion*. New York: Harper and Row.

Mueller, Carol. 1983. In Search of a Constituency for "The New Religious Right." *Public Opinion Quarterly*, 46:213–229.

Smith, Tom W. 1988. Counting Flocks and Lost Sheep: Trends in Religious Preference Since World War II, GSS Social Change Report No. 26. Chicago: National Opinion Research Center.

Wuthnow, Robert. 1976. Recent Pattern of Secularization: A Problem of Generations? *American Sociological Review*, 41:850–867.

Yinger, J. Milton and Stephen J. Cutler. 1982. The Moral Majority Viewed Sociologically. *Sociological Focus*, 15: 289–306.

Table 13.1   Do You Believe in God?--1944-1986

Do you believe in God?

	YES	NO	DK	N	
Nov 1944[a]	97	1	2	2520	AIPO335
Nov 1947[b]	94	3	2	2970	AIPO407
Jun 1952[c]	99	1	0	2987	BG
Mar 1953	98	1	0	1597	AIPO513
Nov 1954[d]	98	1	1	1459	AIPO539
Nov 1965[c,e]	96	2	2	4734	POS671
Aug 1967[c]	98	2	0	3138	AIPO750
1981[f]	95	2	3	1729	AIPOCARA
Mar 1986	95	3	1	1148	ABC/WP

[a]Do you, personally, believe in a God?

[b]Do you, personally, believe in God?

[c]Do you believe in a God?

[d]Do you, yourself, believe in God?

[e]Includes some qualified answers.

[f]Which, if any, of the following do you believe in...God?

Table 13.2   What is Your Religious Preference?--1972-1988

RELIG--What is your religious preference? Is it Protestant, Catholic, Jewish, some other religion, or no religion?

	PROTEST-ANT	CATHOLIC	JEWISH	NONE	OTHER	N	
Mar 1972	64	26	3	5	2	1608	GSS
Mar 1973	63	26	3	6	2	1500	GSS
Mar 1974	64	25	3	7	1	1483	GSS
Mar 1975	66	24	2	8	1	1488	GSS
Mar 1976	64	26	2	8	1	1497	GSS
Mar 1977	66	24	2	6	1	1523	GSS
Mar 1978	64	25	2	8	1	1528	GSS
Mar 1980	64	25	2	7	2	1465	GSS
Mar 1982	65	24	2	7	1	1498	GSS
Mar 1983	61	28	3	7	2	1595	GSS
Mar 1984	64	26	2	7	1	1461	GSS
Mar 1985	62	27	2	7	2	1529	GSS
Mar 1986	63	26	3	7	2	1467	GSS
Mar 1987	65	24	1	7	2	1460	GSS
Mar 1988	61	26	2	8	3	1480	GSS

Table 13.3   How Often Do You Attend Religious Services?--1972-1988

ATTEND--How often do you attend religious services?

	NEVER	LESS THAN ONCE A YEAR	ABOUT 1-2 A YEAR	SEVERAL TIMES A YEAR	ABOUT ONCE A MONTH	2-3 TIMES A MONTH	NEARLY EVERY WEEK	EVERY WEEK	SEVERAL TIMES A WEEK	N	
Mar 1972	9	10	11	14	7	9	6	28	6	1600	GSS
Mar 1973	13	8	14	15	6	8	8	20	7	1495	GSS
Mar 1974	12	7	16	13	8	9	6	22	8	1481	GSS
Mar 1975	14	7	13	14	7	9	7	22	7	1487	GSS
Mar 1976	13	9	14	16	7	7	6	20	9	1492	GSS
Mar 1977	14	8	13	14	7	9	6	21	8	1521	GSS
Mar 1978	15	9	13	13	7	9	7	19	8	1527	GSS
Mar 1980	11	7	15	16	7	8	6	21	7	1462	GSS
Mar 1982	14	7	15	15	7	8	6	20	8	1495	GSS
Mar 1983	14	8	13	12	6	10	6	23	9	1595	GSS
Mar 1984	13	7	12	14	8	8	6	23	9	1460	GSS
Mar 1985	14	7	15	12	7	7	5	25	8	1530	GSS
Mar 1986	14	7	12	12	8	10	6	23	9	1466	GSS
Mar 1987	12	7	14	16	8	10	5	20	8	1454	GSS
Mar 1988	17	7	11	13	8	10	7	19	7	1478	GSS

Table 13.4   How Strong Is Your Religious Affiliation?--
                 1974-1988

RELITEN--Would you call yourself a strong (PREFERENCE NAMED)
or not a very strong (PREFERENCE NAMED)?

IF YOU HAVE A RELIGIOUS PREFERENCE (see Table 13.2)--Base
for the percentages is those with any religious preference.

	STRONG	SOMEWHAT STRONG	NOT VERY STRONG	DK	N	
Mar 1974	43	8	49	1	1373	GSS
Mar 1975	43	11	46	0	1361	GSS
Mar 1976	39	14	46	1	1361	GSS
Mar 1977	41	8	50	0	1414	GSS
Mar 1978	39	8	52	1	1406	GSS
Mar 1980	42	10	48	1	1347	GSS
Mar 1982	43	9	48	0	1360	GSS
Mar 1983	44	7	49	0	1463	GSS
Mar 1984	49	8	42	1	1345	GSS
Mar 1985	44	10	46	1	1379	GSS
Mar 1986	43	11	46	0	1267	GSS
Mar 1987	43	11	45	1	1339	GSS
Mar 1988	42	12	46	0	1202	GSS

Table 13.5 How Often Do You Pray?--1952-1988

PRAY--About how often do you pray? (Categories used as probes.)

	SEVERAL TIMES A DAY	ONCE A DAY	SEVERAL TIMES A WEEK	ONCE A WEEK	LESS THAN ONCE A WEEK	NEVER	DK	N	
Nov 1972	27	27	13	7	21	4	-	1347	NORC5046
Mar 1983	25	30	13	8	20	4	0	1580	GSS
Mar 1984	28	29	14	7	20	1	0	1449	GSS
Mar 1985	27	31	13	8	20	1	-	1511	GSS
Mar 1987	25	31	14	9	20	1	-	1438	GSS
Mar 1988	24	30	16	8	22	0	0	1473	GSS

Do you ever pray to God? [IF YES] About how many times
would you say you prayed during the last 7 days?

	DAILY OR MORE	N	
Jun 1952	81	2987	BG
Nov 1965	71	2783	POS671
Apr 1978	55	1510	GO77121
Jan 1985	60	1528	AIPO249G

256

Table 13.6   What Do You Believe about the Bible?--1963-1988

BIBLE--Which [one] of these statements comes closest to de-
scribing your feelings about the Bible?

   The Bible is the actual word of God and is to be taken
   literally, word for word.

   The Bible is the inspired word of God but not
   everything in it should be taken literally, word for
   word.

   The Bible is an ancient book of fables, legends,
   history, and moral precepts recorded by men.

	WORD OF GOD	INSPIRED WORD	BOOK OF FABLES	OTHER AND DK	N	
1963	65	18	11	6	c1500	AIPO
Aug 1976	37	45	13	5	1553	AIPO958
Apr 1978	37	46	11	6	1523	AGO77121
Aug 1980	39	44	9	8	1538	AIPO160G
Aug 1980	40	45	9	6	1600	AIPO161G
Dec 1981	37	42	11	10	1483	AIPO187G
May 1983	37	44	12	8	1540	AIPO214G
Mar 1984	38	47	14	2	976	GSS
Sep 1984	37	46	12	5	1590	AIPO243G
Nov 1984	40	41	12	7	1509	AIPO245G
Mar 1985	36	49	13	2	746	GSS
Mar 1986[a]	35	49	15	1	1148	ABC/WP
Mar 1987	37	46	15	2	955	GSS
Aug 1987	37	49	11	3	2040	LAT
Mar 1988	34	47	16	3	1478	GSS

AGE:18-24				OTHER	DK		
Mar 1984	37	46	14	2	2	112	GSS
Mar 1985	35	45	20	-	-	49	GSS
Mar 1987	32	53	12	-	3	108	GSS
Mar 1988	36	41	21	1	1	170	GSS

AGE:25-29							
Mar 1984	35	49	15	-	2	121	GSS
Mar 1985	27	53	16	-	4	90	GSS
Mar 1987	30	48	20	-	1	114	GSS
Mar 1988	25	57	15	1	2	186	GSS

AGE:30-49							
Mar 1984	32	50	17	0	1	385	GSS
Mar 1985	29	55	14	0	1	286	GSS
Mar 1987	35	47	17	1	0	401	GSS
Mar 1988	30	49	18	0	2	577	GSS

Table 13.6 (Continued)

	WORD OF GOD	INSPIRED WORD	BOOK OF FABLES	OTHER	DK	N	
AGE:50-64							
Mar 1984	40	45	14	—	1	174	GSS
Mar 1985	43	45	10	—	1	171	GSS
Mar 1987	40	46	12	—	2	169	GSS
Mar 1988	35	47	14	1	3	249	GSS
AGE:65+							
Mar 1984	50	42	6	1	2	179	GSS
Mar 1985	48	40	8	1	3	147	GSS
Mar 1987	48	36	14	1	1	162	GSS
Mar 1988	45	40	12	1	2	292	GSS

[a]"...and moral perceptions [sic]...."

NOTE--"Other" and "DK" were not coded separately in non-GSS studies.

Table 13.7 What Do You Believe about the Bible?--1964-1987

BIBLEY--Here are four statements about the Bible, and I'd like you to tell me which is closest to your own view.

The Bible is God's Word and all it says is true.

The Bible was written by men inspired by god, but it contains some human errors.

The Bible is a good book because it was written by wise men, but God had nothing to do with it.

The Bible was written by men who lived so long ago that it is worth very little today.

	GOD'S WORD	INSPIRED BY GOD	WRITTEN BY MAN	NOT WORTH MUCH	OTHER	DK	N	
Aut 1964	51	41	3	1	-	3	1450	ELEC64
Aut 1968	52	38	6	2	0	3	1538	ELEC68
Sum 1978	37	46	11	0	6		1523	G077121
Aut 1980	46	42	6	2	0	3	1394	ELEC80
Aut 1984	48	40	6	2	1	2	1902	ELEC84
Mar 1984	46	45	6	2	1	1	479	GSS
Mar 1985	44	48	5	1	1	1	770	GSS
Aut 1986	49	39	6	2	1	2	2159	ELEC86
Mar 1987	44	46	7	1	0	1	489	GSS
AGE:18-24								
Mar 1984	40	55	3	2	-	-	95	GSS
Mar 1985	44	44	9	1	1	1	107	GSS
Mar 1987	40	47	6	4	2	-	47	GSS

Table 13.7 (Continued)

	GOD'S WORD	INSPIRED BY GOD	WRITTEN BY MAN	NOT WORTH MUCH	OTHER	DK	N	
AGE:25-29								
Mar 1984	43	51	5	2	-	-	63	GSS
Mar 1985	39	54	4	1	1	1	100	GSS
Mar 1987	28	64	4	2	-	2	47	GSS
AGE:30-49								
Mar 1984	37	52	5	2	2	2	168	GSS
Mar 1985	40	52	5	1	1	1	271	GSS
Mar 1987	41	49	8	1	-	1	202	GSS
AGE:50-64								
Mar 1984	61	28	8	1	-	1	88	GSS
Mar 1985	45	47	4	1	1	1	154	GSS
Mar 1987	49	44	4	1	1	-	88	GSS
AGE:65+								
Mar 1984	58	28	9	3	-	2	65	GSS
Mar 1985	56	37	4	1	1	2	134	GSS
Mar 1987	57	35	7	-	-	2	104	GSS

Table 13.8   Do You Believe There is a Life after Death?--
1944-1988

POSTLIFE--Do you believe there is a life after death?

	YES	NO	DK	N	
Nov 1944	76	13	10	2528	AIPO335
Jun 1952[a]	77	7	16	2987	BG
Mar 1957[b]	74	13	12	1618	AIPO580
Mar 1960[b]	74	14	12	2977	AIPO625
May 1961[c]	74	14	12	1500	AIPOSP
Nov 1965[a]	75	10	15	2783	APOS671
Jun 1968[d]	73	19	8	1536	AIPO764
Mar 1973	70	21	9	1504	GSS
Mar 1975	67	23	10	1488	GSS
Mar 1975[c]	69	20	11	c1500	AIPO
Mar 1976	72	20	8	1498	GSS
Feb 1978[d]	62	33	4	1553	AIPO994
Mar 1978	70	21	9	1529	GSS
Apr 1978	72	14	14	1523	AGO77121
Mar 1980	73	17	10	1462	GSS
1980[e]	67	27	6	c1500	AIPO
1981[d]	71	17	13	1729	AIPOCARA
Mar 1983	68	24	7	1595	GSS
Mar 1984	73	19	8	1463	GSS
Mar 1986	76	17	7	1467	GSS
Mar 1987	72	20	8	1459	GSS
Mar 1988	74	19	7	1480	GSS

AGE:18-24

	YES	NO	DK	N	
Mar 1973	64	27	8	213	GSS
Mar 1975	63	28	9	215	GSS
Mar 1976	65	26	9	203	GSS
Mar 1978	60	28	12	204	GSS
Mar 1980	74	17	10	193	GSS
Mar 1983	69	24	6	163	GSS
Mar 1984	72	21	7	208	GSS
Mar 1986	78	27	5	136	GSS
Mar 1987	66	28	6	155	GSS
Mar 1988	72	21	7	170	GSS

AGE:25-29

	YES	NO	DK	N	
Mar 1973	70	20	9	169	GSS
Mar 1975	68	21	10	190	GSS
Mar 1976	71	21	8	184	GSS
Mar 1978	71	22	7	203	GSS
Mar 1980	70	22	7	162	GSS
Mar 1983	70	23	7	251	GSS
Mar 1984	74	17	9	185	GSS
Mar 1986	80	13	6	190	GSS
Mar 1987	78	14	7	163	GSS
Mar 1988	73	18	9	186	GSS

Table 13.8 (Continued)

	YES	NO	DK	N	
AGE:30-49					
Mar 1973	69	22	9	542	GSS
Mar 1975	70	20	10	511	GSS
Mar 1976	74	18	8	498	GSS
Mar 1978	70	22	8	550	GSS
Mar 1980	74	15	10	528	GSS
Mar 1983	71	22	7	591	GSS
Mar 1984	73	19	7	552	GSS
Mar 1986	76	17	6	584	GSS
Mar 1987	74	18	8	606	GSS
Mar 1988	76	18	6	578	GSS
AGE:50-64					
Mar 1973	70	21	9	358	GSS
Mar 1975	65	24	10	316	GSS
Mar 1976	71	20	9	340	GSS
Mar 1978	77	16	8	312	GSS
Mar 1980	73	20	8	303	GSS
Mar 1983	65	27	8	318	GSS
Mar 1984	75	18	7	265	GSS
Mar 1986	76	18	5	266	GSS
Mar 1987	73	21	6	262	GSS
Mar 1988	72	19	9	249	GSS
AGE:65+					
Mar 1973	75	13	12	217	GSS
Mar 1975	68	23	10	251	GSS
Mar 1976	75	18	8	267	GSS
Mar 1978	68	21	11	254	GSS
Mar 1980	73	14	12	267	GSS
Mar 1983	61	29	10	265	GSS
Mar 1984	74	18	8	249	GSS
Mar 1986	72	17	12	284	GSS
Mar 1987	68	22	10	270	GSS
Mar 1988	72	20	7	293	GSS

[a]Do you think your soul will live on after death?

[b]Do you believe there is or is not life after death?

[c]Do you believe in life after death?

[d]Which of the following do you believe in...life after death?

[e]Do you believe in life after death or not?

Table 13.9   Do You Approve of Required Prayers in Public
Schools?--1971-1988

PRAYER--The United States Supreme Court has ruled that no
state or local government may require the reading of the
Lord's Prayer or Bible verses in public schools. What are
your views on this--do you approve or disapprove of the
court ruling?

	APPROVE	DISAP-PROVE	DK	N	
Oct 1971[a]	28	67	6	1494	AIPO838
Mar 1974	31	66	3	750	GSS
Mar 1975	35	62	3	1487	GSS
Mar 1977	33	64	2	1527	GSS
Mar 1982	37	60	3	1503	GSS
Mar 1983	40	57	4	1595	GSS
Mar 1985	43	54	3	1530	GSS
Mar 1986	37	61	2	723	GSS
Mar 1988	37	59	4	986	GSS
AGE:18-24					
Mar 1974	50	46	4	98	GSS
Mar 1975	48	46	6	215	GSS
Mar 1977	51	48	1	192	GSS
Mar 1982	49	44	7	179	GSS
Mar 1983	52	44	4	164	GSS
Mar 1985	54	46	1	156	GSS
Mar 1986	54	43	3	68	GSS
Mar 1988	53	45	3	114	GSS
AGE:25-29					
Mar 1974	38	59	3	92	GSS
Mar 1975	46	52	3	190	GSS
Mar 1977	51	47	3	176	GSS
Mar 1982	44	54	1	215	GSS
Mar 1983	51	44	5	251	GSS
Mar 1985	59	38	3	193	GSS
Mar 1986	40	57	3	88	GSS
Mar 1988	43	52	5	130	GSS
AGE:30-49					
Mar 1974	28	68	4	253	GSS
Mar 1975	33	64	2	510	GSS
Mar 1977	31	67	2	558	GSS
Mar 1982	37	62	1	509	GSS
Mar 1983	40	58	3	587	GSS
Mar 1985	45	51	4	559	GSS
Mar 1986	44	56	0	286	GSS
Mar 1988	41	56	3	388	GSS

Table 13.9 (Continued)

	APPROVE	DISAP-PROVE	DK	N	
AGE:50-64					
Mar 1974	25	74	1	167	GSS
Mar 1975	31	67	2	317	GSS
Mar 1977	26	72	2	364	GSS
Mar 1982	33	65	2	313	GSS
Mar 1983	35	62	3	319	GSS
Mar 1985	35	62	3	330	GSS
Mar 1986	24	74	2	127	GSS
Mar 1988	31	64	5	155	GSS
AGE:65+					
Mar 1974	26	71	2	136	GSS
Mar 1975	27	71	2	250	GSS
Mar 1977	22	74	4	230	GSS
Mar 1982	30	66	3	275	GSS
Mar 1983	26	68	6	267	GSS
Mar 1985	33	64	3	285	GSS
Mar 1986	26	72	2	150	GSS
Mar 1988	23	74	4	198	GSS

[a]...do you approve or disapprove of this?

14

Family

The American family is undergoing rapid transition, including movement from one major family type--husband, full-time
housewife, several children--to a multiplicity of family
structures (Levitan and Belous, 1981; Glick, 1984), greater
participation of women in the labor force, even those with
young children (Davis, 1984), and declining fertility rates
(Westoff and Ryder, 1977; Westoff, 1986). Most of these
changes have long-term components, extending back to at least
the nineteenth century, as well as short-term elements.
Survey evidence speaks more decisively to the latter, but
there is evidence about some relatively long-term changes as
well.

Ideal Number of Children
(from Table 14.1)

	0-2	3	4-7+			0-2	3	4-7+
Mar 1941	34	28	38		Mar 1972	44	24	25
Aug 1945	24	28	48		Jan 1973	54	25	22
Jan 1947	30	29	41		Feb 1974	55	25	19
Mar 1952	30	29	40		Mar 1974	48	24	19
May 1953	30	29	41		Mar 1975	52	24	17
Feb 1957	21	37	41		Mar 1976	57	20	16
Dec 1959	19	30	51		Feb 1977	61	25	15
Feb 1962	19	26	49		Mar 1977	52	23	19
May 1963	21	29	49		Mar 1978	54	24	17
Apr 1965	22	33	45		Mar 1982	59	20	17
Jan 1966	23	33	43		Mar 1983	55	24	15
Dec 1967	25	33	43		Mar 1985	60	22	15
Jan 1970	40	24	36		Mar 1986	55	25	16
Jan 1971	44	31	25		Mar 1988	55	26	15

Consider the matter of the ideal number of children in a family (see above, from Table 14.1). We sometimes think in terms of linear or at least unidirectional change. Families used to be big; now they are small. Yet attitudes captured since 1941 reveal a pattern of frequent "ups" and "downs," moving more or less in concert with fertility rates (Levitan and Belous, 1981, chap. 3). In 1941, perhaps as a result of the economic hardship of the Depression, a third of the respondents thought that two or fewer children were ideal. After an immediate postwar "blip," there was a steady but slightly higher plateau until the mid-1950s. Then came a decade of still higher ideal sizes. Primarily this was a shift in thinking that three rather than two children were ideal. But larger families were also valued; in 1959 a higher percentage saw five or more as ideal than in any other survey except that of August 1945.

The pattern changed again in the mid-1960s, with a small decline in the perceived value of four or more children and a slight rise in the value of only two offspring. Then, in a two-year period from the end of 1967 to the beginning of 1970, a change occurred that can only be described as dramatic. The combined effects of a rising divorce rate, a rising number of women in the labor force, inflation, environmental concerns, and fear of increasing crime and civil unrest resulted in a large, sudden decline in ideal family size. Additional change occurred in the next three years, so that between 1967 and 1973 the percentage thinking of two children as ideal had more than doubled and the percentage favoring four or more halved. In the last decade and a half attitudes have been relatively stable, though with a further slight decline in the number favoring four or more children.[1]

Judgments about desirable traits for children show little change over the 1973-1983 period (Tables 14.2-14.14). Three characteristics--success, obedience, and responsibility--appear to have become more valued, but the differences are all very slight. There was a significant drop in the importance of role behavior (acting like a boy or girl), all of the change occurring between 1973 and 1975.

If one takes a longer-term view, there is evidence of substantial change in child-rearing attitudes. The 1954 Stouffer study, referred to extensively in Chapter 5, included

---

[1]This is not an obvious subject for question-wording effects, yet the fact that the changes in the mid-1950s and in the late 1960s coincided with changes in the question form raise this possibility. Note, however, that the 1960s form, cited in footnote d in Table 14.1, was used again in 1971, and it reveals a continuation of the extraordinary change observed in 1970.

two questions about children that were repeated twenty years later. They show a sharp increase in the freedom that adults think should be accorded children (14.15-14.16). This change from an emphasis on obedience or conformity to one of automony or self-direction is consistent with changes observed between the late 1950s and early 1980s in Detroit (Alwin, 1984) and between the 1920s and 1970s in "Middletown" (Alwin, 1988; Bahr, 1980).

Substantial changes also occurred over a three-decade period in the frequency of and in attitudes toward divorce (Cherlin, 1981, chap. 2). The largest change occurred in the late 1960s or early 1970s; between 1968 and 1974 many came to feel that getting a divorce should not be so difficult (14.17). Since then, there has been a small redirection of attitudes--paralleling a stabilizing divorce rate (Levitan and Belous, chap. 2; Norton and Moorman, 1987)--as shown by the decline in the percentage thinking that divorces should be easier to obtain. Men have consistently favored easier divorces, but the difference was relatively small fifteen years ago and has declined since. Jews and those claiming no religious identification are more likely to favor easier divorces, but there are no differences between Protestants and Catholics.

The subject of divorce also provides an interesting question-wording effect that we have preserved in Table 14.17. When the status quo was an explicit response category, it was the most popular response in 1978 and presumably would be today. If that response is not made explicit, one would conclude that about a half of the current population favors making divorces more difficult, a considerable misrepresentation of popular sentiment.

Should older people live with their grown children? Table 14.18 shows a major turnabout since the 1950s, and here much of the change has occurred relatively recently. Insofar as we can tell, the 1950s represented the height of feeling that parents and grown children should live separately. By the early to mid-1970s there was increasing uncertainty about this position (the number of "depends" responses doubled), but the ratio of "bad idea" to "good idea" was still substantial. Change since then has altered the balance, so that more felt it was a good idea than a bad idea in four of the five post-1980 surveys.[2] One might expect strong differences by sex because women still bear major responsibility for work in the home. In fact, men are only slightly more favorable (usually

------

[2]The rather large year-to-year fluctuations since 1980 are methodological artifacts caused by the rotation design of recent GSS surveys (Smith, 1988).

3-5 percent), and the differences (not shown) are invariant across time.

Data about evenings spend with family and friends indicate a high degree of stability in recent decades (14.19-14.24). Whether one focuses on the general category of relatives or specifically on parents and siblings, or whether one asks about neighbors or more distant friends, there are no clear trends whatsoever despite measurement back to the turbulent 1960s.

REFERENCES

Alwin, Duane. 1984. Trends in Parental Socialization Values: Detroit, 1958-1983. *American Journal of Sociology*, 90: 359-382.

Alwin, Duane. 1988. From Obedience to Autonomy: Changes in Traits Desired in Children, 1924-1978. *Public Opinion Quarterly*, 52:33-52.

Bahr, Howard M. 1980. Changes in Family in Middletown, 1924-1977. *Public Opinion Quarterly*, 44:35-52.

Cherlin, Andrew J. 1981. *Marriage, Divorce, Remarriage*. Cambridge: Harvard University Press.

Davis, Kingsley. 1984. Wives and Work: The Sex Role Revolution and Its Consequences. *Population and Development Review*, 10:397-417.

Glick, Paul C. 1984. American Household Structure in Transition. *Family Planning Perspectives*, 16:205-211.

Levitan, Sar A., and Richard S. Belous. 1981. *What's Happening to the American Family*. Baltimore: Johns Hopkins University Press.

Norton, Arthur J,. and Jeanne E. Moorman. 1987. Current Trends in Marriage and Divorce among American Women. *Journal of Marriage and the Family*, 49:3-14.

Smith, Tom W. 1988. Timely Artifacts: A Review of Measurement Variation in the 1972-1988 GSS. GSS Methodological Report No. 56. Chicago: National Opinion Research Center.

Westoff, Charles F. 1986. Fertility in the United States. *Science*, 234:534-559.

Westoff, Charles F. and Norman B. Ryder. 1977. *The Contraceptive Revolution*. Princeton, NJ: Princeton University Press.

Table 14.1 What Is the Ideal Number of Children?--1941-1988

CHLDIDEL--What do you think is the ideal number of children for a family to have?

	0	1	2	3	4	5	6	7+	AS MANY AS WANT	N	
Mar 1941a	1	2	31	28	25	7	5	1		2822	AIPO233
Aug 1945b	1	1	22	28	32	9	5	2		2860	AIPO353
Jan 1947c	1	1	28	29	30	5	4	2		803	AIPO389
Mar 1952a	1	1	28	29	28	5	5	2		1977	AIPO488
May 1953a	1	1	28	29	29	7	3	2		1499	AIPO515
Feb 1957d	1	1	19	37	31	6	3	1		1376	AIPO578
Dec 1959d	0	1	18	30	35	8	6	2		1384	AIPO621
Feb 1962d	0	1	18	26	35	6	6	2	7	2768	AIPO655
May 1963d	0	1	20	29	35	7	5	2		3303	AIPO671
Apr 1965d	-	1	21	33	34	6	3	2		2997	AIPO709
Jan 1966d	-	1	22	33	34	4	4	1		2836	AIPO723
Dec 1967d	-	0	25	33	33	5	3	2		1433	AIPO755
Jan 1970a	0	1	39	24	24	6	4	2		1458	AIPO808
Jan 1971d	-	1	43	31	20	3	1	1		1348	AIPO821
Mar 1972	2	1	41	24	18	3	3	1	6	1552	GSS
Jan 1973d	2	2	50	25	16	3	1	2		1417	AIPO862
Feb 1974d	2	2	52	25	14	2	1	2		1423	AIPO890-91
Mar 1974	1	2	45	24	16	2	1	0	8	1444	GSS
Mar 1975	1	2	49	24	15	1	1	0	6	1444	GSS
Mar 1976	2	3	52	20	13	2	1	0	6	1461	GSS
Feb 1977d	2	2	57	25	11	2	1	1		1415	AIPO968
Mar 1977	1	2	49	23	15	2	1	1	6	1500	GSS
Mar 1978	1	2	51	24	13	2	1	1	6	1484	GSS
Mar 1982	1	3	55	20	13	2	1	1	5	1466	GSS
Mar 1983	1	2	52	24	13	1	1	0	6	1556	GSS
Mar 1985	1	3	56	22	11	2	1	1	4	1500	GSS
Mar 1986	1	2	52	25	13	2	1	0	5	1440	GSS
Mar 1988	2	2	51	26	12	2	1	0	5	968	GSS

Table 14.1 (Continued)

a What do you consider is the ideal size of a family--a husband and wife and how many children?
b How many children do you think should be in the family of ideal size?
c What do you think is the ideal number of children for married couples?
d What do you think is the ideal number of children for a family to have?

NOTE--"as many as want" was not a code category in most AIPO surveys.

Table 14.2 Is It Important or Unimportant that a Child Have Good Manners?--1973-1983

MANNERS--Which three qualities listed on this card would you say are the most desirable for a child to have? Which one of these three is the most desirable of all? All of the qualities listed on this card may be desirable, but could you tell me which three you consider least important ? And which one of these three is least important of all?

That he has good manners.

	MOST DESIRABLE OF ALL	AMONG THE THREE MOST DESIRABLE	NOT MENTION-ED	AMONG THE THREE LEAST DESIRABLE	LEAST DESIRABLE OF ALL	N	
Mar 1973	3	21	51	18	6	1500	GSS
Mar 1975	4	22	53	17	4	481	GSS
Mar 1976	3	19	54	19	5	1488	GSS
Mar 1978	3	22	55	16	3	1520	GSS
Mar 1980	4	19	55	18	3	489	GSS
Mar 1983	3	22	53	18	4	1579	GSS

NOTE--In Tables 14.2-14.14, there were two respondents in 1978 and 1 in 1980 who were DK.

Table 14.3 Is It Important or Unimportant that a Child Tries Hard to Succeed?--1973-1983

SUCCESS--Which three qualities...least important of all?

That he tries hard to succeed.

	MOST DESIRABLE OF ALL	AMONG THE THREE MOST DESIRABLE	NOT MENTION-ED	AMONG THE THREE LEAST DESIRABLE	LEAST DESIRABLE OF ALL	N	
Mar 1973	2	11	59	21	7	1500	GSS
Mar 1975	2	10	64	20	4	1481	GSS
Mar 1976	3	10	62	20	5	1490	GSS
Mar 1978	3	12	58	23	5	1520	GSS
Mar 1980	4	12	62	17	4	489	GSS
Mar 1983	3	12	63	18	4	1579	GSS

Table 14.4 Is It Important or Unimportant that a Child Is Honest?--1973-1983

HONEST--Which three qualities...least important of all?

That he is honest.

	MOST DESIRABLE OF ALL	AMONG THE THREE MOST DESIRABLE	NOT MENTION-ED	AMONG THE THREE LEAST DESIRABLE	LEAST DESIRABLE OF ALL	N	
Mar 1973	36	29	33	1	1	1500	GSS
Mar 1975	39	31	28	1	0	1481	GSS
Mar 1976	38	29	31	1	0	1490	GSS
Mar 1978	38	31	30	1	0	1520	GSS
Mar 1980	40	27	31	1	1	489	GSS
Mar 1983	36	32	30	1	0	1579	GSS

Table 14.5 Is It Important or Unimportant that a Child Is Neat and Clean?--1973-1983

CLEAN--Which three qualities...least important of all?

That he is neat and clean.

	MOST DESIRABLE OF ALL	AMONG THE THREE MOST DESIRABLE	NOT MENTION-ED	AMONG THE THREE LEAST DESIRABLE	LEAST DESIRABLE OF ALL	N	
Mar 1973	1	8	55	23	13	1500	GSS
Mar 1975	1	7	55	25	12	1480	GSS
Mar 1976	1	7	54	26	14	1489	GSS
Mar 1978	1	8	56	23	12	1520	GSS
Mar 1980	0	6	54	26	14	489	GSS
Mar 1983	1	6	52	27	14	1579	GSS

Table 14.6 Is It Important or Unimportant that a Child Has Good Sense and Sound Judgment?--1973-1983

JUDGMENT--Which three qualities...least important of all?

That he has good sense and sound judgment.

	MOST DESIRABLE OF ALL	AMONG THE THREE MOST DESIRABLE	NOT MENTION-ED	AMONG THE THREE LEAST DESIRABLE	LEAST DESIRABLE OF ALL	N	
Mar 1973	18	20	55	7	1	1500	GSS
Mar 1975	15	19	59	6	1	1481	GSS
Mar 1976	19	20	52	6	2	1490	GSS
Mar 1978	16	21	55	7	1	1520	GSS
Mar 1980	16	25	52	5	1	489	GSS
Mar 1983	18	19	55	7	1	1579	GSS

Table 14.7 Is It Important or Unimportant that a Child Has Self-Control?--1973-1983

CONTROL--Which three qualities...least important of all?

That he has self-control.

	MOST DESIRABLE OF ALL	AMONG THE THREE MOST DESIRABLE	NOT MENTION- ED	AMONG THE THREE LEAST DESIRABLE	LEAST DESIRABLE OF ALL	N	
Mar 1973	3	15	69	12	2	1500	GSS
Mar 1975	4	15	71	8	2	1480	GSS
Mar 1976	3	15	70	11	2	1490	GSS
Mar 1978	3	16	71	8	2	1520	GSS
Mar 1980	3	12	72	12	2	489	GSS
Mar 1983	3	12	75	8	2	1579	GSS

Table 14.8 Is It Important or Unimportant that a Child Acts Like a Boy (or Girl)?--1973-1983

ROLE--Which three qualities...least important of all?

That he acts like a boy (she acts like a girl).

	MOST DESIRABLE OF ALL	AMONG THE THREE MOST DESIRABLE	NOT MENTION- ED	AMONG THE THREE LEAST DESIRABLE	LEAST DESIRABLE OF ALL	N	
Mar 1973	1	4	41	22	32	1500	GSS
Mar 1975	0	4	31	23	42	1481	GSS
Mar 1976	1	4	32	23	41	1490	GSS
Mar 1978	1	3	29	23	45	1520	GSS
Mar 1980	0	2	32	22	43	489	GSS
Mar 1983	1	2	30	24	43	1579	GSS

Table 14.9 Is It Important or Unimportant that a Child Gets Along Well with Other Children?-- 1973-1983

AMICABLE--Which three qualities...least important of all?

That he gets along well with other children.

	MOST DESIRABLE OF ALL	AMONG THE THREE MOST DESIRABLE	NOT MENTION-ED	AMONG THE THREE LEAST DESIRABLE	LEAST DESIRABLE OF ALL	N	
Mar 1973	2	14	68	12	4	1500	GSS
Mar 1975	2	12	71	12	3	1480	GSS
Mar 1976	1	12	72	11	3	1489	GSS
Mar 1978	2	9	74	11	4	1520	GSS
Mar 1980	2	12	69	14	2	489	GSS
Mar 1983	2	9	76	11	3	1579	GSS

Table 14.10 Is It Important or Unimportant that a Child Obeys His Parents Well?--1973-1983

OBEYS--Which three qualities...least important of all?

That he obeys his parents well.

	MOST DESIRABLE OF ALL	AMONG THE THREE MOST DESIRABLE	NOT MENTION-ED	AMONG THE THREE LEAST DESIRABLE	LEAST DESIRABLE OF ALL	N	
Mar 1973	13	14	65	7	1	1500	GSS
Mar 1975	15	19	60	6	1	1481	GSS
Mar 1976	14	16	64	6	0	1490	GSS
Mar 1978	15	16	63	5	1	1520	GSS
Mar 1980	10	18	64	6	2	489	GSS
Mar 1983	16	18	60	6	0	1579	GSS

Table 14.11 Is It Important or Unimportant that a Child Is Responsible?--1973-1983

RESPONSI--Which three qualities...least important of all?

That he is responsible.

	MOST DESIRABLE OF ALL	AMONG THE THREE MOST DESIRABLE	NOT MENTION- ED	AMONG THE THREE LEAST DESIRABLE	LEAST DESIRABLE OF ALL	N	
Mar 1973	8	23	62	6	2	1500	GSS
Mar 1975	8	24	61	6	1	1480	GSS
Mar 1976	7	26	59	6	2	1489	GSS
Mar 1978	8	25	60	6	1	1520	GSS
Mar 1980	9	25	62	2	1	489	GSS
Mar 1983	7	28	60	5	1	1579	GSS

Table 14.12 Is It Important or Unimportant that a Child Is Considerate of Others?--1973-1983

CONSIDER--Which three qualities...least important of all?

That he is considerate of others.

	MOST DESIRABLE OF ALL	AMONG THE THREE MOST DESIRABLE	NOT MENTION- ED	AMONG THE THREE LEAST DESIRABLE	LEAST DESIRABLE OF ALL	N	
Mar 1973	7	21	62	8	1	1500	GSS
Mar 1975	7	22	64	6	1	1481	GSS
Mar 1976	7	22	66	5	1	1490	GSS
Mar 1978	7	20	66	6	1	1520	GSS
Mar 1980	5	22	67	5	1	489	GSS
Mar 1983	8	22	65	4	1	1579	GSS

Table 14.13 Is It Important or Unimportant that a Child Is Interested in How and Why Things Happen?--1973-1983

INTEREST--Which three qualities...least important of all?

That he is interested in how and why things happen.

	MOST DESIRABLE OF ALL	AMONG THE THREE MOST DESIRABLE	NOT MENTION- ED	AMONG THE THREE LEAST DESIRABLE	LEAST DESIRABLE OF ALL	N	
Mar 1973	4	15	45	22	14	1500	GSS
Mar 1975	3	11	45	27	15	1480	GSS
Mar 1976	3	16	46	23	12	1489	GSS
Mar 1978	3	12	43	28	14	1520	GSS
Mar 1980	4	13	45	26	13	489	GSS
Mar 1983	2	11	41	29	16	1579	GSS

Table 14.14 Is It Important or Unimportant that a Child Is a Good Student?--1973-1983

STUDIOUS--Which three qualities...least important of all?

That he is a good student.

	MOST DESIRABLE OF ALL	AMONG THE THREE MOST DESIRABLE	NOT MENTION- ED	AMONG THE THREE LEAST DESIRABLE	LEAST DESIRABLE OF ALL	N	
Mar 1973	1	4	55	30	10	1500	GSS
Mar 1975	1	4	55	31	9	1481	GSS
Mar 1976	0	4	57	30	8	1490	GSS
Mar 1978	0	4	55	33	8	1520	GSS
Mar 1980	0	5	58	30	7	489	GSS
Mar 1983	1	5	56	30	8	1579	GSS

Table 14.15 Should a Child Be Made to Conform?--1954-1973

If a child is unusual in some way, his parents should get him to be more like other children.

	AGREE STRONGLY	AGREE	DISAGREE	DISAGREE STRONGLY	DK	N	
Jun 1954	9	48	32	5	7	4933	STOUFFER
Apr 1973	3	26	55	12	4	3540	NUNN

Table 14.16 Should a Child Be Allowed to Talk Back to Parents?--1954-1973

A child should never be allowed to talk back to parents, or else he will lose respect for them.

	AGREE STRONGLY	AGREE	DISAGREE	DISAGREE STRONGLY	DK	N	
Jun 1954	20	45	28	3	3	4933	STOUFFER
Apr 1973	13	38	43	5	2	3540	NUNN

Table 14.17   Should Divorces Be Made Easier to Obtain?--
1960-1988

DIVLAW--Should divorce in this country be easier or more
difficult to obtain than it is now?

	EASIER	STAY SAME	MORE DIF- FICULT	DK	N	
Jun 1968	18	15	60	7	1536	AIPO764
Mar 1974	32	21	42	5	1481	GSS
Mar 1975	29	20	46	5	1489	GSS
Mar 1976	27	18	50	5	1496	GSS
Mar 1977	29	18	48	5	1525	GSS
Mar 1978	27	27	42	4	1509	GSS
Mar 1982	22	21	51	6	1505	GSS
Mar 1983	24	19	52	5	1597	GSS
Mar 1985	23	19	53	4	1529	GSS
Mar 1986	27	18	52	4	1468	GSS
Mar 1988	24	22	48	5	982	GSS

WOMEN

	EASIER	STAY SAME	MORE DIF- FICULT	DK	N	
Mar 1974	29	23	44	4	792	GSS
Mar 1975	25	20	50	5	820	GSS
Mar 1976	26	19	50	6	829	GSS
Mar 1977	27	19	49	5	835	GSS
Mar 1978	24	29	43	4	871	GSS
Mar 1982	20	21	53	6	867	GSS
Mar 1983	22	20	54	4	907	GSS
Mar 1985	22	18	56	5	842	GSS
Mar 1986	25	17	54	4	848	GSS
Mar 1988	23	19	53	4	544	GSS

MEN

	EASIER	STAY SAME	MORE DIF- FICULT	DK	N	
Mar 1974	36	18	40	6	689	GSS
Mar 1975	33	20	42	5	669	GSS
Mar 1976	30	16	50	5	667	GSS
Mar 1977	32	16	47	5	690	GSS
Mar 1978	31	25	40	4	638	GSS
Mar 1982	26	20	48	6	638	GSS
Mar 1983	25	19	50	5	690	GSS
Mar 1985	25	21	50	4	687	GSS
Mar 1986	28	18	48	4	620	GSS
Mar 1988	26	26	42	6	438	GSS

PROTESTANT

	EASIER	STAY SAME	MORE DIF- FICULT	DK	N	
Mar 1974	29	22	44	4	951	GSS
Mar 1975	25	21	48	5	975	GSS
Mar 1976	23	17	44	5	950	GSS
Mar 1977	29	18	48	4	1003	GSS
Mar 1978	25	27	44	5	961	GSS

Table 14.17 (Continued)

	EASIER	STAY SAME	MORE DIF- FICULT	DK	N	
Mar 1982	21	20	54	5	967	GSS
Mar 1983	22	17	57	4	970	GSS
Mar 1985	22	18	54	4	954	GSS
Mar 1986	25	16	55	4	919	GSS
Mar 1988	22	21	51	6	595	GSS

CATHOLIC

Mar 1974	27	22	45	6	376	GSS
Mar 1975	26	20	51	4	362	GSS
Mar 1976	30	18	47	6	389	GSS
Mar 1977	23	15	58	4	371	GSS
Mar 1978	24	28	45	3	381	GSS
Mar 1982	20	20	54	6	365	GSS
Mar 1983	23	21	52	4	437	GSS
Mar 1985	20	19	57	3	406	GSS
Mar 1986	25	19	52	3	379	GSS
Mar 1988	24	21	51	4	257	GSS

JEWISH

Mar 1974	48	18	27	7	44	GSS
Mar 1975	48	9	35	9	23	GSS
Mar 1976	30	41	18	11	27	GSS
Mar 1977	41	15	41	3	34	GSS
Mar 1978	34	38	28	–	29	GSS
Mar 1982	22	32	35	11	37	GSS
Mar 1983	37	28	26	9	43	GSS
Mar 1985	28	16	44	12	32	GSS
Mar 1986	32	26	34	8	38	GSS
Mar 1988	35	35	20	10	20	GSS

NONE

Mar 1974	61	12	19	8	101	GSS
Mar 1975	58	19	21	2	113	GSS
Mar 1976	50	22	25	4	113	GSS
Mar 1977	50	19	20	10	93	GSS
Mar 1978	49	30	17	3	118	GSS
Mar 1982	36	32	25	7	109	GSS
Mar 1983	37	26	30	8	117	GSS
Mar 1985	34	21	32	3	109	GSS
Mar 1986	43	29	24	5	98	GSS
Mar 1988	39	26	29	6	85	GSS

NOTE--"Stay same" is a volunteered response.

Table 14.17 (Continued)

DIVLAWY--Should divorce in this country be easier to obtain, more difficult to obtain, or stay as it is now?

	EASIER	STAY SAME	MORE DIFFI-CULT	DK	N	
Feb 1960[a]	9	27	56	8	3122	AIPO624
Mar 1978	23	40	33	4	770	GSS
Dec 1985[b]	14	43	39	4	2308	LAT

[a]Should divorce be made more difficult to get, easier to get, or should things be left as they are now?

[b]Should divorce in this country be easier to obtain, or more difficult to obtain, or stay as it is now?

Table 14.18   Should Older People Live with Their Children?-- 1957-1988

AGED--As you know, many older people share a home with their grown children. Do you think this is generally a good idea or a bad idea?

	GOOD IDEA	DEPENDS	BAD IDEA	DK	N	
Oct 1957	28	7	64	1	2567	NORC383A
Mar 1973	31	11	58	1	1503	GSS
Mar 1975	31	15	53	1	1489	GSS
Mar 1976	36	14	48	1	1498	GSS
Mar 1978	35	17	48	0	1532	GSS
Mar 1980	40	15	43	1	1467	GSS
Mar 1983	43	15	42	0	1597	GSS
Mar 1984	50	13	36	1	1470	GSS
Mar 1986	40	12	47	1	1470	GSS
Mar 1987	50	14	35	1	1464	GSS
Mar 1988	44	14	41	1	995	GSS

Table 14.19 How Often Do You Spend an Evening with Your Relatives?--1964-1988

SOCREL--Would you use this card and tell me which answer comes closest to how often you do the following things

Spend a social evening with relatives?

	ALMOST DAILY	SEVERAL TIMES A WEEK	SEVERAL TIMES A MONTH	ONCE A MONTH	SEVERAL TIMES A YEAR	ONCE A YEAR	NEVER	N	
Oct 1964	5	31	17	17	15	7	8	1973	SRS760
Mar 1974	9	29	19	16	16	8	3	1482	GSS
Mar 1975	7	32	17	16	16	7	5	1488	GSS
Mar 1977	8	29	18	17	16	6	5	1526	GSS
Mar 1978	7	29	19	14	19	8	5	1526	GSS
Mar 1982	8	27	17	17	18	8	4	1497	GSS
Mar 1983	6	26	20	16	19	8	4	1594	GSS
Mar 1985	7	28	19	16	18	7	5	1526	GSS
Mar 1986	10	27	15	17	18	8	5	1464	GSS
Mar 1988	10	27	18	15	18	8	5	984	GSS

NOTE--In Tables 14.19-14.24, there were at most seven respondents in any one year who were DK (less than .5 percent) except for Table 14.22, 1964 (23, one percent), 1974 (18, one percent) and 1975 (10, .7 percent). DKs are excluded from the N.

Table 14.20 How Often Do You Spend an Evening with Neighbors?--1964-1988

SOCOMMUN--Would you...how often you do the following things

Spend a social evening with someone who lives in your neighborhood?

	ALMOST DAILY	SEVERAL TIMES A WEEK	SEVERAL TIMES A MONTH	ONCE A MONTH	SEVERAL TIMES A YEAR	ONCE A YEAR	NEVER	N	
Oct 1964	4	25	12	16	13	6	24	1969	SRS760
Mar 1974	7	23	13	17	11	6	22	1476	GSS
Mar 1975	6	22	13	15	12	8	24	1485	GSS
Mar 1977	6	22	12	16	13	8	24	1524	GSS
Mar 1978	6	23	11	12	13	9	25	1522	GSS
Mar 1982	6	19	12	17	13	10	22	1499	GSS
Mar 1983	6	20	12	14	12	9	26	1592	GSS
Mar 1985	6	18	13	14	13	11	26	1527	GSS
Mar 1986	7	21	11	15	11	9	26	1467	GSS
Mar 1988	5	21	11	15	13	7	28	984	GSS

Table 14.21 How Often Do You Spend an Evening with Friends?--1964-1988

SOCFREND--Would you...how often you do the following things

Spend a social evening with friends who live outside the neighborhood?

	ALMOST DAILY	SEVERAL TIMES A WEEK	SEVERAL TIMES A MONTH	ONCE A MONTH	SEVERAL TIMES A YEAR	ONCE A YEAR	NEVER	N	
Oct 1964	1	17	17	24	21	7	11	1967	SRS760
Mar 1974	2	20	18	22	18	8	11	1478	GSS
Mar 1975	3	18	17	23	18	8	12	1485	GSS
Mar 1977	3	19	20	22	19	7	10	1523	GSS
Mar 1978	2	19	21	16	21	9	12	1526	GSS
Mar 1982	3	18	21	22	19	7	9	1497	GSS
Mar 1983	3	19	21	22	18	6	11	1594	GSS
Mar 1985	3	19	20	21	18	9	10	1529	GSS
Mar 1986	2	20	18	23	20	5	12	1465	GSS
Mar 1988	3	18	21	24	19	6	10	986	GSS

283

Table 14.22 How Often Do You Go to a Bar or Tavern?--1964-1988

SOCBAR--Would you...how often you do the following things

Go to a bar or tavern?

	ALMOST DAILY	SEVERAL TIMES A WEEK	SEVERAL TIMES A MONTH	ONCE A MONTH	SEVERAL TIMES A YEAR	ONCE A YEAR	NEVER	N	
Oct 1964	2	9	4	7	10	10	58	1950	SRS760
Mar 1974	2	10	6	9	12	8	53	1462	GSS
Mar 1975	2	8	7	9	9	10	56	1476	GSS
Mar 1977	3	9	8	10	11	9	50	1525	GSS
Mar 1978	2	9	9	7	12	10	51	1528	GSS
Mar 1982	2	10	6	9	12	11	50	1495	GSS
Mar 1983	2	10	9	8	11	10	50	1593	GSS
Mar 1985	2	8	8	11	11	11	49	1529	GSS
Mar 1986	1	8	6	10	12	10	54	1463	GSS
Mar 1988	1	8	7	10	11	13	51	983	GSS

Table 14.23 How Often Do You Spend an Evening with Your Parents?--1978-1988

SOCPARS--Would you...how often you do the following things

Spend a social evening with your parents?

	NO SUCH PEOPLE	ALMOST DAILY	SEVERAL TIMES A WEEK	SEVERAL TIMES A MONTH	ONCE A MONTH	SEVERAL TIMES A YEAR	ONCE A YEAR	NEVER	N	
Mar 1978	36	3	14	11	7	13	8	7	1526	GSS
Mar 1982	30	7	15	9	12	11	7	9	88	GSS
Mar 1983	31	6	16	10	10	13	8	7	94	GSS
Mar 1985	31	6	11	13	10	12	9	7	27	GSS
Mar 1986	30	7	15	8	10	14	9	7	61	GSS
Mar 1988	25	7	14	9	10	14	8	13	973	GSS

Table 14.24 How Often Do You Spend an Evening with Siblings?--1978-1988

SOCSIBS--Would you...how often you do the following things

Spend a social evening with a brother or sister?

	NO SUCH PEOPLE	ALMOST DAILY	SEVERAL TIMES A WEEK	SEVERAL TIMES A MONTH	ONCE A MONTH	SEVERAL TIMES A YEAR	ONCE A YEAR	NEVER	N	
Mar 1978	11	5	14	12	11	22	16	10	1523	GSS
Mar 1982	9	6	13	12	14	22	15	8	1493	GSS
Mar 1983	11	4	14	13	13	22	13	10	1591	GSS
Mar 1985	9	5	11	15	13	21	17	10	1526	GSS
Mar 1986	8	6	13	11	14	22	16	10	1458	GSS
Mar 1988	8	6	14	11	13	22	15	11	974	GSS

15

Psychological Well-Being/Group Membership

Although social pundits, including President Jimmy Carter at one point, have concluded that the American people from time to time can collectively slump into a condition of malaise, ill-will, or *Westschmerz*, little sign of such notable lapses show up in available public opinion surveys. Chapter 4 suggests that the population's satisfaction with politics, politicians, and political institutions has waxed and waned somewhat over the decades, but questions asking about the respondents' satisfaction with life, marriage, and health, and about their human surroundings have for the most part been quite steady (Tables 15.1-15.9).

   Some of the data extend back into the 1960 and 1950s, but the bulk of it comes from the period since 1973. Quite a few things happened in that era: Watergate, the end of the Vietnam War, inflation, the hostage-taking in Iran, a rise of social concerns over some issues of gender and race, the AIDS epidemic, an economic recovery, the Reagan balm, the Iran-Contra scandal. Throughout, Americans became no more, or less, happy, and they registered happiness ratings at about the same level as in earlier decades (Table 15.1; for more extensive analyses, especially of the earlier period, see Gurin, Veroff, and Feld, 1960; Smith, 1979). Similarly, they said that their marriages were about the same as ever and professed to find no cosmic changes for the better or worse in their health (Tables 15.2, 15.3, 15.9). They found life no more nor less exciting (15.4), and got about the same amount of satisfaction from where they lived, their hobbies, family life, friendships (15.5-15.9), and their work (12.1).[1]

---

[1]A number of efforts have been made to develop sophisticated, multiple-item measures of well-being. See, for example, Andrews and Withey (1976), Campbell, Converse, and Rodgers (1976), and Campbell (1981).

Nor, by and large, have there been major shifts or notable trends in more atmospheric questions about the way things are going in today's world and about the general condition of society and of other human beings (15.10-15.18). However, a degree of cynicism about public officials grew in the 1970s and has receded somewhat since (15.14; compare Tables 4.1-4.3), and there does seem to have been a notable drop after the 1960s in the degree to which people think that other people can be trusted (15.17).

In general, then, data suggest that one should be very cautious about assuming that rises and falls of angst as expressed by political and social commentators reflect similiar trends in the daily thinking of the broad population. For an individual, happiness and discontent may change over time, but in the aggregate these shifts seem to cancel out.

The chapter also includes data about group memberships covering the twenty-year period after 1967 (15.19-15.34). The tables document some decline in the number of people who are members of fraternal groups (15.19), political clubs (15.22), labor unions (15.23), and school service groups (15.26). There has been a possible rise in memberships in sports clubs (15.24) and a quite notable rise (perhaps not entirely beneficial) in memberships in professional or academic societies (15.32).[2] Meanwhile, the popularity of hunting appears to be in decline (15.35).

On another issue, people report that they have been watching television and listening to radio about as much as ever (15.36, 15.37), but that they have been reading newspapers less often (15.38). Perhaps they never got the news of their various slumps into malaise.

REFERENCES

Andrews, Frank M., and Stephen B. Withey. 1976. *Social Indicators of Well-Being*. New York: Plenum.
Baumgartner, Frank, and Jack L. Walker. 1988. Survey Research and Membership in Voluntary Associations. *American Journal of Political Science*, 32:908-928.
Campbell, Angus. 1981. *The Sense of Well-Being in America*. New York: McGraw-Hill.

---

[2]A recent critique of the membership questions (Baumgartner and Walker, 1988) argues that they may have always underestimated group involvement but that underestimation has grown in recent years because of changes in the nature of voluntary organizations. (However, Baumgartner and Walker are in turn soundly criticized by Smith, 1989.) Variations in participation rates among standard demographic groups are documented in Curry (1980) and across the life cycle by Knoke and Thomson (1977).

Campbell, Angus, Philip E. Converse, and Willard E. Rodgers. 1976. *The Quality of American Life*. New York: Russell Sage.

Curry, James Patrick. 1980. Race, Sex, Socioeconomic Status and Participation in Voluntary Associations. Unpublished Ph.D. dissertation, University of Iowa.

Gurin, Gerald, Joseph Veroff, and Sheila Feld. 1960. *Americans View Their Mental Health*. New York: Basic Books.

Knoke, David, and Randall Thomson. 1977. Voluntary Association Membership Trends and the Family Life Cycle. *Social Forces*, 56:48-65.

Smith, Tom W. 1979. Happiness: Time Trends, Seasonal Variations, Intersurvey Differences, and Other Mysteries. *Social Psychology Quarterly*, 42:18-30.

_____. 1989. Trends in Voluntary Group Membership: Comments on Baumgartner and Walker. GSS Methodological Report No. 60. Chicago: National Opinion Research Center.

Table 15.1   How Happy Are You?--1957-1988

HAPPY--Taken all together, how would you say things are
these days--would you say that you are very happy, pretty
happy, or not too happy?

	VERY HAPPY	PRETTY HAPPY	NOT TOO HAPPY	N	
Spr 1957	35	54	11	2452	SRC422
May 1963	32	51	16	1501	NORC160
May 1964	38	48	14	1489	SRS630
Oct 1964	37	52	10	1967	SRS760
Jun 1965	30	53	17	1468	SRS857
Sum 1971	29	61	10	2164	SRC811
Aut 1972	22	67	11	1057	ELEC72
Nov 1972	27	60	14	1459	NORC5046
Mar 1972	30	53	17	1606	GSS
Spr 1972	26	65	9	1254	SRCOMNI
Mar 1973	36	51	13	1500	GSS
Apr 1973	33	54	13	719	CNS1
May 1973	33	55	12	647	CNS2
Jun 1973	33	50	17	642	CNS3
Jul 1973	30	53	18	615	CNS4
Aug 1973	31	51	19	639	CNS5
Sep 1973	29	55	16	630	CNS6
Oct 1973	32	54	14	681	CNS7
Nov 1973	29	55	16	696	CNS8
Jan 1974	23	57	20	692	CNS10
Feb 1974	28	57	15	610	CNS11
Mar 1974	38	49	13	1480	GSS
Mar 1974	33	55	13	656	CNS12
May 1974	27	55	18	693	CNS9
Mar 1975	33	54	13	1485	GSS
Jun 1975	32	50	18	581	NORC5059
Mar 1976	34	53	13	1499	GSS
Sum 1976	31	58	11	2207	SRCMH
Sep 1976	36	52	12	1313	NORC4239
Apr 1976	29	60	11	1520	SRCOMNI
Mar 1977	35	53	12	1527	GSS
Mar 1978	34	56	10	1517	GSS
Sum 1978	30	63	7	3647	SRCQOL
Mar 1980	34	53	13	1463	GSS
Mar 1982	33	54	13	1505	GSS
Mar 1983	31	56	13	1573	GSS
Mar 1984	35	52	13	1446	GSS
Mar 1985	29	60	11	1530	GSS
Mar 1986	32	56	11	1449	GSS
Mar 1987	32	56	12	1437	GSS
Mar 1988	34	57	9	1466	GSS

NOTE--There are virtually no DK responses to this question.

Table 15.2   How Happy Is Your Marriage?--1963-1988

IF CURRENTLY MARRIED (see Table 7.1)--Base for the percentages is those currently married.

HAPMAR--Taking things all together, how would you describe
your marriage? Would you say that your marriage is very
happy, pretty happy, or not too happy?

	VERY HAPPY	PRETTY HAPPY	NOT TOO HAPPY	N	
Jan 1963	64	32	4	1043	NORC458
Mar 1973	68	30	3	1073	GSS
Mar 1974	69	27	3	1061	GSS
Mar 1975	67	30	3	997	GSS
Mar 1976	67	31	2	973	GSS
Mar 1977	65	31	4	970	GSS
Mar 1978	65	32	3	955	GSS
Mar 1980	68	29	3	884	GSS
Mar 1982	65	31	3	849	GSS
Mar 1983	62	34	3	961	GSS
Mar 1984	66	31	3	825	GSS
Mar 1985	56	40	3	864	GSS
Mar 1986	63	33	3	820	GSS
Mar 1987	65	32	2	792	GSS
Mar 1988	62	34	3	787	GSS

NOTE--There are virtually no DK responses to this question.

Table 15.3   How Good is Your Health?--1940-1988

Would you say your health is good, fair, or poor?

	GOOD	FAIR	POOR	N	
Mar 1940	64	30	6	3137	AIPO186K
Mar 1941[a]	74	23	3	3118	AIPO233
Jul 1947[b]	64	31	5	2993	AIPO401
Jul 1950[c]	67	26	7	1355	AIPO457
Sep 1956[d]	65	28	7	1974	AIPO570

[a]In general, would you say your health is good, fair, or poor?

[b]Do you consider yourself to be in good, fair, or poor health now?

[c]What would you say is the state of your health in general--good, fair, or poor?

[d]As in note c except "rather poor" instead of "poor."

HEALTH--Would you say your own health, in general, is excellent, good, fair, or poor?

	EXCELLENT	GOOD	FAIR	POOR	N	
Jan 1957[a]	36	45	17	3	3227	POS397
Oct 1964[b]	36	40	19	5	1970	SRS760
Mar 1972	30	45	20	5	1612	GSS
Mar 1973	32	40	21	7	1501	GSS
Mar 1974	33	40	21	6	1480	GSS
Mar 1975	32	40	21	6	1489	GSS
Mar 1976	31	42	20	7	1499	GSS
Mar 1977	32	41	20	7	1527	GSS
Mar 1980	32	42	20	7	1466	GSS
Mar 1982	32	42	19	7	1505	GSS
Mar 1984	30	48	18	5	1462	GSS
Mar 1985	34	42	18	7	1531	GSS
Mar 1987	34	43	18	5	1465	GSS
Mar 1988	31	45	18	6	976	GSS

[a]Would you say that your own health is excellent, good, fair, or poor?

[b]Would you say your health is usually excellent, good, fair, or poor?

NOTE--There are virtually no DK responses to these questions.

Table 15.4 Do You Find Life Exciting or Dull?--1969-1988

LIFE--In general, do you find life exciting, pretty routine, or dull?

	EXCITING	ROUTINE	DULL	DK	N	
Sep 1969	48	42	8	2	1521	AIPO788
Mar 1973	45	49	5	0	1489	GSS
Mar 1974	43	52	5	1	1450	GSS
Mar 1976	44	51	4	4	1484	GSS
Mar 1977	44	49	7	0	1503	GSS
Mar 1980	46	48	6	0	1468	GSS
Mar 1982	45	49	6	1	1500	GSS
Mar 1984	47	48	5	0	1466	GSS
Mar 1985	48	45	6	1	1530	GSS
Mar 1987	45	50	4	0	1435	GSS
Mar 1988	45	50	5	1	957	GSS

Table 15.5 How Much Satisfaction Do You Get from the Place You Live?--1973-1988

SATCITY--For each area of life I am going to name, tell me the number that shows how much
satisfaction you get from that area.

The city or place you live in.

	VERY GREAT DEAL	GREAT DEAL	QUITE A BIT	A FAIR AMOUNT	SOME	A LITTLE	NONE	DK	N	
Mar 1973	23	24	17	22	6	5	3	0	1504	GSS
Mar 1974	20	27	17	23	7	4	2	0	1484	GSS
Mar 1975	21	29	15	20	6	5	3	0	1485	GSS
Mar 1976	20	30	17	21	7	4	2	0	1497	GSS
Mar 1977	19	28	17	22	6	6	2	0	1528	GSS
Mar 1978	17	30	19	20	7	5	3	0	1526	GSS
Mar 1980	24	31	15	18	6	4	2	0	1468	GSS
Mar 1982	15	25	20	24	8	5	2	0	1505	GSS
Mar 1983	16	31	18	21	7	5	2	0	1596	GSS
Mar 1984	20	33	17	18	6	5	1	0	1467	GSS
Mar 1986	16	27	19	22	8	6	2	0	1456	GSS
Mar 1987	19	31	17	20	7	4	1	0	1457	GSS
Mar 1988	18	31	19	21	6	4	2	0	994	GSS

Table 15.6 How Much Satisfaction Do You Get from Hobbies?--1973-1988

SATHOBBY--For each area of life...how much satisfaction you get from that area.

Your nonworking activities--hobbies and so on.

	VERY GREAT DEAL	GREAT DEAL	QUITE A BIT	A FAIR AMOUNT	SOME	A LITTLE	NONE	DK	N	
Mar 1973	26	29	17	13	5	6	4	1	1498	GSS
Mar 1974	23	31	16	13	6	5	5	0	1484	GSS
Mar 1975	24	32	16	12	6	5	4	1	1486	GSS
Mar 1976	22	35	18	11	6	5	3	0	1495	GSS
Mar 1977	25	29	19	13	5	4	3	1	1528	GSS
Mar 1978	24	34	18	12	4	4	4	0	1526	GSS
Mar 1980	27	34	16	11	5	4	3	0	1467	GSS
Mar 1982	22	30	19	15	6	5	4	1	1504	GSS
Mar 1983	20	32	20	14	6	3	4	1	1596	GSS
Mar 1984	25	36	17	11	4	3	2	0	1464	GSS
Mar 1986	18	34	19	13	5	5	5	1	1457	GSS
Mar 1987	25	35	18	12	4	3	2	1	1457	GSS
Mar 1988	22	36	18	12	6	4	3	0	995	GSS

Table 15.7 How Much Satisfaction Do You Get from Your Family Life?--1973-1988

SATFAM--For each area of life...how much satisfaction you get from that area.

Your family life.

	VERY GREAT DEAL	GREAT DEAL	QUITE A BIT	A FAIR AMOUNT	SOME	A LITTLE	NONE	DK	N	
Mar 1973	43	31	10	9	3	2	2	0	1498	GSS
Mar 1974	43	33	11	7	2	2	1	0	1483	GSS
Mar 1975	44	33	10	7	2	2	2	0	1486	GSS
Mar 1976	38	38	11	6	3	2	2	0	1493	GSS
Mar 1977	42	33	12	7	3	1	2	0	1527	GSS
Mar 1978	39	36	11	7	3	2	2	0	1521	GSS
Mar 1980	44	34	10	6	2	2	2	0	1466	GSS
Mar 1982	49	27	10	6	3	2	2	0	1505	GSS
Mar 1983	38	35	11	7	3	2	2	1	1593	GSS
Mar 1984	45	31	11	6	2	2	1	0	1467	GSS
Mar 1986	37	34	12	9	3	2	2	0	1453	GSS
Mar 1987	42	32	12	7	3	2	1	0	1455	GSS
Mar 1988	44	34	9	6	3	3	2	0	994	GSS

Table 15.8 How Much Satisfaction Do You Get from Your Friendships?--1973-1988

SATFRND--For each area of life...how much satisfaction you get from that area.

Your friendships.

	VERY GREAT DEAL	GREAT DEAL	QUITE A BIT	A FAIR AMOUNT	SOME	A LITTLE	NONE	DK	N	
Mar 1973	33	37	14	11	3	2	1	0	1498	GSS
Mar 1974	32	41	14	8	3	2	1	-	1484	GSS
Mar 1975	29	42	15	9	3	2	1	0	1485	GSS
Mar 1976	29	40	16	9	3	2	1	0	1496	GSS
Mar 1977	30	39	15	10	3	2	1	0	1526	GSS
Mar 1978	27	41	17	10	3	2	0	-	1526	GSS
Mar 1980	34	41	13	8	2	1	1	0	1468	GSS
Mar 1982	28	38	17	10	3	2	1	0	1505	GSS
Mar 1983	27	40	18	9	3	2	1	0	1596	GSS
Mar 1984	36	38	12	9	2	2	0	0	1465	GSS
Mar 1986	24	42	17	11	4	2	1	0	1455	GSS
Mar 1987	33	38	15	9	3	2	1	0	1457	GSS
Mar 1988	29	41	16	8	3	2	1	0	995	GSS

Table 15.9 How Much Satisfaction Do You Get from Your Health?--1973-1988

SATHEALT--For each area of life...how much satisfaction you get from that area.

Your health and physical condition.

	VERY GREAT DEAL	GREAT DEAL	QUITE A BIT	A FAIR AMOUNT	SOME	A LITTLE	NONE	DK	N	
Mar 1973	29	31	12	17	5	3	3	0	1502	GSS
Mar 1974	28	33	13	16	5	3	2	0	1484	GSS
Mar 1975	25	35	15	14	5	4	2	0	1484	GSS
Mar 1976	24	35	15	16	4	3	2	0	1497	GSS
Mar 1977	30	31	14	14	4	4	3	0	1527	GSS
Mar 1978	24	35	15	16	4	4	2	0	1526	GSS
Mar 1980	29	35	13	13	4	4	2	0	1468	GSS
Mar 1982	35	28	14	12	6	3	2	0	1505	GSS
Mar 1983	24	33	17	16	5	4	2	0	1595	GSS
Mar 1984	29	34	14	14	4	3	2	0	1466	GSS
Mar 1986	23	32	16	15	5	5	3	0	1456	GSS
Mar 1987	27	33	16	14	5	2	2	0	1457	GSS
Mar 1988	24	35	16	15	4	4	1	0	995	GSS

Table 15.10   Do You Sometimes Wonder Whether Anything is
Worthwhile?--1963-1976

ANOMIA2--You sometimes can't help wondering whether anything
is worthwhile any more.

	AGREE	DISAGREE	DK	N	
Nov 1963	30	69	0	1379	SRS350
Oct 1964	40	59	2	1969	SRS760
Mar 1973	40	59	1	1501	GSS
Mar 1974	43	56	1	1479	GSS
Mar 1976	40	59	1	1494	GSS

Table 15.11   Should One Live Only for Today?--1963-1976

ANOMIA4--Nowadays, a person has to live pretty much for today and let tomorrow take care of itself.

	AGREE	DISAGREE	DK	N	
Nov 1963	48	51	0	1370	SRS350
Oct 1964	45	53	2	1972	SRS760
Mar 1973	43	56	0	1504	GSS
Mar 1974	44	55	1	1482	GSS
Mar 1976	47	53	1	1498	GSS

Table 15.12   Is the Lot of the Average Man Getting Worse?--
1973-1988

ANOMIA5--In spite of what some people say, the lot (situa-
tion/condition) of the average man is getting worse, not
better.

	AGREE	DISAGREE	DK	N	
Mar 1973	54	43	3	1502	GSS
Mar 1974	59	38	3	1481	GSS
Mar 1976	59	38	3	1497	GSS
Mar 1977	54	42	4	1525	GSS
Mar 1980	67	31	2	1467	GSS
Mar 1982	65	30	5	1499	GSS
Mar 1984	56	42	2	1468	GSS
Mar 1985	48	48	4	1530	GSS
Mar 1987	62	36	2	1463	GSS
Mar 1988	60	36	4	973	GSS

Table 15.13   Is It Fair to Bring a Child into Today's World?
          --1973-1988

ANOMIA6--It's hardly fair to bring a child into the world
with the way things look for the future.

	AGREE	DISAGREE	DK	N	
Mar 1973	36	61	2	1503	GSS
Mar 1974	36	62	3	1482	GSS
Mar 1976	42	55	4	1495	GSS
Mar 1977	38	59	3	1525	GSS
Mar 1980	47	51	3	1466	GSS
Mar 1982	34	62	3	1486	GSS
Mar 1984	40	59	1	1470	GSS
Mar 1985	32	65	3	1530	GSS
Mar 1987	39	58	3	1463	GSS
Mar 1988	38	60	2	975	GSS

Table 15.14   Are Public Officials Interested in the Average
          Man?--1973-1988

ANOMIA7--Most public officials (people in public office) are
not really interested in the problems of the average man.

	AGREE	DISAGREE	DK	N	
Mar 1973	58	40	2	1501	GSS
Mar 1974	64	33	2	1481	GSS
Mar 1976	65	33	2	1494	GSS
Mar 1977	63	34	3	1523	GSS
Mar 1980	71	26	3	1465	GSS
Mar 1982	66	31	3	1491	GSS
Mar 1984	68	30	2	1466	GSS
Mar 1985	63	34	3	1527	GSS
Mar 1987	68	30	2	1461	GSS
Mar 1988	66	31	4	975	GSS

Table 15.15 Do Most People Try to Be Helpful?--1964-1988

HELPFUL--Would you say that most of the time people try to
be helpful, or that they are mostly just looking out for
themselves?

	HELPFUL	DEPENDS	LOOK OUT FOR SELF	DK	N	
Aut 1964	54	4	41	1	1445	ELEC64
Aut 1966	52	2	46	0	1285	ELEC66
Aut 1968	58	3	39	1	1344	ELEC68
Sum 1971	55	4	42	-	2155	SRCQOL
Mar 1972	46	6	46	1	1612	GSS
Aut 1972[a]	47		49	4	2174	ELEC72
Nov 1972	56	3	41	-	1460	NORC5046
Mar 1973	47	4	49	0	1501	GSS
Spr 1973	53		44	3	1411	SRCOMNI
Aut 1974[a]	51		46	3	1529	ELEC74
Mar 1975	56	7	37	1	1488	GSS
Mar 1976	43	6	50	0	1498	GSS
Aut 1976[a]	52		44	4	1898	ELEC76
Mar 1978	59	5	35	0	1527	GSS
Mar 1980	49	4	46	1	1465	GSS
Mar 1983	57	4	38	1	1599	GSS
Mar 1984	52	4	44	0	1470	GSS
Mar 1986	56	5	39	0	1465	GSS
Mar 1987	47	5	47	0	1463	GSS
Mar 1988	50	5	45	1	994	GSS

[a]"Depends" was not a code category.

Table 15.16   Are People Fair?--1964-1988

FAIR--Do you think most people would try to take advantage
of you if they got a chance, or would they try to be fair?

	TAKE ADVANTAGE	DEPENDS	FAIR	DK	N	
Aut 1964	29	3	67	1	1674	ELEC64
Aut 1968	30	3	67	0	1342	ELEC68
Sum 1971	32	3	66	-	2143	SRCQOL
Mar 1972	34	6	59	1	1611	GSS
Aut 1972[a]	37		59	4	2179	ELEC72
Aut 1972	35	3	62	-	1464	NORC5046
Mar 1973	37	5	57	1	1503	GSS
Spr 1973	35		62	2	1401	SRCOMNI
Aut 1974[a]	40		58	3	1545	ELEC74
Mar 1975	31	7	62	1	1488	GSS
Mar 1976	36	4	59	1	1499	GSS
Aut 1976[a]	36		60	5	1899	ELEC76
Mar 1978	30	5	64	1	1525	GSS
Mar 1980	34	4	60	1	1468	GSS
Mar 1983	35	5	59	1	1599	GSS
Mar 1984	34	3	62	0	1470	GSS
Mar 1986	33	4	62	1	1465	GSS
Mar 1987	37	4	58	1	1459	GSS
Mar 1988	34	5	60	1	996	GSS

[a]"Depends" was not a code category.

Table 15.17   Can People Be Trusted?--1964-1988

TRUST--Generally speaking, would you say that most people can be trusted or that you can't be too careful in dealing with people?

	CAN TRUST	DEPENDS	CANNOT TRUST	DK	N	
Aut 1964	54	1	44	1	1679	ELEC64
Aut 1966	53	1	46	0	1284	ELEC66
Aut 1968	55	2	43	-	1343	ELEC68
Sum 1971[a]	48	2	50		2161	SRCQOL
Mar 1972	46	3	50	1	1612	GSS
Aut 1972[b]	46		52	2	2179	ELEC72
Mar 1973	46	3	51	0	1502	GSS
Nov 1972	49	2	49	-	1463	NORC5046
Spr 1973[b]	45		54	0	1421	SRCOMNI
Aut 1974[b]	47		52	1	1556	ELEC74
Mar 1975	39	4	56	0	1485	GSS
Mar 1976	44	4	52	0	1497	GSS
Aut 1976[b]	51		46	3	1907	ELEC76
Mar 1978	39	4	57	0	1532	GSS
Mar 1980	45	4	51	0	1466	GSS
Mar 1983	37	4	58	0	802	GSS
Mar 1984	48	3	49	0	1465	GSS
Mar 1986	37	3	60	0	1470	GSS
Mar 1987	44	4	52	0	1461	GSS
Mar 1988	39	4	56	0	995	GSS

[a]"DK" was not a code category.

[b]"Depends" was not a code category.

TRUSTY--Do you think most people can be trusted?

	YES	NO	DK	N	
Mar 1948	66	30	4	1289	NORC156
Aug 1952	68	30	2	1297	NORC329
Nov 1953	57	39	4	1233	NORC349
Jan 1954	62	34	4	1250	NORC351
Nov 1954	66	32	2	1201	NORC365
Apr 1957	75	22	3	1279	NORC404
Nov 1963	77	21	2	1378	SRS350
Mar 1983	56	41	3	790	GSS

Table 15.18   Do People Get Ahead by Hard Work?--1973-1988

GETAHEAD--Some people say that people get ahead by their own hard work. Others say that lucky breaks or help from other people are more important. Which do you think is most important?

	HARD WORK	BOTH EQUALLY	LUCK OR HELP	OTHER	DK	N	
Mar 1973	65	24	10	1	0	1502	GSS
Mar 1974	61	29	9	1	1	1480	GSS
Mar 1976	62	24	13	-	1	1496	GSS
Mar 1977	61	28	10	-	1	1526	GSS
Mar 1980	63	28	8	-	1	1465	GSS
Mar 1982	60	25	13	-	1	1505	GSS
Mar 1984	67	18	15	-	0	1466	GSS
Mar 1985	66	19	14	-	1	1531	GSS
Mar 1987	66	19	15	-	1	1460	GSS
Mar 1988	67	21	12	-	0	976	GSS

Table 15.19   Are You a Member of Any Fraternal Groups?-- 1967-1987

MEMFRAT--Now we would like to know something about the groups and organizations to which individuals belong. Here is a list of various kinds of organizations. Could you tell me whether or not you are a member of each type?

Fraternal groups.

	YES	NO	DK	N	
Feb 1967	15	85	-	3090	NORC4018
Mar 1974	14	86	0	1465	GSS
Mar 1975	11	89	0	1464	GSS
Mar 1977	10	90	-	1518	GSS
Mar 1978	10	90	0	1516	GSS
Mar 1980	11	89	0	1443	GSS
Mar 1983	9	90	0	1592	GSS
Mar 1984	9	91	0	1454	GSS
Mar 1986	9	91	0	1458	GSS
Mar 1987	9	91	-	1448	GSS

Table 15.20   Are You a Member of Any Service Clubs?--
              1967-1987

MEMSERV--Now we would like to know...whether or not you are
a member of each type?
          Service clubs.

	YES	NO	DK	N	
Feb 1967	6	94	-	3090	NORC4018
Mar 1975	8	92	-	1463	GSS
Mar 1977	11	89	-	1518	GSS
Mar 1978	8	92	-	1520	GSS
Mar 1980	9	91	0	1444	GSS
Mar 1983	10	90	0	1593	GSS
Mar 1984	11	89	0	1451	GSS
Mar 1986	11	89	0	1460	GSS
Mar 1987	9	91	-	1447	GSS

Table 15.21   Are You a Member of Any Veterans' Groups?--
              1967-1987

MEMVET--Now we would like to know...whether or not you are a
member of each type?

          Veterans' groups.

	YES	NO	DK	N	
Feb 1967	7	93	-	3094	NORC4018
Mar 1974	9	91	-	1464	GSS
Mar 1975	8	92	0	1465	GSS
Mar 1977	8	92	-	1518	GSS
Mar 1978	7	93	0	1516	GSS
Mar 1980	7	92	0	1443	GSS
Mar 1983	7	93	-	1591	GSS
Mar 1984	7	93	0	1453	GSS
Mar 1986	6	94	-	1461	GSS
Mar 1987	6	94	-	1447	GSS

Table 15.22   Are You a Member of Any Political Clubs?--
                  1967-1987

MEMPOLIT--Now we would like to know...whether or not you are
a member of each type?

          Political clubs.

	YES	NO	DK	N	
Feb 1967	8	92	-	3091	NORC4018
Mar 1974	5	95	-	1464	GSS
Mar 1975	4	96	0	1461	GSS
Mar 1977	5	95	-	1516	GSS
Mar 1978	3	97	-	1515	GSS
Mar 1980	3	97	0	1445	GSS
Mar 1983	5	95	-	1591	GSS
Mar 1984	4	96	0	1453	GSS
Mar 1986	4	96	-	1461	GSS
Mar 1987	4	96	-	1446	GSS

Table 15.23   Are You a Member of Any Labor Unions?--
                  1967-1987

MEMUNION--Now we would like to know...whether or not you are
a member of each type?

          Labor unions.

	YES	NO	DK	N	
Feb 1967	17	83	-	3092	NORC4018
Mar 1974	16	84	-	1465	GSS
Mar 1975	16	84	0	1461	GSS
Mar 1977	17	83	-	1519	GSS
Mar 1978	15	85	0	1520	GSS
Mar 1980	13	87	0	1447	GSS
Mar 1983	14	86	0	1593	GSS
Mar 1984	14	86	0	1452	GSS
Mar 1986	11	89	0	1461	GSS
Mar 1987	13	87	-	1448	GSS

Table 15.24   Are You a Member of Any Sports Clubs?--
1967-1987

MEMSPORT--Now we would like to know...whether or not you are
a member of each type?

Sports groups.

	YES	NO	DK	N	
Feb 1967	12	88	-	3093	NORC4018
Mar 1974	18	82	0	1465	GSS
Mar 1975	19	81	0	1465	GSS
Mar 1977	19	81	-	1517	GSS
Mar 1978	20	80	-	1520	GSS
Mar 1980	17	83	0	1446	GSS
Mar 1983	21	79	-	1593	GSS
Mar 1984	21	78	0	1455	GSS
Mar 1986	21	79	-	1461	GSS
Mar 1987	19	81	-	1449	GSS

Table 15.25   Are You a Member of Any Youth Groups?--
1967-1987

MEMYOUTH--Now we would like to know...whether or not you are
a member of each type?

Youth groups.

	YES	NO	DK	N	
Feb 1967	7	93	-	3085	NORC4018
Mar 1974	10	90	-	1464	GSS
Mar 1975	10	90	-	1462	GSS
Mar 1977	10	90	-	1518	GSS
Mar 1978	9	91	0	1516	GSS
Mar 1980	8	92	0	1443	GSS
Mar 1983	11	89	-	1591	GSS
Mar 1984	9	90	0	1453	GSS
Mar 1986	11	89	-	1460	GSS
Mar 1987	9	91	-	1446	GSS

Table 15.26   Are You a Member of Any School Service Groups?
             --1967-1987

MEMSCHL--Now we would like to know...whether or not you are
a member of each type?

             School service groups.

	YES	NO	DK	N	
Feb 1967	17	83	-	3091	NORC4018
Mar 1974	18	82	0	1463	GSS
Mar 1975	14	86	0	1462	GSS
Mar 1977	13	87	-	1516	GSS
Mar 1978	14	86	0	1516	GSS
Mar 1980	10	90	0	1441	GSS
Mar 1983	14	86	-	1592	GSS
Mar 1984	12	88	0	1453	GSS
Mar 1986	14	86	-	1459	GSS
Mar 1987	12	88	-	1447	GSS

Table 15.27   Are You a Member of Any Hobby or Garden Clubs?
             --1967-1987

MEMHOBBY--Now we would like to know...whether or not you are
a member of each type?

             Hobby or garden clubs.

	YES	NO	DK	N	
Feb 1967	5	95	-	3093	NORC4018
Mar 1974	10	90	-	1462	GSS
Mar 1975	9	91	0	1458	GSS
Mar 1977	9	91	-	1516	GSS
Mar 1978	9	91	-	1517	GSS
Mar 1980	9	91	0	1444	GSS
Mar 1983	10	90	-	1592	GSS
Mar 1984	9	91	0	1454	GSS
Mar 1986	9	91	-	1457	GSS
Mar 1987	9	91	-	1446	GSS

Table 15.28   Are You a Member of Any Fraternities or
              Sororities?--1967-1987

MEMGREEK--Now we would like to know...whether or not you are
a member of each type?

         School fraternities or sororities.

	YES	NO	DK	N	
Feb 1967	3	97	--	3094	NORC4018
Mar 1974	5	95	0	1463	GSS
Mar 1975	4	95	0	1461	GSS
Mar 1977	4	96	--	1518	GSS
Mar 1978	4	96	--	1516	GSS
Mar 1980	4	96	0	1439	GSS
Mar 1983	5	95	0	1592	GSS
Mar 1984	6	94	0	1452	GSS
Mar 1986	5	95	--	1460	GSS
Mar 1987	5	95	--	1446	GSS

Table 15.29   Are You a Member of Any Nationality Groups?--
              1967-1987

MEMNAT--Now we would like to know...whether or not you are a
member of each type?

         Nationality groups.

	YES	NO	DK	N	
Feb 1967	2	98	--	3090	NORC4018
Mar 1974	4	96	0	1464	GSS
Mar 1975	3	97	0	1456	GSS
Mar 1977	3	97	--	1518	GSS
Mar 1978	3	97	--	1514	GSS
Mar 1980	3	97	0	1439	GSS
Mar 1983	4	96	--	1592	GSS
Mar 1984	3	96	0	1452	GSS
Mar 1986	5	95	--	1460	GSS
Mar 1987	2	98	--	1445	GSS

Table 15.30   Are You a Member of Any Farm Organizations?--
1967-1987

MEMFARM--Now we would like to know...whether or not you are
a member of each type?

Farm organizations.

	YES	NO	DK	N	
Feb 1967	4	96	-	3089	NORC4018
Mar 1974	4	96	0	1463	GSS
Mar 1975	4	96	0	1461	GSS
Mar 1977	4	96	0	1516	GSS
Mar 1978	4	96	-	1514	GSS
Mar 1980	4	96	0	1439	GSS
Mar 1983	4	96	-	1590	GSS
Mar 1984	4	96	0	1451	GSS
Mar 1986	4	96	-	1459	GSS
Mar 1987	4	96	-	1447	GSS

Table 15.31   Are You a Member of Any Literary, Art,
Discussion or Study Groups?--1967-1987

MEMLIT--Now we would like to know...whether or not you are a
member of each type?

Literary, art, discussion or study groups.

	YES	NO	DK	N	
Feb 1967	4	96	-	3090	NORC4018
Mar 1974	9	90	0	1463	GSS
Mar 1975	9	91	0	1459	GSS
Mar 1977	9	91	-	1518	GSS
Mar 1978	9	91	-	1513	GSS
Mar 1980	9	91	0	1440	GSS
Mar 1983	10	90	0	1592	GSS
Mar 1984	9	91	0	1453	GSS
Mar 1986	9	91	0	1461	GSS
Mar 1987	7	93	-	1446	GSS

Table 15.32   Are You a Member of Any Professional or
Academic Societies?--1967-1987

MEMPROF--Now we would like to know...whether or not you are
a member of each type?

Professional or academic societies.

	YES	NO	DK	N	
Feb 1967	7	93	–	3090	NORC4018
Mar 1974	13	87	0	1464	GSS
Mar 1975	12	88	0	1462	GSS
Mar 1977	13	87	–	1517	GSS
Mar 1978	13	87	–	1515	GSS
Mar 1980	13	87	0	1440	GSS
Mar 1983	16	84	0	1593	GSS
Mar 1984	16	84	0	1454	GSS
Mar 1986	15	84	0	1462	GSS
Mar 1987	15	85	–	1446	GSS

Table 15.33   Are You a Member of Any Church Groups?--
1974-1987

MEMCHURH--Now we would like to know...whether or not you are
a member of each type?

Church-affiliated groups.

	YES	NO	DK	N	
Mar 1974	42	58	–	1475	GSS
Mar 1975	40	60	0	1467	GSS
Mar 1977	39	61	–	1518	GSS
Mar 1978	36	64	–	1524	GSS
Mar 1980	30	69	0	1448	GSS
Mar 1983	38	62	–	1592	GSS
Mar 1984	34	66	0	1455	GSS
Mar 1986	40	60	–	1462	GSS
Mar 1987	30	70	–	1448	GSS

Table 15.34   How Many Groups Are You a Member of?--1974-1987

Now we would like to know...whether or not you are a member of each type?

MEMNUM--Number of memberships.

	0	1	2	3	4	5	6	7+	
Mar 1974	25	26	19	12	8	2	3	5	GSS
Mar 1975	28	28	18	11	7	3	3	3	GSS
Mar 1977	28	28	16	11	7	4	2	4	GSS
Mar 1978	28	27	18	13	7	3	2	2	GSS
Mar 1980	34	25	16	11	6	3	2	1	GSS
Mar 1983	27	26	19	11	7	4	3	1	GSS
Mar 1984	32	24	17	11	6	4	2	1	GSS
Mar 1986	28	25	18	11	9	4	3	2	GSS
Mar 1987	32	26	17	9	6	4	2	2	GSS

Table 15.35   Does Someone in the Household Hunt?--1959-1988

HUNT--Do you go hunting? Does your (husband/wife) go hunting?

	HUSBAND	WIFE	BOTH	NEITHER	N	
Jul 1959	31	1	5	63	1530	AIPO616
Jan 1965	30	1	5	64	1679	AIPO704
Aug 1966	32	1	5	62	1491	AIPO733
Mar 1977	24	2	3	71	1527	GSS
Mar 1980	21	2	4	74	1465	GSS
Mar 1982	20	2	3	75	1501	GSS
Mar 1984	21	2	3	75	1467	GSS
Mar 1985	20	1	3	76	1531	GSS
Mar 1987	19	2	3	76	1464	GSS
Mar 1988	17	1	2	80	976	GSS

HUNTOTHR--Does any other member of this household go hunting?

	YES	NO	DK	N	
Mar 1977	26	74	0	674	GSS
Mar 1980	20	79	1	666	GSS
Mar 1982	23	76	1	546	GSS
Mar 1984	22	78	0	634	GSS

Table 15.36 How Many Hours a Day Do You Watch TV?--1964-1988

TVHOURS--On the average day, about how many hours do you personally watch television?

	0	1	2	3	4	5	6	7	8	9+	N	
1964[a]	7	30[b]	28	16	10	4	3	2[c]			1940	SRS760
1975	4	17	27	20	15	8	5	1	2	2	1476	GSS
1977	4	21	25	20	13	6	5	1	2	2	1520	GSS
1978	6	21	27	19	13	6	4	0	2	2	1524	GSS
1980	8	18	24	19	13	9	4	1	2	2	1440	GSS
1982	4	21	25	19	14	6	4	2	2	3	1502	GSS
1983	6	19	25	20	13	6	6	1	2	2	1591	GSS
1985	5	18	26	20	14	8	4	1	2	2	1512	GSS
1986	4	18	26	20	13	7	4	1	2	3	1462	GSS
1988	3	19	25	19	14	8	6	1	2	3	979	GSS

[a]On the average, how many hours a day do you watch television?

[b]Includes responses of less than one hour and one hour.

[c]Seven hours or more.

313

Table 15.37 How Many Hours a Day Do You Listen to the Radio?--1957-1983

RADIOHRS--Do you ever listen to the radio? IF YES: On the average, about how many hours a day do you usually listen to the radio?

	0	1	2	3	4	5	6	7	8	9+	N	
1957[a]	19	19	24	16	6	7	3	4			1919	SRCMEDIA
1978	10	36	19	8	7	4	4	1	6	6	1516	GSS
1982	9	33	19	10	7	5	4	2	4	7	1496	GSS
1983	10	33	18	9	7	4	4	1	6	7	1591	GSS

[a]0, less than 1, 1-2, 2-3, 3-4, 4-6, 6-8, 8+.

Table 15.38   How Often Do You Read a Newspaper?--1967-1988

NEWS--How often do you read the newspaper--every day, a few times a week, once a week, less than once a week, or never?

	EVERY DAY	FEW TIMES A WEEK	ONCE A WEEK	LESS THAN ONCE A WEEK	NEVER	N	
Feb 1967	73	12	6	4	5	3093	NORC4018
Mar 1972	69	15	8	4	4	1611	GSS
Mar 1975	66	16	8	5	4	1488	GSS
Mar 1977	62	17	10	7	5	1527	GSS
Mar 1978	57	20	10	7	5	1528	GSS
Mar 1982	54	22	12	7	6	1503	GSS
Mar 1983	56	21	11	8	5	1599	GSS
Mar 1985	53	21	13	8	6	1530	GSS
Mar 1986	54	20	13	8	6	1468	GSS
Mar 1987	55	21	13	7	5	1459	GSS
Mar 1988	51	24	12	9	5	988	GSS

Index of GSS Mnemonics

(Non-GSS variables have no mnemonic)

Index

About the Authors

RICHARD G. NIEMI is Professor of Political Science at the University of Rochester. He is coauthor of *Generations and Politics, The Political Character of Adolescence,* and *Vital Statistics on American Politics,* and has published articles and chapters on voting behavior and other topics in political science.

JOHN MUELLER is Professor of Political Science at the University of Rochester. His publications include *War, Presidents and Public Opinion, Astaire Dancing, Retreat from Doomsday: The Obsolescence of Major War,* and numerous articles and commentaries on politics, foreign policy, and related topics.

TOM W. SMITH is Research Associate and Director of the General Social Survey at the National Opinion Research Center, University of Chicago. He has published numerous articles, chapters, and reports dealing with social change, public opinion, and trend analysis.